Commercial Real Estate Investing

COMMERCIAL REAL ESTATE INVE$TING

A STEP-BY-STEP GUIDE TO FINDING AND FUNDING YOUR FIRST DEAL

FIND → FIGURE → FUND → FIX
→ FILL → FINANCIALS → FREEDOM

MIKE SOWERS, CCIM

Commercial Real Estate Investing:
A Step-by-Step Guide to Finding and Funding your First Deal

Hardcover ISBN: 978-1-5445-2098-8
Paperback ISBN: 978-1-5445-2097-1
Ebook ISBN: 978-1-5445-2096-4
Audiobook ISBN: 978-1-5445-2099-5

I dedicate this book to God.

Thank you for saving me and giving me these gifts, so that I may share them with others that they may walk the path to freedom.

Thank you to my students, partners, and Scribe Media for encouraging me to write this book.

To my wife Lisa, and children Andi and Brody, I developed this system so I could spend the best hours of my life with you. You are my sunset I could sail off into forever and never leave.

Contents

A NOTE FROM MIKE xi

INTRODUCTION xiii

PART 1
STRATEGY 1

    Chapter 1
    How to Face Your Fears 3

    Chapter 2
    Why Commercial? 11

    Chapter 3
    Active vs. Passive Investing 17

    Chapter 4
    Value-Add Strategy 25

    Chapter 5
    Choose an Asset Class 37

PART 2
SYSTEM 45

    Chapter 6
    Case Study 47

STEP 1: FIND 51

Chapter 7
Create Prospecting Lists 53

Chapter 8
Make Contacts 63

STEP 2: FIGURE 85

Chapter 9
Tour the Property 87

Chapter 10
Conduct Market Research 99

Chapter 11
Calculate the MACO 113

Chapter 12
Determine Creative Offers 153

Chapter 13
Present Your Offers 171

STEP 3: FUND 183

Chapter 14
Conduct Due Diligence 185

Chapter 15
Structure the Partnership 205

Chapter 16
Raise the Capital 233

Chapter 17
Secure the Debt 243

Chapter 18
Close the Deal 253

STEP 4: FIX 261

Chapter 19
Estimate Repair Costs 263

Chapter 20
Gather Firm Bids. 283

Chapter 21
Sign Construction Contracts 293

Chapter 22
Complete Construction Draws 301

STEP 5: FILL 309

Chapter 23
List the Property 311

Chapter 24
Generate Leads 319

Chapter 25
Conduct Showings. 327

Chapter 26
Screen the Tenants 335

Chapter 27
Negotiate and Sign Leases 339

STEP 6: FINANCIALS 359

Chapter 28
Select Management Company 361

Chapter 29
Onboard the Property 369

Chapter 30
Stabilize the Financials 377

STEP 7: FREEDOM 385
   Chapter 31
   Refinance the Property 387
   Chapter 32
   Sell the Property 395

CONCLUSION 407

APPENDIX 411

A Note from Mike

Dear reader,

I'm including a complimentary resource bundle for this book at the link below. I hope this system will help you achieve true freedom in your life.

https://www.CREInvestingBook.com

Sincerely,

Mike Sowers

Introduction

I have a secret for you.

   All these years you've spent investing in residential properties, you could have been making ten times more. It doesn't matter if you are wholesaling, flipping, buying junior liens, or doing rentals, the process for commercial investing is almost identical to residential, but the returns are exponentially higher.

I know what you're thinking: *the process might be the same, but it's still a change.*

I'm willing to bet you haven't gotten into commercial because:

- You don't have enough cash or credit.
- You don't know how to raise capital from other people.
- You don't know where to find a good deal.
- You can't figure out how much you should pay for a property.
- You don't know how to lease commercial spaces.
- You believe commercial is too risky.

Here's what you may not realize: These are beliefs that are not real. They are just fears that stem from a lack of understanding. How do I know this?

Because I had all of the same fears keeping me in my comfort zone doing residential deals, until one day I unlocked a secret that changed my investing strategy for good.

With this secret, I jumped from averaging $50,000 per flip to doing deals where I was making several million dollars per deal. The best part is, it allowed me to do an *unlimited* number of these deals and turn up the faucet as high as I wanted to go, and it didn't require any more work than flipping a house did.

The secret is simple: You can partner with other people who have good credit and lots of cash to fund your deals. If done properly, you can scale up exponentially, taking on no more risk than residential, getting ten times the results with the same amount of effort.

I know what you're thinking: *why would anyone ever want to partner with me?* To be honest, maybe they wouldn't. But that's only because you don't have a strategy or an investing system yet—and that's what you bought this book for. Stick with me to the end, and you are going to be able to bring quality deals to them that give them better risk-adjusted returns than they would ever get anywhere else. In return, they will compensate you greatly for doing all of the work, allowing them to remain passive in the investment. That's it. No gimmicks, no missing pieces. Just a complete investing system that you can put into use right away.

Who This System Is For

You don't have to stop doing what you're doing to implement this system. In fact, maybe your residential investing system is working fine right now. But let's face it: you're getting bored. You can't do this transactional stuff forever. You fantasize about being able to do one large deal per year to make your entire year's income instead of having to crank out the numbers, over and over again. You're getting outbid on properties by rookies who watched an HGTV show, attended a seminar, and overbid because they were so desperate to do a deal.

Guess what! These rookies don't exist in the commercial game.

Maybe you're sick of dealing with unreliable contractors and deadbeat tenants and are ready to spend your time interacting with business owners and entrepreneurs all day.

Maybe you just want the prestige of getting into the big leagues and being able to cash your first million-dollar check. You know you need a new strategy for that, because the only way to scale up with your current system would be to take on more headaches.

Maybe you are working as a real estate agent or contractor for other people who are investing in real estate. Why are you working for the tip, when you could be sitting down and eating the meal? Making a commission or a contractor fee is nice, but the real profits are made by the investor.

Maybe you own a successful business and have lots of capital you want to smartly put to work. You understand marketing, sales, and operations, but you haven't figured out how to use those skills to get your cash working for you, earning double-digit returns.

Maybe you've never invested before, but you know you can't keep doing what you're doing. You have wanted to get into real estate for a while, but you can't figure out how to get started. You know there is a better life out there for you, but you don't know how to obtain it.

No matter what your background or current situation, the first thing you need to do is **retire the idea of retirement.**

Let it go. Even though our society is built around it, the human spirit is not designed to retire. To retire is to die. Sometimes literally. Death rates in the early years of retirement are staggering. We are not meant to stop providing value to society, and retirement should *not* be your goal.

Your goal should be FREEDOM.

Imagine your life with complete freedom over time because your residual income exceeds your cost of living. You could travel the world with your family and return home with more money in your bank account than when you left. You could wake up Monday morning and decide whether you want to go to the lake, play with your kids, or work on your business.

You'd feel excited to get out of bed again—to have a real challenge that forces you to stretch your abilities, without consuming every waking hour. You would only have to do one deal a year, and each year your residual income would snowball. You only need to do a few commercial deals to be set for life. In this book, I give you the exact recipe so you can buy back your time and focus on the things that truly matter to you.

If you implement the steps in this book, you will buy your first commercial property in the next twelve months, with about the same amount of capital that you would need for the down payment on a house.

The best part is, this system will only add to what you are already doing.

If you can only invest part time, don't worry. You don't have to quit your day job. This system only takes about ten hours per week to implement.

You don't need to sell your other investments either. You'll only need enough working capital to fund your marketing system and the due diligence on your first deal—$20,000 to $60,000 in total capital to get your first deal done. Some people take it out of their IRA or borrow it from a family member. Others just use what they set aside to invest in their next rental property and decide to buy a commercial property instead.

What You'll Learn

This book is divided into two parts—strategy and systems.

In the first half, you will form your strategy and create a plan. You'll shed your limiting beliefs that have been holding you back and open your eyes to why commercial is so much better than residential. Then you will learn all of the different ways to make money in this business, but you'll learn how to do it in a way that reduces or eliminates risk. We will end the first part of the book by choosing what types of properties to target and where to target them.

In the second half, you will learn the system—the 7 Steps to Freedom—which gives you a roadmap to doing your first deal and implementing the plan you put into place in the first half of the book.

With this information, you will be able to duplicate my success in your market. With a winning strategy and a proven system to implement it, you can maximize profit while minimizing the amount of risk you will take to earn it.

Here's a summary of what you will learn in each of the seven steps.

THE 7 STEPS TO FREEDOM

STEP 1—FIND: Learn how to find and focus on properties that have problems you can solve. This includes creating a list of prospective properties and rolling out a proven marketing strategy to get brokers and property owners calling you. You'll learn how to pre-qualify the deal and schedule the tour.

STEP 2—FIGURE: Learn to figure out exactly how much you can pay for a property to achieve your desired cash flow and equity growth. To accomplish this, you will tour the property, do market research, review the seller documents, and calculate your Max Allowable Cash Offer. You'll be able to present three different offers, negotiate the deal, and determine exactly how much profit you will make on the deal.

STEP 3—FUND: Learn to fund a deal by partnering with other investors. You will learn exactly how to find and secure equity partners and split the profit with them. You'll be able to secure bank financing, even if you have no credit, and properly underwrite the deal to structure away the risk.

STEP 4—FIX: Learn to fix a property up to make it shine like a new coin. You'll be able to evaluate what repairs make sense and what ones don't. You'll learn how to use our renovation cost worksheet to estimate the cost of those repairs, then find good contractors to verify your assumptions and get the updates in motion.

STEP 5—FILL: Learn to fill the property with quality tenants. You'll know how to create a world-class listing and deploy a marketing strategy to generate leads. You'll be able to conduct showings, screen tenants, and structure creative lease agreements to get your spaces filled quickly.

STEP 6—FINANCIALS: Learn to stabilize the financials. You'll know how to source and secure the best property management firms and structure their compensation to get them to think like an owner. You'll maximize your net operating income (commonly called NOI, more on that later) by automating rent collection, eliminating wasteful spending, and ensuring your billing procedures are airtight.

STEP 7—FREEDOM: Learn how to free up your time, capital, and profit. Once you've established a history of improved financial performance, you can either flip the property for a big profit, or refinance, pay your partners off, and hold the property for long-term cash flow. You'll know how to analyze which one makes more sense and make smart decisions to maximize your cash flow and equity growth over time.

The seven steps are not necessarily linear, so first read the entire book to understand the process as a whole. Then come back and work through each step one at a time, as needed, while you move through your first commercial deal.

There are spreadsheet versions of every worksheet you see in this book that you can download on my website at www.CREInvestingBook.com. The spreadsheets have the formulas built-in, which will save you considerable time.

You probably already have a deal analyzer spreadsheet tool, but try using mine as you work through the book. I have a different way of analyzing deals than most other systems. Working in the spreadsheet as we go through the case study will help you digest the numbers, and you'll see how the moving parts interact with each other. Plus, when it comes time to use them for your first deal, you'll have some practice under your belt already.

I know what you're thinking: *if this strategy really works, why isn't everyone doing it?*

Because it's simple, but not easy.

Everyone thinks they want a change, but almost nobody wants to do the work.

It'll be new territory, and you'll have to stretch outside of your comfort zone. It also takes time—it can take a few months to get your first deal under contract and another three to four months to fund and close on that deal. You'll get paid at closing and begin implementing your business plan, which can take another one to two years before you sell or refinance. Here is what the timeline looks like.

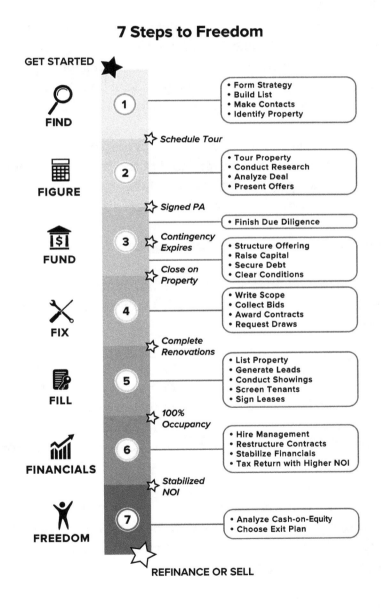

7 Steps to Freedom

GET STARTED

FIND
1
- Form Strategy
- Build List
- Make Contacts
- Identify Property

☆ *Schedule Tour*

FIGURE
2
- Tour Property
- Conduct Research
- Analyze Deal
- Present Offers

☆ *Signed PA*

- Finish Due Diligence

FUND
3
☆ *Contingency Expires*
- Structure Offering
- Raise Capital
- Secure Debt
- Clear Conditions

☆ *Close on Property*

FIX
4
- Write Scope
- Collect Bids
- Award Contracts
- Request Draws

☆ *Complete Renovations*

FILL
5
- List Property
- Generate Leads
- Conduct Showings
- Screen Tenants
- Sign Leases

☆ *100% Occupancy*

FINANCIALS
6
- Hire Management
- Restructure Contracts
- Stabilize Financials
- Tax Return with Higher NOI

☆ *Stabilized NOI*

FREEDOM
7
- Analyze Cash-on-Equity
- Choose Exit Plan

☆ REFINANCE OR SELL

You are going to feel like quitting at various stages throughout the process, but seeing this journey through to completion will mean a new life for you—your ideal life. And this isn't just about you, is it? You are doing this for your family, to spend the best hours of your life with them. You are doing this for the people you can serve.

Why I Made the Switch

Back in business school, I started a remodeling business and used the profits to buy my first rental property at the age of twenty-one. Over time, I scaled that remodeling business into a multimillion-dollar operation and kept acquiring more and more properties with the profits. In my first decade of investing, I rehabbed over a thousand properties and built the organization to over fifty people.

On the surface, it looked like I was crushing it, but deep down something was missing. I wasn't excited anymore, and I was tired of the grind. Every month, I had to start back at zero. I wanted to create a snowball that kept getting bigger instead of melting every month.

Then the unthinkable happened: my mom hung herself.

Her fear of retirement and financial failure pushed her over the edge, so she tossed her final thoughts on a pad of paper and signed off without saying goodbye.

I crumbled.

I had worked my entire life to save enough to finally take care of her, and now no amount of money would give me the opportunity to at least say goodbye.

I had more money in my bank account than I'd ever had, but I felt more bankrupt than I'd ever been.

After that, I took a hard look in the mirror and committed to never again do things just for the sake of money. I decided it was time to begin stepping into my purpose and do something that excited me again, so I sold my construction company and tried doing some commercial deals.

I had avoided commercial real estate before because I thought you needed hundreds of thousands of dollars to do these big deals, and I didn't know how to raise equity capital from other people. Now that I had funds from the sale of my company, I gave it a try.

It was tougher than I thought it would be, but only because I didn't have a system. I didn't know how to tell what a good deal looked like. To be honest, I had no clue what I was doing! I read as many books and talked to as many people as I could. They all covered some awesome concepts, but they all lacked one thing: specific first steps that I needed to take to get my first deal done. Each book left me with *more* knowledge but *less* of an understanding of what actions I should actually take.

I didn't need more concepts; I wanted specific tactics and a roadmap to success. I wanted to know the best way. The proven way. The pathway that, if I just stayed on it, would lead me to get my first deal done.

Out of this frustration, I started the *"CREative Commercial Real Estate Podcast"* just to have a forum to get some of these top investors in my market to open up. To my amazement, it worked! I was able to uncover some of the industry's tightest-held secrets, and over the years, I've continued assembling these secrets into a proven system that anyone can implement.

I used that system to buy my first commercial property, and I've continued refining the system ever since. At some point, I had all of my money invested and started raising capital from other people. That's when I realized that I never needed capital to do this in the first place. As soon as I realized how much more exciting and rewarding commercial could be, and forming these partnerships to fund deals, I sold the rest of my residential properties, broke off the rearview mirror, and never looked back.

The concepts I'm going to give you are not new. What *is* new is how I've assembled them into a roadmap so you know what to do, step by step, until you have bought your first property.

Using this system, I have created millions in equity and tens of thousands in residual income per month in just a few short years. I don't say that to impress you, but to impress *upon you* that this system works for anyone who chooses to use it. The only way to fail is to quit. Which you won't do, because seeing this through to completion means a new life for you—a life with true freedom.

Just remember to do this for the right reasons.

When money is your god, the work is all about you. But when the work is about purpose, God provides the money. Be grateful for the things you have now and the journey you're taking. Maintain your humility. Never stop learning, continue asking questions, and always challenge your mindset.

After losing my mom, my scoreboard changed from how much money I could make to how many lives I could bless by seeing both people and properties not for what they are today, but for what they could become tomorrow.

I believe God has a plan for you to realize the potential within yourself and make an impact on the world that is truly remarkable. Will you commit to doing this program with me? Will you commit to your freedom and finally step into your purpose?

Good. Let's get started.

Part 1
Strategy

The first half of this book is meant to give you a strategy that helps you maximize cash flow and equity growth while minimizing risk.

It'll start by uncovering fears you may have about commercial real estate and help you overcome them. Then it covers why I moved into commercial real estate, and why you should consider doing it too. We help you figure out if you want to be an active investor or a passive investor, and then we show you why the Value-Add strategy is the best overall strategy that balances cash flow and equity growth.

Then we cover the three different ways you can exit out of any particular deal: wholesale it, flip it, or refinance it and hold it long term. We end the first half of the book by helping you select an asset class to focus on so you can become an expert in your chosen market.

If you adopt the investing strategy I propose here, you can replicate my success in your market and be on your way to cashing your first million-dollar check.

Chapter 1

How to Face Your Fears

Deals are like babies: Your first one is the hardest. You're nervous and afraid you will blow it. But when the next one comes around and you know what you're doing, you realize it wasn't that bad after all. Perspective makes (at least some of) the fear dissipate.

Shifting from residential to commercial—or from passive investing to active—is the same way. If you're feeling those first-time jitters, don't worry. It won't last forever. All you need is a desire to change your life, a commitment to take action, and the rest of this book.

I know—I've been there. I avoided commercial real estate for a long time because I didn't think I had enough connections, money, or experience. I'm willing to bet you feel the same way. The numbers feel too big, the language is too complicated, and the steps are unfamiliar.

If you've flipped a house or invested in residential property at all, it can be difficult to imagine investing in something worth ten or twenty times what you've already purchased. We think of commercial real estate in terms of the deals we've already done, and have no frame of reference for the financing, funding, or structuring of the deal. And if we don't know how to do it yet, we can't picture anyone else trusting us with their money.

These first chapters are all about dispelling myths, learning the truth, and facing your fears of investing commercially. You don't need corporate connections, and you're not going to buy something that sits empty and rots away. It may surprise you to know that I'm not talking about apartments either. There are better properties, purchased the right way, that will keep your job exciting and lucrative—without taking up all your time.

> Tucker Max taught me how to overcome my fear of writing this book. He showed me that our bodies can't tell the difference between excitement and anxiety. They both have the same physical symptoms—heightened awareness, increased heart rate, and sweaty palms. The only difference is how you position the symptoms in your brain and what action you take as a result.

The shift into Value-Add commercial properties is absolutely worth it—and yes, we'll learn what that term means and so much more. You just need to face some fears first. Let's take a minute to identify them, validate them, and then learn how to overcome them.

Fear: I Don't Have Enough Experience.

You may have read some books or attended a seminar but emerged even more confused than when you started. Starting on your own is tough. You don't know how to find an off-market deal, so you look at stuff online. You don't understand how to tell a good deal from a bad deal, so you get frustrated. You don't understand how to put a system in place to generate consistent leads or have a way to figure out how much you should offer.

The reality is that you probably *don't* have enough experience. That's why you need to leverage someone else's. This book will give you a system, and that system will show you how to partner with other people who *do* have the experience.

Fear: I Could Lose Everything I've Worked so Hard for.

Once again, it's true. But you could also lose everything you worked so hard to earn by simply getting behind the wheel of your car. That doesn't stop you from driving, does it?

This is really an extension of the previous fear—knowledge gaps create anxiety. You fear you will make a mistake and a million-dollar mistake at that. But what most people don't know is that you can structure away most, if not all, of your long-term risk with the right strategy and underwriting process.

Risk is not the same as fear. You should avoid risk and overcome fears. The key is knowing the difference.

Fear: I Don't Have Enough Money or Credit.

It's common to think you need a ton of cash to get into commercial. Most investors begin with residential properties, and the shift to larger purchases can be intimidating. That's because you don't know how to find an equity partner who brings the down payment. After all, why would someone want to partner with you on your first deal?

I've sat right next to investment planners, commercial real estate brokers, and residential house flippers who couldn't believe they could buy a piece of commercial real estate with *very little* of their own money. But you can and you will. This book will show you how to do it by forming a partnership where you raise the down payment from other investors. You will only need approximately $20,000–$60,000 in working capital to set up your system and do your first deal.

Here is a breakdown of typical working capital needs for your first deal.

Start-Up Capital

Item	Low	High
Business Set-Up	$1,000	$5,000
Marketing	$3,000	$6,000
Inspection	$1,000	$3,500
Phase I	$2,000	$3,500
Survey	$3,000	$6,000
Appraisal	$3,000	$6,000
Legal	$2,000	$10,000
Earnest Money	$5,000	$20,000
Total	**$20,000**	**$60,000**

You can use capital from your IRA, 401(k), and other liquid reserves. Or you can borrow the money from a friend or partner to fund your operation on the front end. When you close on your first property, the partnership you form will not only reimburse all of your hard costs as shown above, but they will also pay you an acquisition fee of 1–2 percent of the purchase price. The reimbursement will replenish your capital supply and ensure you have enough capital to keep repeating this process. You can live off the acquisition fee, or you can reinvest it back into the deal.

Fear: I Don't Have the Right Connections.

This is probably true as well. Growing your network is a key part of growing your real estate business. This industry is ripe for disruption, but the reality is that it is still very much an industry where if you aren't on the inside, you are "less-than" in their eyes. Don't get frustrated if you encounter the good-old-boys mentality when you start playing in this space.

You'll rely on these brokers to bring you premarket opportunities, so you have to show them you are in the fraternity with them. Instead of fighting the elite club mentality, learn to embrace it.

> I remember my first networking session with other commercial real estate brokers. Everybody was wearing suits and talking in a language I couldn't quite understand. Somebody mentioned financing their deal using mezzanine debt. I didn't know what mezzanine debt was at the time, so I asked if there were people networking up on the mezzanine level as well. They chuckled, and I felt like a complete idiot.
>
> Throughout this book, I'm going to use industry jargon so you can talk the talk and not get caught with your pants around your ankles like I did. Study the terms and understand them, so you at least sound like you know what you're doing.

Fear: I Don't Have Enough Time.

Of course you are afraid to quit your day job. If this investing thing doesn't work out, you won't be able to provide for your family. But that's okay. You can continue doing what you are doing to earn money as you learn to invest in commercial properties.

You only need five to ten hours per week to do this until you close on your first deal and get paid. Yes, you have to be willing to invest that time and a small amount of money into building this system, but that's the price you pay for long-term financial freedom. If it were easy, everyone would be doing it.

Fear: I Don't Know How to Lease Commercial Properties.

Why is it that every property you see has a For Lease sign out front for long periods of time? You've heard horror stories about buildings sitting vacant for years, and you conclude that leasing commercial properties must be tough! That sounds like a risk, doesn't it? What you don't realize is that they are probably full—agents leave their signs out either because they are lazy or because they still generate leads for other properties off them.

You might also have a misconception of what a commercial tenant is. Sure, there are downtown office tenants for Fortune 500 companies, but those aren't the tenants I'm going to teach you to target. You are going to look at suburban properties with relatively small units, around one thousand to five thousand square feet. That means you don't need corporate connections to fill these vacancies. All you need to be able to do is put an ad on Craigslist and a sign out front. That's it. It's really no different than finding renters for an apartment.

You may not realize that there are lots of multi-tenant buildings with small spaces. This will help you diversify your risk over multiple, smaller tenants, who are easier to find and negotiate with.

Fear: Is Now a Good Time to Invest?

I love this one. This is the number one question I get. My answer is, "If the day ends in y, it's a good time to invest!"

Speculative investing is about getting in at the right time and getting out at the right time. I don't do speculative investing, and you shouldn't either. Unless you are God, you will never know how to time the market.

I'm not saying you shouldn't study the market to see what's going on and examine where you are at on the market cycle. What I'm saying is you can use that information to help you predict the future value of the property and take that into account when drafting your offers. You can adopt a strategy that allows you to win in *any* market.

When the market is improving, I find deals. When the market is declining, I find even better deals. And when the market has completely tanked, I find the very best deals. Don't let the fear of what the market will do hold you back from investing.

> **Instead of trying to find the *right time* to invest, focus your energy on finding the *right deal* to invest in.**

Action Cures Fear.

When you feed these fears, it convinces you that commercial is too risky, complicated, and out of your reach. I won't lie to you. You may not have the credit, connections, money, or experience, but I'm going to let you in on a little secret:

None of that matters.

The only thing holding you back from investing in real estate, particularly commercial real estate, is *you* and your own limiting beliefs.

You don't need any of those things to buy a property. I'm not saying a *bank* doesn't prefer credit, connections, money, and experience. What I'm saying is *you* don't need to have them. What you need is a system that shows you how to partner with other people who *do* have those things.

7 Steps to Freedom is that system.

Zig Ziglar said, "It's your stinking thinking" that is holding you back, and Henry Ford said, "Whether you thought you could, or you thought you couldn't, you are probably right." Nothing more. Nothing less.

Try saying this out loud to yourself:

"I am a commercial real estate investor."

Say it again. And again. Until you believe it.

Then go order some business cards that say it.

Start introducing yourself as a "commercial real estate investor who finds off-market deals, funds them using money partners, then fixes them up, fills them with great tenants, and manages the financials for long-term cash flow."

You'll still feel fear, but instead of letting it debilitate you, let it spring you into action!

Invite the anxiety into your life, but reposition it in your mind as an alarm to go call some property owners or set up some property tours. You'll begin replacing fear and anxiety with healthy actions that produce positive results.

In this book, I'm going to give you the STRATEGY and the SYSTEM. Then the only thing between you and setting your family up for generations to come will be your decision to adopt the strategy and take ACTION on the system, and your GRIT to see it through until you get your first deal done.

Trust me; the first baby will survive, and so will you.

Now, let's discuss why I moved from residential into commercial investing, and why you should too.

Key Reader Takeaways

☐ Your fears are real to you until you overcome them.
☐ Reposition anxiety as excitement in your mind and let it spring you into action.
☐ Action cures fear.

Chapter 2

Why Commercial?

Even after you've faced your limiting beliefs, you might still be on the fence about whether you should move into commercial or not. I invested in residential for over a decade before moving into commercial. When I finally made the leap, my heart started beating fast again, and I will never go back!

You may have found, like I did, that the world of residential eventually loses its excitement. If you want to be challenged again—to get out of being so transactional and to find more freedom of time—then commercial might be the right move for you.

Benefits of commercial over residential:

- Challenge
- Scalability
- Bankers' Hours
- Less Competition
- Quality of Interactions

Challenge

Doing houses got boring for me. I yearned for a challenge and to be better respected at cocktail parties. Commercial real estate is much harder if you don't have a system, but if you do have a system, it is simple yet challenging.

The biggest skills you need to learn are how to analyze commercial deals, raise equity capital, and negotiate commercial leases. Once you have those three down, you can start crushing it in commercial.

Whether you are flipping houses, wholesaling, or doing residential rentals, you can modify your strategy to move into commercial and get your heart beating fast again. It's the equivalent to buying thirty, fifty, or even a hundred homes on one deal. You only need to do one deal a year to make a killing. For me, that got me excited again!

Scalability

I remember the very first seminar I held for commercial real estate investing. One of my students told me they weren't investing in commercial real estate because it was too big for them and was a lot more work. I responded, "It's all the same work—just add a zero!"

Doing a thirty thousand-square-foot commercial roof requires the same amount of project management as doing a three thousand-square-foot residential roof—you are only hiring one roofing contractor.

Here is something interesting though: often, the larger projects cause fewer headaches because commercial contractors run larger operations. If one employee of the firm is sick or has issues, you never even hear about it. They just send a guy from a different crew. With smaller home projects, you are typically working with mom-and-pop type contractors, and an issue with any one person can dramatically impact the whole job.

The reality is that finding, funding, fixing, or filling a commercial building is only more complicated because the numbers are larger. And the scale really becomes evident when profit starts rolling in.

Let's compare the typical profits from commercial and residential deals I've done, which all required similar effort.

Commercial and Residential Profit Comparison

Strategy	Residential	Commercial
Wholesale	$5K–$20K per Deal	$50K–$200K per Deal
Flip	$30K–$100K per Flip	$300K–$1M per Flip
Rental	$300–$500 per Month	$3K–$5K per Month

Need I say more?

If you want to be like everyone else, keep flipping houses. But if you have bigger aspirations, #addazero and join the big leagues.

Bankers' Hours

"On the seventh day, he rested" clearly wasn't written about residential real estate agents and investors. One of the things I hated about being a residential agent was having to work nights and weekends. You're dealing with renters, homeowners, and home buyers, and most of them work during the day. That means you are going to work at night and on the weekends, or you have to build a team that does.

If your goal is freedom of time, residential will contradict that reason for investing in the first place. At least it did for me. Today, you won't find me at open houses on Sunday mornings. You will find me playing electric guitar in the worship band at church and spending the day with my family.

Just today, I called a broker who said to me, "Mike, I'm just pulling in the driveway. Let's chat at 10:00 a.m. tomorrow."

This is a $3.85M deal we are negotiating—and it's *industry standard* for professionals to shut it down after hours. I appreciate that so much, and so does my family!

Less Competition

If you have self-doubts as to whether you are good enough, smart enough, or have enough resources to break into the commercial world—then you are *normal*. It's natural to feel that way, just like everyone wants to run away from a burning building, not toward it. Only a few people with hard hats and balls of steel run toward the danger.

The question is whether you want to be the firefighter of commercial real estate.

The other investors in your market have the same gaps in knowledge and resources as you. Your limitations are a benefit—as long as you're willing to act in spite of them. Once you fill in those gaps with action, something spectacular will happen. Your fear will begin to dissipate. Your courage will build, and you will be ready to run toward the fire when everyone else is rushing out toward residential property.

Yes, you'll be competing against some sophisticated investors, but not like the residential rush. The commercial game isn't filled with a bunch of rookies artificially driving prices up. Competition exists, but just by stepping up, you'll have an edge.

Quality of Interactions

At some point in life, your scoreboard will change from the number of deals you've done to the number of people's lives you can bless. I find that my interactions with business owners, property owners, vendors, and equity investors provide far more meaning to me than my surface-level discussions I would have with homeowners and renters.

You are in the people business. See people and property not for what they are today, but for what they can become tomorrow. Have eyes like Jesus did and always see the best in people and properties, and make it your mission to help unlock that potential using your creative capacity.

- **Commercial Vendors** are business savvy compared to those in the residential game who don't even know how to fill out an invoice properly.
- **Commercial Tenants** are business owners and entrepreneurs, just like you! I love talking to these people and having the privilege of providing a home for their business. They are winners, and they lift me up in the world with their knowledge, attitude, and trajectory in life.
- **Commercial Property Owners** are super successful investors who always seem to have a great story. I love learning from them.
- **Commercial Investors** are high-net-worth individuals who have extra cash and turn to me as their trusted commercial real estate advisor who can help them deploy their capital. I appreciate partnering with them so I can do larger deals, and they appreciate the passive returns I deliver.

The interactions I have with people in the commercial world add value to my life, and at the end of the day, that means far more to me than any amount of money could.

With your fears faced and some of the benefits of getting into commercial real estate in hand, let's figure out if you want to be an active investor who executes the strategy or a passive investor who just puts money into the deals.

Key Reader Takeaways

- ☐ Commercial gives you ten times the results for a similar effort.
- ☐ You will have a higher quality of life if you do commercial deals instead of residential deals.
- ☐ The time spent learning commercial will pay off big for you.

Chapter 3

Active vs. Passive Investing

I f you've decided to explore commercial for its benefits, the next decision you need to make is whether you want to be an active or passive investor.

Active investors do the work and may or may not bring money to the deal. Passive investors only bring money to the deal. In this chapter, you will decide which one you want to be.

Active Investors

We refer to the active investors throughout this book as deal sponsors, general partners, developers, or managing members, and there may be one or more active investors in the deal. Memorize these different naming conventions because they are important.

To be a successful deal sponsor, you'll need to learn how to find and value property, estimate rehab and leasing costs, structure partnerships, raise capital, manage projects, lease vacancies, and manage the financials. You may be good in some areas, and not so good in others, so consider bringing in another general partner or hiring a coach to fill in the gaps where you are weak. Just be careful about giving up equity to people who you can outsource to.

There's a difference between a "strategic partnership" and an actual partnership. A strategic partnership is where you hire someone to perform a certain task for you, whereas a true partnership is where you give someone ownership in the company that owns the property. I highly recommend you outsource your construction, leasing, and property management, and not bring those people in as equity partners.

However, you may want to give up equity to someone if they have a deal under contract that you want to buy, or if they can raise the equity funding for you. You may also need to use their income or credit to qualify for the debt. I also like to partner with tenants who will occupy the building as a tenant if they have capital to bring to the deal.

Understand that as the general partner, you will do a lot of work for a payday that may or may not come. It can take up to a year's worth of work to close and create value in your first deal. If you focus on how much you are earning moment by moment, you will stunt your growth.

> **Focus on how much you're learning, NOT how much you're earning.**

If you have cash to put into a deal, it will make it easier for you to raise money when other people see you putting "skin in the game." If you don't have any capital to put in, don't sweat it. You can bring in limited partners to raise the down payment. This system is designed for you to raise 100 percent of the capital from outside partners for the down payment. You'll need approximately $20,000–$60,000 in working capital for due diligence and earnest money, but you'll get that money back when you close the deal.

Passive Investors

We refer to passive partners in a lot of different ways throughout this book—limited partners, money partners, equity partners, or investors. The passive partners put up the cash. They desire passive income.

> **If you are looking to be a limited partner, your only job is to pick the right general partner to invest your capital with.**

As a limited partner, you put up your cash in exchange for a return. You should select your deal sponsor wisely. By reading this book, you can understand the process a good deal sponsor should be using, so you know what questions to ask when selecting one.

Getting Paid

There are different ways to get paid as both the active and the passive investor.

Different Ways the General Partner Gets Paid

Active

- Acquisition Fee
- Assignment Fee
- Brokerage Fee
- Construction Management Fee

Residual

- GP Distributions from Rental Operations
- Asset Management Fee
- Property Management Fee

Passive

- LP Distributions from Rental Operations

Net Worth

- Distributions at Refinance
- Distributions at Sale

Active Cash Flow is the income you live off of. You have to work for it, and you only cash the check once. Examples include an acquisition fee for putting the deal together, an assignment fee if you assign your contract, a brokerage commission from the seller if the property is listed and you are licensed, and a construction management fee if you oversee the construction. Active income is important because without it, you are living off your savings and decreasing your net worth (like most people do in retirement). You can use active income to invest back into your own or other people's deals, which can create a snowball effect.

Residual Cash Flow is the income that keeps on paying in a recurring fashion, but you have to work for it as the general partner. You cash the check more than once. The two big ones are your ongoing asset management fee and your cut of the cash flow from your rental operation. This is not passive cash flow, because good asset managers are never passive. However, with my plan, you will put good systems in place so that eventually the property runs on autopilot, and this income will require less effort long term. This income is important because it is the income that continues paying you each month, so it's how you replace your active income over time and achieve financial freedom quickly.

Passive Cash Flow is the income that keeps on coming in each month *without* you doing any work. I call it mailbox money—you just open your mailbox each month and there it is. If you contributed capital to the deal, you'll get a passive return on that capital. As you do more deals, you will be able to contribute more capital to the deals and get more and more passive income. You can also invest in other people's deals as a passive investor if you choose to do so.

Net Worth is your personal balance sheet. Your net worth depends on the equity in the properties that you haven't tapped into yet. By utilizing the Value-Add strategy I show you in the next chapter, you can increase your net worth significantly. Then you can decide if and when to free up that equity by refinancing or selling. We cover when and how to tap your equity in the Freedom step.

> ## Pro Tip
>
> Have you ever calculated your net worth? You should be doing this on a regular basis. Here's how you do it. If you sold everything you own and paid off all the debt, how much would you have left over? Most people have no idea what their net worth is.

If you enter into a deal and implement all seven steps, you get to have your cake and eat it too. You will earn all four types of benefits. You get paid an acquisition fee at closing, you get monthly cash flow from asset management fees, you get your cut of the profit for being a general partner, and you get monthly cash flow on your limited partner units if you contributed capital. Plus, you get a big backend payday when you sell or refinance. Don't be shortsighted because you are afraid of the operational process of the business.

Wholesale, Flip, or Rental

So far, we have been talking about high-level strategies. Now we are going to talk about deal-specific strategies and how you should always begin with the end in mind, because the way you analyze the deal depends on it.

The deal sponsor(s) will decide when and how to exit from the property, and those decisions will determine how much active income, residual income, and net worth they will achieve in the process. The four main exit strategies are wholesaling, quick flip, long flip, and refinance to hold long term.

Chances are good that you are familiar with all of these strategies, but I'm going to show you how each strategy is different in commercial than it is in residential. Then, I'll show you why you should always start a deal with the intent to hold it as a long-term rental property.

WHOLESALING

Wholesaling is when you sell your position in the purchase agreement to another person for a fee, and they step into your shoes and close on the property. You are out.

If you own a residential wholesaling business and want to start wholesaling commercial, understand that you can lose a lot of money if you get properties under contract with no intention of closing. Let me explain.

I already showed you that you may need to spend up to $60,000 in due diligence costs and that it can take up to eight weeks to complete. If you don't start due diligence right after you get the property under contract, you risk not leaving enough time to complete due diligence. If you *do* start due diligence right away and can't find someone to assign the contract to, you could end up leaving a lot of money on the table. Either way, you will earn a reputation as a flake in your market.

The commercial arena is very small, and your reputation is important.

Here's how you should position your wholesaling operation: enter into deals with the goal of getting the big payday! Why settle for a small fee for finding and freezing the deal up when you can make a million if you do all seven steps?

As you start raising capital, try to solve the problems early on. Take notice if one of your partners shows signs that they really want to hog the deal for themselves. Perhaps one of your other offers gets accepted, so now you have too many deals to do at once—that's a good time to ask if your partners want to buy you out of the deal. The partner who bought you out will close on the deal and execute the business plan, and you'll walk away with a very handsome fee.

How much of a fee should you charge? I usually shoot for 15–20 percent of the profit the sponsor stands to make. If they stand to make a million dollars, then $150K–$200K is not unreasonable. Your fee should always be based on what you are giving them, and that's how it should be positioned. You are not *taking* a fee—you are *giving* them a deal with the majority of the meat still on the bone.

Don't enter into a purchase contract with no intention of closing, but be open to an early buyout from your partners. Be reluctant to wholesale, plan to close, and you will see success (with better fees) as a result.

FLIP TO OWNER-USER VS. FLIP TO FINANCIAL BUYER

Flipping commercial properties can be done two ways.

You can renovate the building and sell it to an "owner-user" who will buy the property to move their business into. I call this the quick flip because it can go extremely quickly, just like flipping a house can. This strategy works well for single-tenant buildings that are smaller in size, like under twenty thousand square feet.

The other option is to fix the building up, fill it with great tenants, and then sell the building to an investment group that is looking to buy fully stabilized properties for long-term cash flow. We call investors who buy properties for financial reasons "financial buyers" (more on this later in the Figure step).

The investor that buys the property from you will request the financials for the building. If you haven't held it long enough to show a history of improved performance on the financials, then they may not see your property as valuable as it actually is. To get around this and to avoid paying the higher income taxes on the sale, I recommend you hold the property for a year or two, and then once you have a history of improved financials, you sell the property at the highest price. We cover all of these strategies in much greater detail in the Freedom step at the end of this book.

REFINANCE AND HOLD LONG TERM

Instead of selling after a year or two, you can refinance. By doing this, you can harvest some of the equity you have gained in the building and use it to pay off some or all of your limited partners.

We cover this strategy later in the book, but when you pay off expensive equity partners using cheap debt, your cash flow position increases dramatically. What most people don't think about is that their net worth is directly tied to the amount of residual income that they have created. Active income from flips and wholesaling is super sexy, and everyone loves cashing a big check. However, creating a stream of residual income has a far more dramatic impact on your net worth because that income stream can be sold at a high multiple to a financial buyer. Therefore, it's an asset that increases your net worth substantially.

I hope now you can see that the fastest way to increase your net worth and achieve financial freedom is to buy income-producing properties and hold them long term. However, sometimes it makes sense to sell. In the Freedom step, you will learn a concept called cash-on-equity, which will help you calculate if it makes sense to sell or not. Of course, if you need to eat along the way or you want to mix things up a little bit, you can mix in some wholesaling and flipping too.

Now that you are starting to get an idea of the kind of investor you are, let's look at the different investing strategies you can use.

Key Reader Takeaways

☐ General partners do the work and get paid active and residual income for it.

☐ Limited partners put up the cash and get passive income for it.

☐ Never give up equity for something you can outsource.

☐ Always enter into contracts with the intent to hold long term but be open to a wholesale or flip if the price is right.

☐ Focus on how much you are learning, not on how much you are earning early on. The cash flow and net worth will come faster if you do.

Chapter 4

Value-Add Strategy

Risk is inherent in any deal, but there are different kinds of risk that you can build a strategy around. This chapter aims to help you reduce, and in some cases eliminate, risk by helping you adopt the right investing strategy. We are going to show you why the Value-Add strategy reigns supreme, balances cash flow and equity growth, and is the strategy that you will learn in this book.

There is long-term risk, and there is short-term risk, and we are going to learn how to minimize both.

Long-term risk is the risk that comes from shifts in the ratio of supply and demand in your market. These changes can impact rent rates, occupancy rates, cap rates, debt rates, property taxes, commission rates, and skilled labor rates over time. These metrics dramatically impact your cash flow and subsequent equity position in the property.

You can't control long-term risk, but you can dramatically reduce it by choosing the right investment strategy that ensures the value of your property far exceeds the total dollars you have invested into it. That way if the market changes, you will have a big enough cushion to maintain a healthy cash flow and a large equity position in the property.

Short-term risk is the risk that comes from not executing your business plan well. This is what I call inexperienced investor risk, and it usually stems from a lack of systems, knowledge, or both. You can eliminate most of this risk by learning, adopting the right system, repetition, and ensuring you have a team of advisors that double-check your work.

Here are just some of the most common mistakes I see rookie investors making:

- Not knowing the market rent rates or vacancy rates
- Having trouble figuring out what operating expenses should be
- Not knowing how to measure a building properly
- Using the wrong cap rate
- Underestimating construction costs
- Forgetting to factor in leasing commissions
- Not accounting for negative cash flow as a "cost"
- Not being thorough enough in due diligence

Messing any one of these items up could lead to a multitude of problems, such as reduced cash flow, cost overruns, overpaying for a property, canceling a deal, never getting a deal in the first place, or the cardinal sin, losing your investors' money.

Here is a chart that shows you a cause-and-effect relationship from different types of risk and how to avoid them using this strategy and system.

How to Lose Money in Real Estate

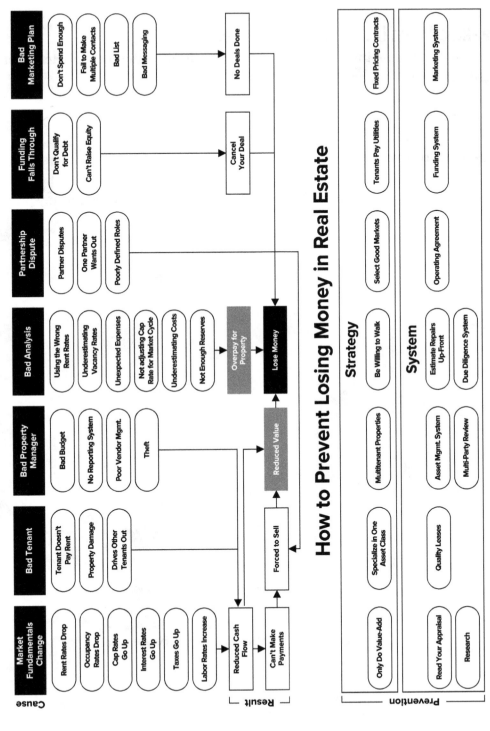

How to Prevent Losing Money in Real Estate

Breaking Down Investment Strategies

There are three main investing strategies. Each one has different short-term versus long-term risks. They are:

- Stabilized
- Value-Add
- Opportunistic

Let's talk about each one, and about why I use a Value-Add strategy as my primary strategy.

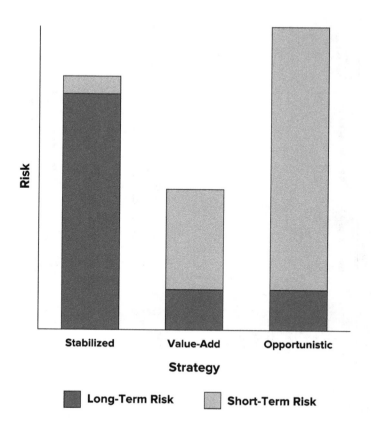

Investing Strategy Risks

STABILIZED

The stabilized strategy is all about cash flow.

A stabilized property has market-rate occupancy at market-rate rents and is usually well maintained. The primary metric that a stabilized investor cares about is cash-on-cash return or yield as measured by the internal rate of return (IRR) on their money. These properties seem low-risk to the untrained investor but actually pose the highest long-term risk, because you are going to pay top dollar for them. If the market takes a dip, the value could drop below the total investment you have put into the property. Of course, if you're cash-flow positive and you can hang onto the property until the market recovers, you'll be fine.

If you have a few million sitting in the bank and don't want to take on a project, then you should probably consider investing in pretty properties that are fully occupied and very well run. For the rest of you who don't have that kind of cash lying around, let's talk about other options.

VALUE-ADD

The Value-Add strategy is for value creation.

The top two reasons people invest in real estate are to generate cash flow and increase their net worth. The Value-Add strategy focuses on creating equity in properties by stabilizing them. Once they are stabilized, you can choose to harvest that equity by selling the asset or refinancing it and hanging onto it for long-term cash flow.

It's called the Value-Add strategy because it's all about buying distressed properties and then improving the financial performance of them to force appreciation. This creates equity which increases your net worth. Increasing your net worth early in your investing career has a much larger impact than generating cash flow. Let me explain how this works in more detail.

The income approach to valuation suggests that a piece of commercial real estate is worth a multiple of its net operating income, or NOI, and it's the most important term you need to know when doing commercial real estate. To calculate it, you simply add up all the income for the property and then subtract all of the expenses. The result is the net operating income. It's usually shown as an annual number.

Net Operating Income = Total Income – Total Expenses

This next part is very important, so listen up. **You don't factor balance sheet items into the NOI.**

Balance sheet items are things like mortgage payments, distributions to partners, and capital costs. It's important to distinguish between capital costs and operating expenses.

Capital costs are things you depreciate over time instead of expensing right away—major improvements, leasing commissions, and closing costs.

Operating expenses are things you expense right away—taxes, utilities, maintenance, property management, insurance, repairs, and administrative costs.

Another way to think of NOI is that if you paid all cash for a property, the NOI is the amount you would put in your pocket each year.

IMPORTANCE OF NOI

The NOI impacts you about as much as your spouse will—it's that important!

It determines your cash flow during the holding years, refinance, and at disposition. It also determines how much you pay in taxes. Here is a modified version of the three financial statements you are probably used to seeing that shows how the NOI impacts them all. Here you can see how to calculate your cut on the cash flow as the general partner (GP).

The Three Financial Statements

Statement of Cash Flows

CF from Operations

Rental Income
− Operating Expenses
= **Net Operating Income**
− Debt Service
− Other Debt Service
= **Cash Flow to Partnership**
− Reserve Replenishment
= **Distributable Cash Flow**
− Preferred Return
− Return of Capital (optional)
= **Distributable Upside**
× Sponsor Upside Split(s)
= **Cash Flow to GP**

Reserve Calculations

Beginning Reserves
− Capital Improvements
− Leasing Commissions
− Unforeseen Capital Costs
+ Reserve Replenishment
= **Ending Reserves**

Income Statement (P&L)

Rental Income
− Operating Expenses
= **Net Operating Income**
− Interest
− Depreciation
− Amortization
= **Taxable Income**
× GP Ownership Percentage
= **Taxable Income for GP**

Balance Sheet

Net Operating Income
÷ Market Cap Rate
= **Market Value of Asset**
− Cost of Sale
= **Net Proceeds from Sale**
− Bank Debt Balance
− Other Debt Balance
= **Sales Proceeds Before Tax (SPBT)**
− Return of Capital (Balance)
= **Distributable Upside**
× Sponsor Upside Split(s)
= **Cash Flow to GP**

> **The Value-Add strategy is all about increasing the underlying NOI and the multiple of that NOI that the market will pay.**

This is why Value-Add investors target rundown or poorly managed properties. These properties usually look tired and have vacancies, but not always. Sometimes they just have very poor property managers. It's like the We Buy Ugly Houses® strategy, but we are just doing it for commercial buildings.

Getting a good Value-Add deal is not necessarily about buying properties under market value either. It's about ONLY targeting properties with problems where you can solve those problems to increase the value significantly more than what it costs to do so. For example, if you can fix the building up and fill it with great tenants and increase the value by $500,000 but it only costs you $200,000 to do it, then you've created $300,000 in equity.

That's why the primary metric a Value-Add investor cares about is equity multiple—that is, to what extent did they multiply the capital the partnership put into the deal. If the partnership put up $300,000 and later sold and pulled out the $600,000, the project equity multiple is 2.0. I'm going to show you how to raise money from other partners and then double their money and split that profit with them.

In this case, you would each get $150,000 profit. You, as the general partner, get $150,000 for doing the work and they, as the limited partners, get $150,000 for putting up the cash.

If you can increase the NOI by at least 20 percent, I would consider it a Value-Add deal. This is how I invest and what this book focuses on. If you want to buy something pretty that has no upside potential because you don't want a "project," then close this book right now and look up your local brokerage office. I'm sure someone there will help you. If you are willing to put in the blood, sweat, and tears it takes to make it big, stick with me.

OPPORTUNISTIC

The opportunistic strategy is for development profit.

These are major construction projects—either ground-up new construction or a significant overhaul of an existing building where you are changing the use or zoning in some way. The primary metrics a developer cares about are cap rate spread and developer fees.

Opportunistic deals are riskier than Value-Add in the short term because they introduce the elements of political risk and market-shift risk. You have to go through what's called the "entitlement process" to build new or change the zoning for a building. This is where you get approval rights from the city to do what you want to do. I can tell you from experience, there are larger political elements at play on these deals that create risk. Because the timelines are usually very long, sometimes several years, you can run the risk of construction costs or market metrics changing dramatically.

I would recommend waiting until you have a few Value-Add deals under your belt before you try to do an opportunistic project. If you uncover one early in your investing career, you may just want to sell the opportunity for a finder's fee.

Investing Strategy Overview

Strategy	Definition	Condition	Goal	Metrics	Risk Elements
Stabilized	Market-Rate Occupancy at Market-Rate Rents	Pretty	Cash Flow	Cash-on-Cash Return	Value Drops below Cost Basis
Value-Add	Existing Building where the Net Operating Income Is Depressed	Ugly	Equity	Equity Multiple	Missing Construction and Lease Up Projections
Opportunistic	Ground-Up Development or Change in Use of Existing Structure	Nonexistent or Conversion	Development Profit	Cap-Rate Spread and Development Fee	Political Risk, Entitlement Process Risk, Construction, Lease Up, Market Shift

Why Value-Add?

You tell me what's riskier. Buying a fully stabilized asset at an aggressive cap rate or buying a Value-Add property, fixing it up, filling the vacancies, and then having a cushion of 30–40 percent equity above your total investment basis?

The added value comes from solving problems.

No money, no problem. But if there's no problem…no money!

You can do deals without any of your own money, but you *can't* do deals without a problem. Not if you want to make any money. Think of the seller as your ally here rather than your adversary. If you can't solve their problem, then you won't create any value.

Human decisions are driven by the pursuit of pleasure or avoidance of pain. Find the pain, then use your God-given creativity to solve the problem. I see new students spending way too much time looking at deals where there isn't a clear problem to be solved. Learn how to uncover problems and then solve them.

Two Kinds of Problems

Look for both people problems and property problems. People problems require some digging, whereas property problems are more obvious. Here are some of the most common problems I find for each:

People Problems
- Headache tenants
- Bad lease language
- Bad management
- Poor utility or net rent billing practices
- Due on sale issues with the underlying loan
- Foreclosure
- Divorce
- Inherited property
- Partnership disputes

Property Problems
- Environmental issues
- Hazardous materials
- Zoning change
- Deferred maintenance
- Bad floor plan
- Not the highest and best use

Value-Add deals avoid the long construction timelines of new construction and the political risk of the entitlement process while still giving you a tremendous amount of upside potential. The main risks you take on a Value-Add deal are that you blow it during your remodel or lease-up, or that you hire a shitty management company. That's it. And the Fix, Fill, and Financials steps will help you get it right.

In the next chapter, you are going to select an asset class to focus on, which will dramatically impact the way you go about your investment business.

Key Reader Takeaways

- ☐ Long-term risk comes from shifts in the market which could result in a reduction in cash flow or value of your property.
- ☐ Short-term risk is risk that you don't execute your business plan properly.
- ☐ Value-Add is a term used to describe an investing strategy where we target properties we can add value to by increasing the underlying net operating income (NOI).

Chapter 5

Choose an Asset Class

Some people refer to the four types of commercial real estate properties as the "four food groups." They are called asset classes, and they include:

- Multifamily
- Retail
- Office
- Industrial

They all have their benefits, but chase two squirrels and get none. It seems counter-intuitive, but the tighter your focus, the easier getting your first deal done will be.

In this chapter, I am going to help you choose one of the four asset classes to focus on.

If you focus on learning one area of expertise, you will know the net rent rates, vacancy rates, and market cap rates to help you analyze deals with ease. But if you try to be an expert in all of them, you will fail in all because you'll have to start your market research all over again every time you look at a new property.

Redefining Commercial

Technically, apartments are considered commercial real estate, but the business processes for apartments vary dramatically from those of the other three commercial asset classes. The default position for newbies is multifamily—apartment complexes—because it is the most familiar, and they are afraid of commercial leasing. Before you skip this chapter to keep pursuing apartment deals, let me tell you a story to help you see things differently.

At one of my Commercial Investing Bootcamps where I teach new students how to apply these principles, I was driving a van full of students and could hear them discussing strategy in the back of the van. One guy was very dominant about why apartments were the best asset class, hands down, because of the "lower risk." He asserted that everyone will always need a place to live. Then he went on to talk about how he always sees commercial properties around town with For Lease signs out in front of them for long periods of time, and that he knew a "friend" who had a single-tenant commercial property that sat vacant for a couple years and ultimately put him into bankruptcy.

I have to admit his arguments seemed sound. I didn't jump in because I wanted to let him finish his argument, but I was smiling ear to ear. He could not have set me up any better for the material I was presenting after lunch! After lunch, we all arrived back at the workshop space in our headquarters, and I asked everyone what asset class they were doing. Almost every single one of them said multifamily. By the end of that day, I only had one student who still wanted to do multifamily as their primary focus.

Before I reveal the secret I told these students that changed their minds, let's discuss the four asset classes so you can understand them better.

Multifamily

These are buildings people live in.

Apartments with five or more units are commercial assets that seem like the best place to start after you've worked residential. They are solid opportunities if you can find them and create enough value in them, but you will have to work much harder than you think. The competition is brisk. You will most likely need to expand your reach into other markets to do these types of deals, so be ready to fly around the country to keep up.

Retail

These are buildings people buy things in.

Strip malls, restaurants, gas stations, or anywhere people go shopping are retail properties. Location is the most critical element for this asset class since the discretionary income of people in the area is the main thing that drives demand for this type of product. Other important things to look at are signage options, visibility, access, traffic count, and parking.

In general, I'm not a fan of retail because retail is by far the hardest asset class to value since rent rates vary dramatically. You can have two identical buildings across the street from each other renting at drastically different rates. The key to doing retail deals is having a vision and a tenant-in-tow, which means having a tenant lined up already before you close on something.

I avoid retail deals unless I can get them for pennies on the dollar, and if I do look at retail, it's usually small strip malls with multiple mom-and-pop type tenants because finding Value-Add deals with large credit tenants in place is nearly impossible.

Office

These are buildings people do white-collar work in.

Office complexes range from suburban professional buildings to downtown skyscrapers. Amenities and parking are critical here. Make sure you evaluate the parking ratio—I shoot for one car per 250 square feet as a baseline.

Location matters as well, but I like to focus on suburban Class B and C offices with multiple tenants. Having multiple tenants diversifies the risk of any one tenant defaulting—the same benefit of having an apartment complex with multiple tenants. Class B and Class C are usually older buildings that tend to be more outdated, and thus it is easier to find opportunities to do a renovation and increase rent rates and subsequently value.

Office rates will vary slightly by city, with generally higher rates in cities that have a higher median income and much higher rates as you move toward and into downtown. People care about the name of the city their business resides in. The demand driver for office space is new job creation in the area.

Industrial

These are buildings people make or store things in.

Industrial properties include warehouses, manufacturing, research and development, and flex. These buildings may have one or more space types within them that each rent at a different rate. Different space types include:

1. Warehouse
2. Production/Manufacturing
3. Office/Showroom

Office or showroom space costs the most to build out because it has framed walls and drop ceilings, so it rents for a higher price per square foot. The production or manufacturing space is just a warehouse that is heated and cooled year-round, so it rents at slightly higher rates than the warehouse space that is usually just heated in the winter.

The demand driver for industrial properties is new blue-collar jobs. Critical elements are the availability of labor and freeway access. The farther from the freeway it is, the less desirable it will be for tenants.

I've owned properties in all four asset classes, but my favorite product is the multi-tenant industrial flex space. I call it the mullet of real estate: showroom or office in the front and warehouse in the back. These small-bay warehouse spaces are easy to fill with great tenants like contractors, car service companies, or anyone who has outgrown their garage and wants a warehouse they can drive their truck into and do office work out of as well. If you're undecided, go with this type of product.

Pro Tip

Retail, office, and industrial buildings are generally priced per square foot. Apartment properties are generally priced per door. This price per unit method is often referred to as "price per pound" in the industry.

Mixed-Use

A building can have more than one type of asset class. That is called a "Mixed-Use" property. The different asset classes will have a clear delineation, like retail on the first floor and apartments or offices above. Please note that an industrial flex building is not a mixed-use building because there are not multiple asset types clearly delineated from each other. It's just that any one given space can be modified to be a warehouse or office within that space itself.

I love mixed-use properties because other people really struggle to evaluate them, and therein lies the opportunity to buy properties for significantly less than their true value. Evaluating these mixed-use properties is actually quite simple: divide and conquer! Each space type will have a different rent rate, vacancy rate, and market cap rate. Break the building into its different space types, evaluate each type independently, and then add them together at the end.

Don't Mistake Comfort for Opportunity

So what did I say to those students who had decided on multifamily?

"You're blinded by your knowledge gap and mistaking comfort for opportunity."

The reality is that you are comfortable filling apartments because you know how to rent to individuals. Most of you have flipped or rented a house, so renting a building with fifty houses inside it seems comfortable too. In order to fill commercial buildings, you imagine needing a commercial network. And if you're a small entrepreneur who hates the idea of having to suck up to corporate bigwigs, you want to opt out of commercial as much as possible.

Here's what made the difference for that class: because apartments have a higher demand, you have to pay a lot more than you would for a warehouse or office building with the same NOI. Because you pay more for the same NOI, you have to take on far more debt with the same income to pay that debt. And *this* means the apartments actually pose more real risk from a financial standpoint, even though they are perceived as less risky from a demand standpoint.

You can usually absorb 30–50 percent vacancy on warehouse and office buildings and still have enough cash to pay your mortgage. Whereas you may only be able to absorb 10–20 percent vacancy on an apartment before you can't pay your mortgage.

I also reminded them that you can either spend all day working with cool entrepreneurs and business owners, or spend all day dealing with deadbeat renters.

I could see the bells going off in their heads, as I imagine is happening for you right now. If everyone is walking east, you can either join the crowd and fight to see the same scenery as everyone else...or you can look west and find the opportunity everyone else is walking away from.

Selecting a Market

Selecting a market to invest in is easy: invest in the metropolitan area closest to where you live.

For your first deal, I recommend you stay close to home for a variety of reasons. When you invest close to home, you can visit the property, meet the owner or broker, and see for yourself what renovations need to be done. When you start investing outside your market, you have to put systems in place to get other people to inspect the property and estimate your repairs. This requires effort and creates risk if not done effectively. I think it's important you start by investing in your local market, and then you can expand geographically, if and when you have the systems in place to do so.

Conclusion of Part 1

In the first part of this book, you created an investing strategy. You threw out your limiting beliefs and learned why commercial is so much better than residential. You adopted the strategy of targeting multi-tenant, Value-Add commercial properties in the industrial and office sectors in your local market and are convinced that buy and hold is the best long-term strategy for wealth and cash flow. Of course, you'll remain open to a flip or wholesale if it makes sense.

It's okay if you choose to be a passive investor and just put your money into deals or if you want to go after retail or apartments—whatever fits your needs best.

Now that you have your strategy clearly defined in your head, let's learn the system to go out and execute on it.

Key Takeaways

- ☐ Choose one asset class to focus on and your market research will go further.
- ☐ Don't mistake comfort for opportunity. Apartments are sexy, but that means you'll pay more for the same income, have a harder time finding deals, and take on a higher risk of default.
- ☐ Multi-tenant industrial and suburban office buildings provide the greatest opportunity and are the asset classes Mike focuses on.
- ☐ By choosing a market close to home, it will be easier to become an expert.

Part 2
System

You learned to face your fears of commercial real estate and decided if you wanted to be an active investor doing all the work or a passive investor who just puts money into deals. You learned why the Value-Add strategy is the fastest way to increase your net worth and create a steady stream of income. You learned that the smartest investors wholesale, flip, and do rentals so they can get active income to eat today and create residual income to achieve financial freedom. Lastly, you chose an asset class and market to focus on.

Congratulations! You have the foundation of a strategy! Now let's dive into the seven steps to apply that strategy toward a new challenge that will ultimately create freedom. They are:

1. Find
2. Figure
3. Fund
4. Fix
5. Fill
6. Financials
7. Freedom

The second half of the book goes beyond these steps as concepts and gives you the exact process I have used to buy multiple assets and create millions in equity. Each of the seven steps has its own components, and they are not always linear. Here's the best way to use this system without getting lost in it.

First, read the whole book. Bounce around as you need to, but make sure you read and understand every chapter, but skip the action items. Then come back and read the book again. This time, read it one chapter at a time and actually do the action items for each chapter before moving on to the next. The Center Drive property can serve as your template as you work through the spreadsheets and exercises that accompany each step.

You don't need a $50,000 course from a guru to go do your first deal. All you need is a good strategy and this system. If you follow it, you will own a commercial real estate asset that replaces your full-time income by the end of this year.

Chapter 6

Case Study

We are going to follow a real property as we move through the seven steps so that you can see how each step applies to a real-world property.

The Center Drive property is the very first deal I ever did in commercial real estate. As we go through the seven steps, we'll reference this case study throughout them all, so you can see how each step applies to this real-world example.

I will take you through this deal step by step, and you will emerge with a mastery level understanding of the seven-step process.

Let's talk about the basics of the deal.

It was a twenty thousand-square-foot industrial flex building that had showrooms and offices in the front and drive-in doors in the back. As I mentioned before, this is by far my favorite type of product because there are so many different types of businesses that want to rent these spaces. The demand is insane.

My partner found this property listed on the MLS, of all places. It had ten units that ranged in size from one thousand to three thousand square feet (SF) each, and they were all occupied. The owner was an elderly gentleman who only had a few months left to live (God rest his soul).

The leases were all short-term leases: either month-to-month or less than a year left on them. The lease documents stated that the landlord was supposed to pay all of the expenses except the utilities, but the owner wasn't enforcing this clause well and was paying the water bills for the tenants.

At first glance, you could see that the property needed a roof and looked very tired on the outside. The electrical was all messed up. Wiring and plumbing ran between units so tenants were fighting over who should be paying for what meters. After interviewing the tenants, we found out that some tenants wanted more space, and some wanted out of their leases.

The average gross rent rate on the leases was $5.50 per square foot per year, which generated $110,000 each year in income. The expenses were $70,000 so the current NOI was around $40,000. It was being offered at $800,000 which was a 5% cap rate.

The market cap rates for this type of property in this area were 7–9% depending on the financial condition and tenant mix. So the 5% cap rate it was being offered at was very low for the market, making it appear to be very overpriced (we cover cap rates and the numbers in the Figure step, so don't worry if you don't know what it is yet or how to calculate it).

Set the numbers aside for a minute. Can you see the problems here that can be solved to create value in the property?

What I saw that the other investors didn't was that the lease rent rates were at an average gross rate of $5.50 and the market was $8.00. The goal is to buy properties that are NOT stabilized. Stabilized means market-rate occupancy at *market-rate* rents. Even though this property was fully occupied, it was not yet stabilized because the rents were very depressed. I also realized the tenants were supposed to be paying the utilities, but the landlord was not collecting.

I paid $700,000 for the property and spent $75,000 cleaning it up, so I was all in at $775,000. I increased the NOI from $40,000 to $100,000 in two years. The increase in the NOI that we achieved came from driving the rent rates up as leases renewed, billing the utilities back to the tenants, and fixing major problems so the annual repairs and maintenance budget decreased significantly.

I refinanced with an appraisal value of $1,250,000 and got all of my money back out of it and now enjoy a residual income of around $50,000 per year on that property, with no capital into it. Plus, if I ever sell it, I will walk away with a half-million-dollar paycheck.

Everyone else kept telling me I overpaid and got screwed on the deal because I bought it at a 5.7% cap rate when the market cap rates were 7–9%. If that's what getting screwed means, I hope it happens again soon!

Most investors in our market politely took a pass on Center Drive, and I would have too, if my partner didn't help me out with it. I can't emphasize how important having a coach or a mentor is, especially when you are getting started.

I have to be honest; at the time, I had no clue what a deal even looked like. I remember bringing a small twenty-four hundred-square-foot vacant condo listed at $100 per square foot to that first partner and asking if it could have potential. He laughed at me and said, "Dude, you have no clue what you're doing, do you?"

I bowed my head, found my humility, and said, "No, I don't. Please show me how you filter the good ones out from the garbage."

I knew I had to create a method for valuing properties quickly, and I left his office determined to create a system that allowed me to do that.

It took three years, but it's the system I have now. It revolutionized my ability to create equity and cash flow from commercial real estate. It's the 7 Steps to Freedom, through commercial real estate investing, and I'm going to unlock its secrets to you right now.

Step 1
Find

The Find step is the first and most important because it's all about finding properties to make offers on. Without leads, you don't have a business.

Find is broken down into two parts:

- Create Prospecting Lists
- Make Contacts

You'll identify lists of property owners, business owners, and brokers in your market. Then, you will contact the owners and brokers to schedule tours for properties you are interested in making an offer on.

If you are looking to buy only one property, you may just want to hire a broker to find you that one deal, and you'll skip this step altogether. However, if you want to be able to consistently find deals on your own—if you want to set up a real estate investing business—this marketing step is critical.

Chapter 7

Create Prospecting Lists

FIND

Objective: Create Property Owner and Broker Prospecting Lists

Two lumberjacks had a contest to see who could cut down more trees in a day. One went out and started chopping down trees right away. He did quite well, but he grew weary throughout the day. The second lumberjack sat down for the first two hours of the day and sharpened his axe. Although he spent much less *time* cutting down trees, each tree only took a fraction of the effort and he was able to cut down many more than the first lumberjack did that day.

When I first set out with the goal of buying a commercial building, I was like the first lumberjack with regard to analyzing properties, and I suspect up until now, you have been too.

You're running around like a chicken with your head cut off. You have no process. You might look at multifamily one day and warehouses the next. You'll surf the endless trenches of the internet scouring for a deal or read any offering a broker sends you.

It's great that you're doing the activity. There's only one problem: you have no clue what a good deal even looks like! You just know you want to buy *something*.

Eventually, I learned to be more like the second lumberjack, and you should too.

In this chapter, I'm going to show you how to create a property prospecting list with the mailing addresses, phone numbers, and emails of property owners and brokers so you can roll out a direct marketing sequence to them. Creating a contact list of all the commercial properties and brokers in your area is a critical first step if you want to fast-track your results. A solid list is worth a million dollars—literally.

Prospecting Software

There are tons of services out there you can use to help you prospect for owners, but I don't recommend them. There is one major problem with software for prospecting: they have a limit on the number of records you can export at any one time, usually 500.

Why? Because they make their money off your monthly subscription. They know if they let you download the entire database, you would do that on day one and cancel the subscription. It makes sense for *them*, but it creates a problem for *you*. You can't do mass marketing with only 500 records. Sure, you could do 500 per month, but that's not enough contacts to get your first deal. If you choose to use one of these systems, such as CoStar or Reonomy, you'll be stuck calling one owner at a time and not being able to track your data very well.

In short, you won't own your success and you won't be able to scale up.

Instead, here is a process to get the list for *all* of the properties in your county that match your criteria:

1. Obtain the parcel data in spreadsheet format.
2. Combine your lists into one.
3. Filter your lists.
4. Append the data with a manager name.
5. Skip trace the manager for phone, email, social media links, and mailing address.
6. Scrub your list to remove any bad numbers or bounce-back emails.

This process will allow you to own your own data and it will unlock your ability to take massive action.

Pro Tip

You can hire someone on fiverr.com or upwork.com to do the data entry and manipulation for you, or you can hire a list broker to do it for a fee.

---

1. OBTAIN THE PARCEL DATA IN SPREADSHEET FORMAT

It's the age of technology. Did you know that most counties in the country have gone to digital land records—that is, you can usually get a spreadsheet with the relevant data for every single parcel in that county for free?

Merry Christmas!

Google, "_____ County parcel data." You *might* find a downloadable version of the parcel data in .xls or .csv format right on the county website, though most counties make it a little more difficult than that! They normally have GIS data, so you would need to buy a GIS mapping software, pull the data in, and then export it to spreadsheet format.

If you pull half your head of hair out before getting results, then try this method: Call the county information line and ask who handles the GIS open parcel data. Then send that person a gift card to Starbucks, and they will be your best friend. (Only slightly kidding.) Get that person on the phone or email and ask them how you can get your hands on a spreadsheet version (.xls or .csv) of the public county parcel data. Not the GIS data. Most times this information is free, but if they charge you a small fee to help you get it, be glad to pay it. Do not pre-filter the data before you download it. Have them send you the entire dataset for now.

2. COMBINE YOUR LISTS INTO ONE

Keep working with the county until you get your hands on a spreadsheet file. If your list for your primary target county doesn't contain at least two thousand commercial properties, get another county and combine the lists using copy and paste. Be sure to not screw up the data when you do this by getting the columns intermixed or by sorting the data without selecting all of the records first. If you only sort one column without having the whole dataset selected, all your data will get jumbled.

Sometimes the data doesn't come through the exact same for each county. One county might have city, state, and zip all in one column, and one might have separate columns. I recommend organizing the data into easy columns and eliminating any columns you don't need, to make your file smaller and more manageable.

A spreadsheet program like Google Sheets or Microsoft Excel will work to get you started, but a true database software is the best option.

Most CRMs like Hubspot, MailChimp, ActiveCampaign, and Salesforce are just glorified spreadsheets. They are not true database applications where you can set up complex relationships between data. For example, you may have one owner that owns multiple properties (one-to-many), or you may have multiple owners for multiple properties (many-to-many).

A spreadsheet will work, but if you have the same owner who owns multiple properties, you'll have duplicates of that owner's information. That in itself can create issues later on when you are skip tracing. So if you really want to set yourself up for long-term success, I recommend you consider a true database application. I custom built a database software for my team and franchisees that pulls the data directly from the county, because I wasn't happy with having to go through this process over and over.

Whether you use a spreadsheet, a basic CRM, or a true database application doesn't matter—what does matter is that you do the work. If you are on a budget, just use a spreadsheet, but if you want to set yourself up now so you don't have to redo any work later, then spend more time sharpening your axe here, and find a custom database where you can set up the complex relationships between the properties, the LLCs that own those properties, and the asset managers who manage those LLCs that you ultimately need to contact.

Property → Ownership Entity (LLC) → Manager of LLC

3. FILTER YOUR LISTS

Filter your spreadsheet using key metrics: property type and tax assessed value.[1]

Earlier in this book, you identified which asset class you wanted to focus on. Asset class, zoning, and classification are all similar, but not the same.

For most cities, the property *zoning* is set at the city level. Each city uses different naming conventions for zoning codes. Light Industrial I-1 zoning in one city may have a very different set of permitted and conditional uses than that same zoning in another city.

Your county data will likely have a column that says something like property classification, property type, or use type that won't fit nicely into any of the four asset class buckets, nor will it match the zoning type that the city actually has for the property, which is what really matters. You will get frustrated. Expect it.

What's important is that you learn what your city and county's naming conventions are and then filter your list by them as best you can. For example, in my target county, they simply have C—Commercial, R5—Multifamily, and I—Industrial.

Since my primary asset class is Industrial, I filter by that property type in my spreadsheet to remove the single-family houses, apartments, and commercial properties.

---

1   If you don't know how to set up a data filter on a spreadsheet, there are lots of tutorials on the internet for how to do it. This is worth learning to do well—your job will be much easier with this skillset.

The C—Commercial classification includes office buildings and retail, so you can't decipher between retail and office properties using my county data; I would need to target both or neither.

Next, what size of property are you going to go after? Most county data will not include the property square footage for commercial buildings. If they don't, be sure to add that column so you can start tracking the size of these assets. What they will include is the assessed value, so you can sort by that instead.

I recommend starting with properties assessed between $500,000 and $2,000,000. Anything smaller than that will probably yield you the same results as flipping a house, and anything larger than that might overwhelm you on your first deal.

4. APPEND DATA WITH THE MANAGER NAME
Add columns for these items in your spreadsheet or database:

- Manager First Name
- Manager Last Name
- Manager Phone
- Manager Email
- Manager Mailing Address
- Manager Facebook Page Link
- Manager LinkedIn Page Link

Most commercial properties are owned by an LLC. Even though the IRS views an LLC as a person, it can't answer the phone or respond to your email. Therefore, you need to figure out who is really in charge. Sometimes the taxpayer name on the parcel spreadsheet is a real person. If it is, use that. If it isn't, go to the Secretary of State website for the state your property is in. Beware, your state may have a different way of organizing the public business filings, so figure out how they do it in the state you are targeting.

Do a business search for the name of the LLC or corporation that owns the property. If the business was formed in your state, then there *will* be a record. Beware of spelling or grammar differences, and make sure you look at active and inactive records. Click through to the details and see if there is an individual named as the "registered agent" or "manager" or something like that. Copy their name and address to your spreadsheet.

If you can't locate the LLC in your state records, it may have been formed in another state or spelled differently than it shows on the county data you have in your spreadsheet. If that happens, have your skip tracer look up the LLC and get the manager's name for you.

5. SKIP TRACE THE MANAGER

Skip tracing is the process of locating an individual and obtaining their contact information. You can skip trace the registered agent for a home address, phone number, email, and social media links using a reputable skip tracing software or a virtual assistant. I batch process them using a virtual assistant or a bot I had created to automate this process. We skip trace so that we can actually contact these people by phone, text, email, and social media. Without this step, you'll be limited to contacting them by direct mail.

6. SCRUB YOUR LIST

Skip tracing will yield a lot of potential numbers and emails. It's not an exact science. You should use a mailing address, phone, and email list scrubbing service to remove any duplicate owners, undeliverable addresses, disconnected numbers, and bounce-back emails. This part will reduce wasted money on mail sent to a bad address and increase your overall success when you contact them.

> ## Pro Tip
>
> Download a screen recording app for your computer and do a narrated screen record of you completing this process where you explain what you are doing as you go. Use that video to find a good virtual assistant to do this task for you. It's much easier to *show* them what to do through a narrated video than it is to *tell* them what to do in a written scope of work.

You can use a similar process to create a broker list. You can pull the data from your local commercial association of Realtors® or have a VA (virtual assistant) find a way to pull the list. Keep a list of every real estate agent/broker in your area with a mailing address, phone number, email, and social media links, especially LinkedIn.

Creating this list is your way of sharpening the axe. Spend time and money here to make this as good as possible. With a solid list, you will have the power to get property owners and brokers calling you directly versus having to call them. It will also allow you to take massive action with little effort.

> **Small Action = Small Results. Massive Action = Massive Results.**

Based on the law of averages, my studies show that you need around two thousand people on your list to get your first deal done. I'll show you why in the next chapter. Once you have a full list of at least two thousand properties with owner contact information, and you have a list of every broker and agent in your market, then you are ready to start contacting them.

In the next chapter, I'm going to give you a proven direct marketing sequence that works. But in order to implement it, you have to build your own list in a spreadsheet or database. You can't achieve that by renting someone else's data. So if you want small results, rent someone else's data, start making one-off contacts, and skip all of this. If you want to be able to send mass communication to get thirty, forty, or fifty property owners calling you every month trying to sell you their property, start making your list today.

Key Reader Takeaways

☐ Build a list from scratch using county parcel data instead of renting someone else's data.

☐ Use Virtual Assistants, Bots, Jobbers, or List Vendors to help do the "busy work."

☐ Have at least two thousand filtered records with phone, email, address, and social media links.

Action Items

☐ Get the county parcel list spreadsheets.

☐ Find a VA to combine, filter, skip trace, and scrub the list for you.

☐ Do a similar process to create a broker prospecting list.

☐ If you want bonus points, have your VA make a list of every small business in town with owner name and contact information. It will come in handy in the Fill step.

Chapter 8

Make Contacts

Objective: Schedule a Tour with a Property Owner

I was with my wife waiting for the elevator to reach our floor when the phone rang. We were going to tour some condos and had strongly considered moving to Florida to start fresh. Minnesota winters wear on you.

I looked down at the screen and instantly recognized the name that popped up. It was the same business broker who had called me three times before. The first time he called me, I told him he was nuts. Who in their right mind would ever want to buy a small remodeling company?

The second time, he caught me right as I was walking into a meeting, and I simply said, "No, thank you" and hung up. The third time, I think I said something along the line of, "Dude, take me off your list."

This was his fourth call. His pitch was the same, but my motivation wasn't the same because I had my mind set on moving to Florida.

I asked, "How much do you think you can sell my company for?" He gave me some ballpark figures. I thought he was full of shit, so I told him I'd sign the listing agreement right now if he could get me that kind of money, and I set the appointment with him.

That appointment resulted in me listing my remodeling business for sale, and it sold for seven figures seven months later. That sale gave me the nudge I needed to transition from residential to commercial real estate. I'm grateful he made the fourth call. His perseverance paid off. Big time. For me and for him.

What's interesting about this story is that he didn't change his pitch. I changed my motivation!

You will be calling on property owners, and they may treat you just like I treated this guy. They will tell you they are not interested. Don't believe them. Don't take them off the list, and most importantly, don't take it personally. Thank them for their time and set a reminder to call them back on a different day.

Maybe you will catch them standing at an elevator someday.

> **A no is not a no forever. It means not right now, or not the way you presented it.**

Sustenance Strategies

I know what you're thinking: *Mike, I was really liking your book until you told me I would have to cold call.*

I hear you, buddy, and I've got great news for you—you *don't* have to cold call! You *do* have to roll out a proven marketing sequence that allows you to make massive contacts, and all in a sustainable way.

> **Taking consistent, massive action on your lists is the key to filling your deal pipeline.**

In this chapter, I'm going to give you a strategy that has worked for me to get millions of dollars of properties under contract. I call this the sustenance strategy, and it's one you'll be able to tweak to meet your needs.

Why sustenance? Because you need to eat. Food, in this case, is a meeting with a property owner who is motivated to sell, and there are four ways to eat:

1. Gather food
2. Go hunting
3. Catch a fish
4. Plant seeds

Let's cover these four basic sustenance strategies, then the top tactics you can use to roll out this plan.

Marketing Strategy Overview

Strategy	What	Who	Tactics
Gathering	Listings	Brokers	Listing Sites Yard Signs Direct Marketing
Hunting	Prospecting	Property Owners	Direct Marketing
Fishing	Advertising	Property Owners	Signs Social Media
Farming	Relationships	Existing Tenants Bankers Attorneys CPAs Financial Advisors	Golf Broker Events Broker Opens Direct Marketing

GATHERING (LISTINGS)

Someone else already created this meal, and you just have to pick it up. Gather the low-hanging fruit—properties that are listed for sale by the property owner or their brokers. Analyze these properties first, since you already know the owner wants to sell. Our case study, Center Drive, was listed for sale by another broker and sat on the market for several months. Roughly half of the properties I purchase are formally listed for sale, while the other half never hit the market.

Set up auto searches on listing platforms like LoopNet, Craigslist, and the MLS to be notified whenever new properties hit the market. Make friends with one really good broker who will also set you up on auto searches for your local commercial exchange (the equivalent of the commercial MLS) if you have one in your area.

Call every For Sale sign in town and see what's happening with them. You can even roll out a direct marketing sequence (I'll show you this sequence in a minute) to your broker list to become top of mind for them so they start bringing you premarket opportunities.

The key here is knowing what kind of food to gather and what kind of food to skip over, then convincing brokers you are the real deal. Being able to write offers quickly and actually close on those offers with as little pain as possible will work in your favor.

Pro Tip

If you come across a listing that says, "Great owner-user opportunity," that will typically mean the building is overpriced for you as a financial buyer and won't pencil out well.

HUNTING (PROSPECTING)

Here, you will hunt property owners down to secure off-market deals. This happens using a proven direct marketing sequence of direct mail, ringless voicemail, text, and email campaigns to get property owners coming to you directly and allowing you to leverage the lists you built to take massive action.

Hunting takes more time and money than gathering but generates the best deals out of all four tactics. The key is having the right weapon and doing enough activity that the numbers fall in place. If you catch the right people at the right time and show them how you can save them a commission, the hunt will pay off.

FISHING (ADVERTISING)

As you grow, fishing for property owners via advertising will amplify your deal pipeline. If you have a lot of cash, this is a good strategy. If you don't, you may skip this one.

Consider a billboard or newspaper, TV, and radio ads. You can also start advertising on Facebook, LinkedIn, and Google to try to catch property owners.

The key is having a shiny lure and being in the right place at the right time (multiple times, so they finally pick up the phone and call you). This strategy doesn't typically generate as many direct leads, but it creates a brand for your company and increases the success ratio of the other tactics.

FARMING (RELATIONSHIPS)

Cultivate relationships with anyone who advises or provides service to commercial property owners. These include bankers, attorneys, CPAs, and financial advisors, but could also include lots of other types of professionals. I call these people channel partners.

Roll out a proven, direct marketing sequence to them or network with them at other events that they might attend. The key to this strategy is showing them how you can solve problems for their clients, and in doing so, make them look good.

Sustenance Tactics

The sustenance strategy is a powerful marketing strategy, and you might have noticed that it employs different tactics to generate leads. Let's go through each of them and see how they apply to the four strategies to generate leads.

LISTING PLATFORMS

Get inside the brain of a motivated seller. Where do they go when they want to sell their property? They either list it for sale themselves or hire a broker. This is low-hanging fruit to gather up because you already know they want to sell. The question is whether they are motivated and if there is a problem you can solve—that's it.

Owners who have distressed properties often don't want to admit they are having issues, so they try to rent the vacancies or list their property for-sale-by-owner. There are ways to fish for these owners, such as searching the For Sale section of Craigslist. It seems counterintuitive, but check the For Rent section too. Call to see if they have ever considered doing a master lease, contract for deed, or just selling outright.

For the MLS, Craigslist, and LoopNet, set up auto searches for properties that meet your criteria so you're notified when new listings hit. Call the agents for each listing and introduce yourself. Get on their buyers list and give them your buying criteria. Take advantage of every call to every broker as an opportunity to start developing a relationship for them to bring you premarket deals, and for you to pay them a commission in return.

SIGNAGE

Drive around the areas you want to buy in and call all of the For Lease and For Sale signs to see what people have going on. Don't sound too eager to buy something, but let them know you are the real deal, have capital, and can close quickly if you can arrive at a fair agreement that works for both sides.

SOCIAL MEDIA

I have to be honest—the social media strategy works, but only sparingly. You will not get massive results. With limited time each day to make a difference, will you have more impact spending two hours calling property owners and brokers, or spending two hours noodling around on Facebook? You already know the answer! Change your title and let people in your sphere know what you do, but don't waste too much time here.

NETWORKING EVENTS

Networking is a great farming tactic for long-term results but rarely yields an immediate return. I use networking events to find limited partners and tenants and to network with people who know other property owners.

Show up and join a networking group. Show up and play a random round of golf with someone you don't know. They may also have capital they want to invest in your deals.

Don't spend all of your time here. Farming yields a long-term harvest. Grow your network with people, stay in contact with them, and send them business proactively whenever possible. Networking is giving, not getting, and it's promised in the Bible that a harvest will come eventually if your heart is for helping others.

DIRECT MARKETING

Direct marketing is nothing more than directly contacting your target customer. You will use these tactics to target property owners, brokers, referral partners, and eventually tenants.

There's a magic sequence I use that you can use to hunt for property owners:

- Direct mail (wait thirty days)
- Second piece of direct mail
- Connection request on LinkedIn with Message (wait thirty days)

- Email (wait fifteen days)
- Text (wait fifteen days)
- Ringless voicemail (wait three days)
- Call

Most people make one or two contacts and then give up. Remember the business broker who got the meeting with me on the fourth call? It's a valid strategy. A Harvard study showed that the response rate increases at an increasing rate with each subsequent contact. This means your chance of getting a response increases dramatically as you hit a person the fourth, fifth, and sixth times. Wait some time in between, but definitely hit them multiple times.

In addition to consistency, you have to be able to take massive action to hit lots of people with little effort. Making five calls a week isn't going to get you there. Sending out a thousand pieces of direct mail, two thousand emails, and five hundred ringless voicemails every month might—and you can do all of those in just a few hours each week. There are various tools you can rent to do these tasks, but the best ones allow you to do all of them under one software so your data is organized, and you can track your activity across multiple platforms.

DIRECT MAIL

A top broker in our market once called to say he had just received a copy of a piece of mail I had sent several of his clients (I didn't know they were his clients). I said, "Great! Are the properties listed for sale?" He said no, and that he would appreciate me not reaching out to his clients ever again. Then he proceeded to explain to me that there is a gentlemen's agreement in town about not contacting other people's clients. Had I known they were his clients, I would not have contacted them, but that's when I knew my strategy was good. It was so good that this guy took time out of his day to try and scare me into stopping my marketing campaign. Challenge accepted! I'm sending out twice as much mail now and getting more leads than ever before.

This is why you need to put a direct mail campaign in place:

- You can hit everyone on your list with one round of mailers.
- It gives you a reason to call later.
- They are calling you, so you hold the power.
- You are using a strategy of attraction, not promotion.

You are probably wondering what to write on the piece of mail itself. Keep it simple—one page—and make it look professional.

> Dear Bill,
>
> I'm contacting you because land records show you own the property at _____. I'm an investor who buys properties, and I'm easy to sell a property to. We can pay all cash and close quickly, or structure a deal on the terms that work best for you.
>
> When you sell to me, you save a commission. I will have an offer to you within forty-eight hours of you requesting one, guaranteed. It will be in plain language. Call me or go to our webpage to request your offer.
>
> Sincerely,
>
> Your Name

Don't overcomplicate it. Make it compelling and simple.

Send a second piece of direct mail about a month later with a similar message, this time telling them you are following up because you haven't heard from them. I also recommend requesting to be added to their network on LinkedIn at the same time, so they can research you to provide an additional level of comfort. Make sure your LinkedIn page looks professional, has a nice headshot, and contains some real estate-related posts at the top of your feed.

Online services cost around $1.00 per piece of mail, and you'll need to send two thousand pieces of mail to do your first deal. If you do it yourself, you can cut the cost in half, but it's a ridiculous amount of work. I only recommend printing yourself if you or your neighbor has a child who wants to earn some extra cash for the bike they've had their eye on. I'm sure the child labor people are going to come after me, but I'm okay with you teaching our youth how to make an honest buck.

If you do want to do it yourself, get a printer that can fold the letters too. Buy envelopes with the windows on them and just print the addresses on the letter so you don't have to address the envelope. Learn how to use the Mail Merge feature in Microsoft Word so you can write one letter but print them as personalized letters from the data in your property owner list. A bulk mail permit will save a ton of dough as well.

MASS EMAIL

If they haven't responded after two letters, I hit them with an email. And don't worry—nobody wants to read your perfectly formatted email. HTML formatting looks like spam. Just send a normal email from Gmail or whatever you use, and copy your email list right into the bcc field so none of them can see the other people on the email.

Your email should be a follow-up on the letters you sent, using no more than two sentences.

> Hi _____,
> I'm following up on the commercial property you own that I sent you a couple letters about. We were interested in making you an offer. Did you get my letters?
> Your Name

As long as it looks like you wrote them a personal email in simple text format, you will get a high response rate. I use this tactic to blast email my broker list as well, saying something like:

> Hi _____,
> We just sold some assets recently and are in a position to take down another deal in the next ninety days. I'd love to pay you a commission. Do you have anything we should be looking at?
> Mike

MASS TEXT

Text messages are money! Studies show people respond to text messages at much higher response rates than regular mail, email, or even a phone call.

Did you know you can send an email to someone's phone as a text? I recommend subscribing to a text messaging platform to send out text messages. All you need to do is upload your property owner prospecting spreadsheet and then craft your message—keep it simple, same as the email—and it will do all the behind-the-scenes work for you.

RINGLESS VOICEMAIL

You can make fifty calls per day, or you can make 5,000 calls with the click of a button. I use a ringless voicemail service and send this out to the property owner and broker lists with slightly different messages. It costs a small fee, but what is your time worth?

I prerecord a voicemail that says something along the lines of:

> Hi, it's Mike Sowers. I was calling to follow up on that letter I sent about the offer we have for you on your building. I haven't been able to reach you. Please call me back so we can talk about this offer we have for you on this building.

CALLING

When all else fails, pick up the phone! Calling will put you on the map. If all you have is time and no money, make your list and start calling right away. If you load your list into a dialer service, you will spend more time on the phone and less time dialing and waiting.

I'm going to add something that sounds counterintuitive here: leave your sales hat at home! Success comes from making *enough* calls, not from what you say when you call. If your heart is in the right place, your words will come out in a way that communicates it.

Why are you calling this person? Because your group wants to acquire another asset in the next ninety days, and you think their property might be a great fit. Have they ever considered selling?

Don't try and beat around the bush. This is business-to-business sales here—not at all like working with homeowners. They will appreciate your candor and brevity.

Volume Wins in the End

My book writing mentor, Tucker Max, told me the story of a ceramics teacher who split his class in half and told them he was going to grade them each differently. The first half would be graded on the quality of their best pot. The second half would be graded on the weight of all of their pots combined.

At the end of the semester, he flipped the script and told everyone that they were all actually being graded the same way—based on quality. To the teacher's amazement, the second group had far better pots, because they had made a lot of them and gotten good at it. But the first group was so concerned about the quality of their pots, they spent the whole semester trying to make one pot perfect. The moral of the story is that if you get too caught up in the quality of your strategy or your calls, you will be like the first group.

Think like the second group and judge your performance on the sheer volume of outreach you do.

Set a small, obtainable goal first—like talking to five owners each day, Monday through Friday. Commitment is much more important than skill at this point in the game. If you just did that, you would be a winner in the end. You will naturally get better as you go. It is all about quantity, and the quality will come with time.

Tips for Making Calls

If you're still worried, let me give you a few pointers on how to do an effective call so you don't blow it completely:

- Read the property details from your database or spreadsheet before you call and maybe even take a look at the building on Google Earth.
  - Who owns it?
  - When did they buy it and for how much?
  - What's the tax-assessed value?
  - How many square feet is it?
  - What type of building is it?

The Calling Script

OPENING

Hi, is this Bill? You own the property at 8409 Center Drive, right?

REASON FOR CALLING

My name is Mike Sowers. I'm an investor with Commercial Investors Group, and I'm calling to follow up on the letter I sent you. Did you get it?

QUICK RAPPORT

Okay, great! (Or "okay no worries" if they didn't.) Well, we are looking to acquire one more asset here in the next ninety days, and I was wondering if you had ever considered selling?

DISCOVERY

Objection 1: "Yes, it's listed."

   "Cool, who is your broker?"

   "Okay, can I have their contact information? (Schedule through broker.)

Objection 2: "Yes, for the right price."

"I can appreciate that for sure."

- Is it listed with a broker?
- How many square feet?
- Who are the tenants?
- Any vacancies?
- Any major repairs you know of?
- What were you hoping to get out of it?
- What were you realistically expecting to get for it?
- If I got you all cash and a quick closing, what is the lowest you would take?

"Okay, it looks like it might be a fit..." (Go to close.)

Objection 3: "No, we are cash flowing."

"That's awesome! How long have you owned it for?"

"Well, say, Bill, I drum up off-market opportunities all the time. Are you ever looking for off-market deals?"

If yes—get their details and put them on the wholesale buyer's list, or see if they have any additional capital they are ever looking to get into deals. (Some of my best investors come from calling sellers.)

If no—say, "Well, I appreciate your time. If it's okay, I will send you my contact information in case your situation ever changes. Can you confirm your email address?"

Objection 4: "No, and don't ever call me again."

"Okay, no worries. We have other properties we are looking at. I just thought you might want to chat about it. How about I send you my information in case your situation ever changes and you want to do an off-market deal and save a commission?"

Yes—send an email.

No—Thank them politely and hang up.

CLOSE AND SCHEDULE THE APPOINTMENT

"I tell you what, Bill. How about I come out there and take a quick peek at the property? You can show me any work that needs to be done, I can grab a little info from you, and then I can get a real, solid offer in your hands. Then you can decide if it makes sense or not. How does your week look?"

No, just send me an offer and I'll consider it.

"I could do that, but then I'd be wasting both of our time because I would have to change the offer once I get the information I need to actually evaluate the deal. I want to get you a real offer at a real price that I can close at. Let's just meet and see what I can do. How does your week look?"

CONFIRM DETAILS

Ask the seller to send you a copy of the floor plans, rent roll, and historic expenses in advance so you can be prepared for the meeting. If they refuse your request, don't push too hard for it. It's more important to get the meeting than it is to get the data at this point in the process.

Create a calendar event and send a pre-appointment email confirmation. The pre-appointment email you send them should set expectations for what will happen when you arrive for the property tour (we cover this in a bit). Be sure to enter their data into your database/spreadsheet, especially an email address, because then you can upload those lists to Facebook for Facebook-targeted ads.

Tips for Scheduling Tours

My marketing manager was training a new appointment setter at my construction company. The appointment setter was down on his luck and had gotten some rude "nos" on his first day.

Robert simply said, "No worries, **SW³N**." The appointment setter looked up at him confused.

Even I didn't know what he was talking about, so I poked my head around the corner to see how this one would play out.

Robert looked him dead in the eye and said, "Some Will. Some Won't. So What? Next Call!"

You have to learn how to be resilient to the word NO, because your journey will be filled with them. Reframe them as invitations to ask questions, learn, and try again on a different day. This is why I try to set activity-based goals instead of results-based goals. You can control how many calls you make, how many emails you send, and how many envelopes you make the neighbor kid stuff your letters into—you can't control the responses. Do what you can and leave the rest to God.

HAVE A CLEAR REASON FOR CALLING.

This is why I like sending the piece of direct mail first, so I can simply follow up on the mail I sent. Other reasons you could use for contacting them are:

- We own some property in the area.
- We live in the area.
- We have some extra capital we are looking to deploy.
- I saw the For Lease sign out front.
- We have a mutual friend _____ (use LinkedIn to find mutual friends).
- I have extra tenants (you will, after you have a property with a For Lease sign out front).

MAKE IT CLEAR YOU ARE NOT A BROKER.

Brokers are good at calling. It's likely they have gotten a bunch of calls from brokers, but that you are their first call from an actual investor. Make it clear to them you are not a broker looking to list their property.

PRICE CONDITION, BUT GENTLY.

At this stage, your primary objective is to schedule a tour. Then simply ask questions like: What did you hope to get out of it? Why? How did you arrive at that number?

Throw the assessed value out there, and see if they think the value is more or less than that number. Ask "How much more?" Then say, "That sounds good. Once I have all of the information, I can tell you what we can do. I'm looking forward to seeing you."

If you find yourself arguing with them over valuation, you are going down the wrong path.

BE RELUCTANT.

I was at a real estate conference we hosted in Minneapolis, and one of the speakers made a very powerful illustration. He had someone come on stage, face him, and push their hands against his. People respond in kind. The harder he pushed, the harder the other person pushed back. Then he did something that left an impact on me. He stopped pushing. When he did, the other person almost fell on top of him.

Push your message onto people, and if they push back, then pull back a little bit and let them come to you. You don't need to buy that property. You will do fine without it. You have other properties you can buy. This is not about convincing someone against their will. It's about finding people who were already thinking about selling and setting a tour with them.

Sometimes you catch people at the wrong time, and they are rude to you. This is normal. You've probably gotten angry with someone who called you out of the blue too. It doesn't mean you're a bad person. Pull back if they are rude and keep it real with them.

> "Bill, I'm not calling to sell you anything. I'm calling to give you something. An offer on your property. We are real buyers, but we have other properties we are looking at too. I just thought I'd check to see if you had thought about selling direct to avoid paying a commission. If you do, great. If not, no big deal."

CONVERT NOS TO WHOLESALE BUYERS OR EQUITY PARTNERS.

If they respond with a no, that's okay. Ask them why they don't want to sell. They will tell you how great the property has been for them. Say, "That's awesome. Are you ever looking for other properties to buy?" Tell them you come across off-market deals from these marketing efforts all the time and that you can add them to your database. Ask them what they are looking for. Some of my best equity partners were sellers I called on who said no. These people already own property, so who better to pitch a partnership to?

HIRE A CALLER.

I encourage hiring a caller to automate this process if you have the funds to do so. Pay them hourly plus a bonus per appointment. Set a quota of one appointment every eight hours worked or whatever you find it takes you. I'm a firm believer in knowing how to do something yourself first, before hiring someone, so you can train them effectively.

Pro Tip

When to Involve the Broker

Brokers are like dessert—they are delightful when you have a good one, but too much of them will make you sick to your stomach. Sometimes it's appropriate to skip them altogether! Always involve the broker if they have a substantial pre-existing relationship with the owner, regardless of whether they have a formal listing agreement signed or not. You want to call the broker before the seller does. They will appreciate your gesture, and it will establish a positive working relationship. If they ever think you are trying to cut them out, they will go out of their way to kill your deal.

If the seller tells you they are not working with anyone, then don't invite an outside broker into the deal. Not all brokers are created equal, and the broker mindset is different than the investor mindset. Some will be exactly what a property owner needs to get the deal across the finish line, and some will ruin your deal. Plus, if the seller has to pay a commission, it will be harder to put a deal together at the price you both want.

PLAY THE NUMBERS GAME

When it comes to marketing and generating leads, you can either throw money at it or put effort into it, or both. If you don't have money, you better be willing to make twenty calls a day instead of five. And the key is simply making enough calls until you find someone who has already thought about selling—not to convince someone to sell who wasn't already considering it.

Remember how I said you needed two thousand contacts to do your first deal? Here is an example Investor Action Plan showing you why:

Acquisition Funnel

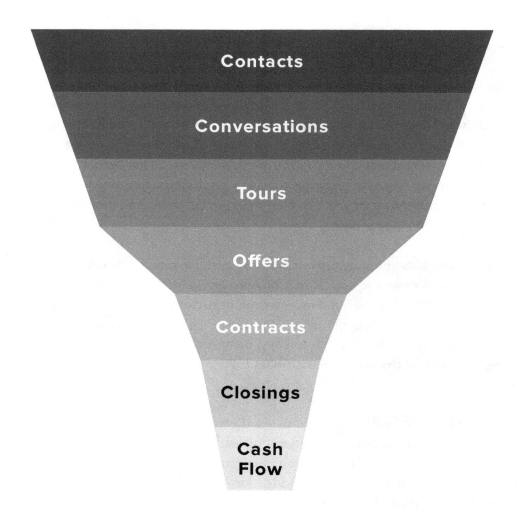

- **2,000 contacts**
- **200 conversations**
- **30 tours**
- **15 offers**
- **3 contracts**
- **1 closing**
- **$5K per month cash flow**

The raw activity at each level measures your commitment; the conversion ratios measure your skill. Focus on your commitment, and your skill will slowly improve with time.

If you track your contacts, conversations, and appointments, you will have some powerful data at your fingertips to see how you are doing. If you aren't getting enough properties to the closing table, you may be lacking in raw numbers or conversions (or both). Tracking your numbers helps you see where you need to engage a coach to help you get better.

The mistake I see many investors making, especially ones just starting out, is spending too much time networking or researching properties online and never actually touring properties. They wonder why they can't find a deal!

Whether you are calling on listed properties, calling on owners to see if they would sell, or trying to create a network that gives you referrals, don't put your results in someone else's hands. Sure, look at listed properties first but you also have to start hunting for your own meals. If you are just getting started, spend 80 percent of your time on hunting and gathering tactics and you will do just fine.

Key Reader Takeaways

☐ A no just means not right now.

☐ A good sustenance strategy includes gathering, hunting, fishing, and farming.

☐ Time can save you money and money can save you time.

☐ Be systematic and take massive action.

☐ Roll out a direct marketing sequence to your broker list too.

☐ Involve the broker if the seller has a substantial preexisting relationship with one.

☐ Track your numbers and see the law of averages come to life.

Action Items

☐ Create an investor action plan for yourself.

☐ Create a calendar with key dates for each element of your strategy.

☐ Send your first direct mail campaign.

☐ Call property owners until you have one to three tours scheduled.

Step 2
Figure

This is where you figure out how much to offer for the property and get it under contract. There are five parts:

- Tour the Property
- Conduct Market Research
- Determine Valuation Approach
- Analyze the Deal
- Present Your Offers

When you tour the property, you'll systematically gather key property data that you need to analyze the deal. You will also learn what the seller's motivations are and uncover problems you can solve to create value.

Then you'll conduct market research to better understand the rent rates, vacancy rates, and cap rates for the submarket this property is located in.

Next, you'll review the different options for the property—wholesale, quick flip, long flip, or refinance and hold—and use that information to better analyze the deal.

You'll analyze the deal by projecting the future value of the building (once you execute your business plan) and then deduct your costs and desired profit to back into what you can pay for the property today.

Finally, you'll draft and present your offers to the seller or their broker with the goal of getting a signed purchase agreement.

If you love math and spreadsheets, this step is going to be your favorite. If you don't, do not despair. I made it as simple as possible so you understand every step along the way and won't need to do any complicated math.

Chapter 9

Tour the Property

Objective: Gather the Key Property Data You Need to Analyze the Deal

On my first tour, I knew it all. I positioned myself as the expert contractor. I boasted about selling my remodeling company and how great my processes were.

Then the seller told me he had moved a demising wall.

I about shit my pants. I had no idea what he was talking about.

If you want the seller to like you, humility is the key. Especially on your first deal.

People get a feeling of power in two ways: by proving *their* dominance or by helping *you* out. Position yourself as competent but humble. The Bible says in 1 Corinthians

3:18 (KJV), "Let no man deceive himself. If any man among you seemeth to be wise in this world, let him become a fool, that he may be wise."

Humility doesn't mean self-deprecation. They don't need to know if you haven't done any deals before. If they ask how long you've been investing, say, "We do pretty well for ourselves. My partners are very experienced, and we have cash and the ability to perform if we can come to a fair deal." Then go back to asking them a question about the property. Memorize this progression and practice it in a mirror.

On the first tour, a lot of my students get tripped up like I did. You don't have experience yet, and it's easy to fall apart when a seller asks an unfamiliar question. But you have the power. You are the paycheck they are seeking. Position yourself not as an expert but as a representative of a group of investors who have cash. Your job is to get it invested, and you want to see if their property is it. You can be the son or daughter they never had that they want to see succeed, not some cocky little investor who thinks their shit doesn't stink.

At the end of the day, they don't need to know what you have done in the past—they need to know what you can do for them in the future.

Pre-Tour Process

- Measure the building footprint using Google Earth Pro.
- Get as much data into the MACO worksheet as you can.
- Collect and review the floor plan, rent roll, and historic expenses.
- Identify discrepancies and gaps. Make a list of questions you want answered.
- Print these documents so you can make notes on them.

Tour Process

Having a clear process makes you look like you know what you are doing even if you don't. This is the basic tour process I use. Let's go through each part of this process, then you can make it work for you.

Part 1: Tour the property with the seller and ask questions

- Set the Agenda
- Build Rapport
- Ask Tenant Questions
- Vendor and Property Questions
- Hot Button
- Probing
- Price Condition
- Schedule a Time to Present Your Offer
- Trial Close

Part 2: Stay and gather property data

- Measure the Building
- Renovation Cost Worksheet
- Finish Up

FIGURE

SET THE AGENDA

The person asking the questions is in control. Make sure that's you. Laying out an agenda puts you in control of the situation and puts them at ease. If a broker is present, honor them. Ask if the agenda is acceptable to them.

BUILD RAPPORT

Build rapport, but don't overdo it at the beginning. Jump into things as quickly as you can. These people value their time and will appreciate you getting right down to business. As the tour progresses, you can build more rapport. You'll know you built the right amount of rapport if you get them to smile or warm up to you somehow.

ASK TENANT QUESTIONS

Verify the rent roll details. The first time someone told me they were going to send me the rent roll, I pretended I knew what they were talking about. I'm going to save you this embarrassment! A rent roll is just a spreadsheet that shows the details of each unit in the building and a summary of the leases in place.

Make sure you review it and understand who is who. Does the rent roll show lease end dates? If they don't have a rent roll, have them send you the actual leases so you can create one. Here are some questions I ask discretely about the tenants as we tour:

- Who is good/bad?
- Anyone not current?
- Any renewals or new leases in the mix?
- Who does the leasing?
- How are they finding tenants?
- Are these net or gross leases?
- What expenses do the tenants pay and what expenses does the landlord pay?
- What rates are you advertising at as opposed to signing leases at?
- Do you have a standard lease you are using?

VENDOR AND PROPERTY QUESTIONS

Figure out the inner workings of the maintenance and utilities.

- What meters serve what spaces?
- What are the heating systems? Rooftop units, unit heaters, or furnaces?
- Who are the vendors for cleaning, lawn, snow, etc., and what do they do?
- How are you contracted with the vendors? Fixed rates or pay per visit?
- Do you do an annual roof, mechanical, or other inspections?
- What repair items do you know of that need to be done?

Begin noting the property condition items and vendor names/roles on your renovation cost worksheet and vendor contact list as you go. Keep it moving, because this is seller time, and you will check all that stuff on the second round. If you sense they are getting overwhelmed, start walking again and ask simple questions about something you are looking at before coming back to your property and vendor questions. Be an inquisitive twelve-year-old, not an annoying toddler.

HOT BUTTON

The hot button is the number one reason they are selling. They will have multiple reasons, but there is a core driver for wanting to sell. You need to know what it is and show them how your offer will address that primary motivation.

There are three core reasons somebody would want to sell, with underlying hot buttons for each:

- Financial
  - Lock in a strong market price
  - Want cash now for something
  - Want cash over time for retirement
  - Avoid paying taxes
- Freedom
  - Eliminate stress from management
  - Bad tenant or management
  - Reduce risk
  - Don't want kids to have to deal with it
- Forced
  - Negative cash flow
  - Foreclosure
  - Divorce
  - Partner dispute
  - Lack of capital for improvements needed

Your job is to listen, ask follow-up questions, and clearly define which of the three core reasons is their primary reason for selling.

PROBING

My favorite statement to keep people talking is, "Tell me more." Then I ask specific questions based on what they told me, like "What do you plan to use the cash for?" "Who on your advisory team would you need to run this deal past before you make a decision?" and "If I came up with a creative deal structure that would help you avoid paying taxes and net you more cash, would I be crazy for showing you something like that?"

The thing to realize is people seldom tell you the real reason for making their decisions until they like you and trust you. Work toward it slowly.

Another trick I learned is that if you are going to ask a person a sensitive question, lower your voice almost to a whisper. It works like magic. Lean in and whisper, "Jim, what's the real reason you are selling this?" Keep at it until you feel confident you know what pain they are trying to eliminate or what pleasure they are trying to seek.

PRICE CONDITION

Sellers always want all cash—or at least they think they do—until you help them realize that they don't. A lot of times, they want certainty, duration, or elimination of headaches more than they want cash. What they really want is to achieve a goal they have in their head. The cash is not the goal—it's just a means to achieving that goal.

If you don't ask them the following line of questioning, you will never find out what their real needs are:

> *Why are you selling?*
> *Tell me more about that.*
> *Who weighs in on the decision to accept an offer or not?*
> *In a perfect world, what did you hope to get out of this?*
> *How much do you realistically expect to get?*
> *If I gave you all cash with no contingencies, what's your bottom line?*
> *I can appreciate that, and we can do all cash, but as you know, equity is expensive. Usually, we can pay a much higher price for terms. If I were to bring an all-cash offer and a couple of creative offers with higher prices that will net you more cash and help you avoid paying capital gains tax, would I be crazy for putting something like that together?*

Now you planted the seed. Mission accomplished. Hopefully, they gave you a number they would sell at, but if they didn't, don't worry. People have a fear of putting the price out for two reasons. The first is they don't want to name a price too high and sound like an idiot and scare you off, and the second is they don't want to name a price too low and cut their own throat.

Sellers are very sensitive on the price issue, but I've learned a few tricks to get it out of them. I can ask, "What do you have into it?" and I can ask, "It's assessed at $_____. Would you sell it for that?"

If they say they want more than the assessed value, then I can ask them, "How much more?" If they still don't give in, I throw out three ranges, with the assessed value plus $100K per range.

For example, if the property is assessed at $1.2M, I might say something like "Would you be looking at like $1.2–$1.3M, $1.3–$1.4M, or $1.4–$1.5M?" Now they are picking a range instead of a number, and for some unconscious reason, it alleviates their fear. It gives them enough wiggle room. Try it out; it really works!

SCHEDULE A TIME TO PRESENT YOUR OFFER

Do not leave without setting a firm time to present, ideally at your office or by video call. Don't present at the building or their office. They are in the position of power at these locations.

Make sure everyone who needs to approve this decision is going to be there. For that reason, I like video calls to present offers. "When would be a good time to do a video call with the partners and your team of advisors so we can present our offers? How does the same time, same day next week sound?"

TRIAL CLOSE

Ask, "So when I meet with you and your partner Jim tomorrow, is there any reason other than price or terms that we wouldn't be able to put a deal together?"

Take note of what they say. If it's, "No, as long as your price is a good price," or "Let's just see what you have." Then you say, "Great, I'm looking forward to it." And wrap up the meeting.

If they offer an objection like "I need to run this by my accountant" or some higher authority gambit, then you should say something like "So your CPA's advice would weigh heavily on your decision?"

If they say yes, make it part of the next steps of the offer. "If that's the case, would it make sense to have your CPA on the call so they can fully understand what I'm offering, and then you guys can discuss it among yourselves after to make a decision?" Use this same line of reasoning for presenting your offer directly to the seller in the first place if the broker is trying to gatekeep you from presenting directly.

Here's what I say to brokers to help convince them it's in their best interest to let me present to them AND their client: "I don't just send offers blindly and hope they work. In the past, people have misunderstood my terms, and I'm genuinely interested in getting a deal done with you so we can both get paid on the deal. I am going to spend a fair amount of time analyzing this property and drafting one or more offers for you. I would appreciate it if you would give me the opportunity to at least go over them with you and your client directly, even if we are just doing a video call together. Fair?" If they push back and say no, honor that decision and just present it to them.

Start removing roadblocks to getting your deal done before it even begins.

Now you are done with the seller, and/or their broker, at the property. Ask if it's okay if you just add up some numbers and measure a couple of things on the outside of the building. If you set the expectation during the setup call and at the beginning of this meeting, this shouldn't be an issue.

MEASURE THE BUILDING

This is critical for two key reasons.

1. You use the total building size to estimate your rental income.
2. You use measurements and quantities to estimate repairs.

Everything we do is based on the total square footage of the building, yet less than 5 percent of buyers actually measure the building!

You use the building's total square footage times the market rent rate to project the potential rental income, so having the building's total square footage is critical. The good news is you can measure the building footprint prior to arriving in about sixty seconds, using Google Earth Pro, a free aerial measuring tool from Google. Beware of overhangs on office and retail buildings, and make sure you only measure from where the walls are. If your building is only a single story, you're done! If all stories are the same, just multiply the footprint size by the number of stories. If some stories are different sizes, you may have to also use a laser tape measure to measure those floors and add those to the total. This is when you do it. You are not measuring individual units at this point. We don't do that until the due diligence part of the Fund step.

You can either be pleasantly surprised if you measure the building and it's quite a bit bigger than everyone thought it was, or severely disgruntled when you find out it's less than everyone thought it was. I've been on both sides of the coin.

I once got an office building under contract. The rent roll had it at 90,000 square feet. I measured the building using a combination of Google Earth and a laser tape measure and figured out the building was actually 110,000 square feet.

I about fell out of my chair in excitement. The building had recently appraised at $9M based on ninety thousand square feet. That's $100 per square foot. This meant the building I got under contract at $8.2M was probably worth closer to $11M. Unfortunately, COVID-19 hit while I had that deal under contract, and the owner wouldn't make a price concession, so we left our due diligence money on the table and walked.

But then there was another property I got under contract from one of my mailers that was showing as thirty-six thousand square feet on CoStar. I made the offer based on that assumption without measuring. I got the property under contract at

FIGURE

$1,600,000 on a master lease with the option to purchase, on a ten-year deal with $100,000 down at master lease commencement.

Then I found out the building was only thirty thousand square feet when I measured it three days later. I realized they had been counting the mezzanine square footage in the total. Don't ever pay for mezzanine square footage! I asked for a price concession and the seller wouldn't budge, so I canceled the deal.

RENOVATION COST WORKSHEET

Now it's time to figure out the quantities of the renovation items you will need to complete. You will estimate repairs by plugging these quantities into the renovation cost worksheet, so it's important you spend the time here to be accurate. For example, if you want to recarpet the building, you have to figure out what areas have carpet and which ones don't while you are at the property. If you plan to update the bathrooms, it's important to count the number of fixtures and toilet stalls, and measure the square footage of tile to be replaced. If you can get blueprints that are to scale from the owner, you can download and use a takeoff software to shortcut this process.

It's best to fill out the renovation cost worksheet while still at the property. Otherwise, you will miss things and guess on the quantities. Jump to the "Estimate Repair Costs" chapter in the Fix step to understand how to plug these quantities into the renovation cost worksheet to estimate costs. You'll want to go line item by line item while at the property and ask yourself, does this need to be fixed, replaced, updated, or overhauled in some way? If so, measure or count it, and plug the quantity into the renovation cost worksheet.

FINISH UP

Before you leave the property, make sure you have everything you need to analyze the deal or make a checklist of anything you need to follow up to get. The next chapter covers how to take all the raw data you collected and put it into your MACO worksheet to figure out exactly how much you should offer.

Key Reader Takeaways

- ☐ Be prepared.
- ☐ Set an agenda and honor any brokers present.
- ☐ Be the one asking the questions.
- ☐ Measure the building.
- ☐ Complete the renovation cost worksheet while at the property.

Action Items

- ☐ Buy a laser tape measure and try measuring a building on Google Earth before the tour.
- ☐ Tour your target property and write down the seller's hot button.
- ☐ Complete the renovation cost worksheet for that property.

FIGURE

Chapter 10

Conduct Market Research

Objective: Determine the Market Metrics for This Property

After touring the property, you will have lots of property-specific data that you can use to analyze the deal. The next step is to figure out what's happening in the local real estate market to see how the rent rates at the property compare to what's happening in the market. If I had skipped this step with the Center Drive property, I would not have uncovered a major opportunity.

There are four market metrics you need to know in order to analyze your deal with supreme confidence:

- Rent Rates (Gross and Net)
- Vacancy Rates (Occupancy Rates)
- Cap Rates (Multiples)
- Absorption Rates

Your goal should be to have a high degree of confidence in what you can rent each space for, what percentage of that rent you can actually expect to collect, and what multiple the market will pay for that income stream. Let's talk about what each metric is and then I'll show you how to get them.

Rent Rates are the rates per square foot that things lease at. They can either be stated as a gross rent rate or a net rent rate. A gross rent rate is a rate that includes the landlord paying most, if not all, of the expenses, whereas a net rent rate is a rate where the tenants pay the expenses on top of that rate. The rate you will use for your analysis will depend on the type of leases that are in place when you analyze the deal and the type of leases you plan to put into place if you buy the property. We go into the difference between net leases and gross leases in more detail in the Fill step, but for now, that's what you need to know.

For Center Drive, the leases in place were gross leases (the landlord was supposed to pay everything except utilities) that had an average rental rate of $5.50 per square foot per year. I uncovered in my market research that the average market rate people were renting these spaces for was actually closer to $8.00 per square foot per year gross.

Rent rates can vary by property because of specific advantages or disadvantages the building has compared to the other buildings in the market.

What features make a property more valuable?

- Windows/light
- More clear height of ceilings
- Longer clear span between pillars
- High quantity and size of drive-in or dock doors
- Quality and quantity of bathrooms
- Electrical upgrades
- Heating and cooling system
- Parking
- Signage
- Access

- Access to skilled labor
- Access to highways
- Conference rooms
- Workout facilities
- Elevators
- Common area features like waterfalls and artwork

Start thinking like a tenant. Knowing what makes a space more valuable is a big part of predicting the rent rates. Make sure you also think about what renovations you are going to do and factor that into the equation. Bottom line, you need to be able to look at a space and know with certainty what it will rent for.

Vacancy Rates are the market averages for how much space is vacant in the overall market within the report. They will indicate how strong a market is. The stronger the market, the lower the vacancy rate. An occupancy rate is the opposite of a vacancy rate. To calculate it, you take 100% minus the vacancy rate. So a vacancy rate of 5% is the same as an occupancy rate of 95%.

Cap Rates are nothing more than a mathematical relationship between a property's net operating income (NOI) and its value (or sale price). "Cap rate" is short for "Capitalization rate," and the *market* cap rate is the unleveraged rate of return that the market demands based on the perceived risk of the investment.

$$\text{Market Cap Rate} = \frac{\text{NOI}}{\text{Value}}$$

Pro Tip

Commercial real estate is filled with finance guys from Wall Street. They use the term "trading" when referring to trading stocks, so they refer to the sale of a property as a "trade." You will hear phrases like "What did that one trade at?" or "What cap rate are buildings trading at?" Trading simply means selling or trading hands. The terms are synonymous.

If multifamily apartments are trading at a 5% cap rate and warehouses are trading at a 7% cap rate, then investors in your market perceive warehouses as having more risk and would therefore pay less for the same income stream.

How Asset Class Impacts Value

Sign	Metric	Apartment	Warehouse
	NOI	$100,000	$100,000
÷	Market Cap Rate	5%	7%
=	Price/Value	$2,000,000	$1,428,571

Divide the NOI by the cap rate to get the market value. In this example, both properties have the same NOI, but the market would pay $2M for the apartment and just over $1.4M for the warehouse. Remember when I told you that apartments actually pose a higher risk of default? This is why. You would have a much larger mortgage payment to make with the same $100K NOI to pay it with. Note that the credit of the tenant impacts the market cap rate too.

What would *you* rather have—a long-term lease with a corporate tenant who has rock solid credit or a month-to-month lease with a mom-and-pop shop? Which one would you perceive to have more risk? Probably the mom-and-pop shop, right?

If both leases produce the same exact NOI, most investors would pay a lower cap rate (or higher multiple) for the high credit corporate tenant. This equates to a higher valuation for the same NOI.

How Tenant Credit Impacts Value

Sign	Metric	National Credit	Local Credit
	NOI	$100,000	$100,000
÷	Market Cap Rate	6%	8%
=	Price/Value	$1,666,667	$1,250,000

Real estate is a business. Valuing a piece of real estate is exactly like valuing a company. I sat down with a business broker in 2017 to list my remodeling company for sale. He asked me how much I made on average for each of the last three years. He jotted a few numbers on a napkin, slid it over, and said, "I can sell your company for that."

I was kind of pissed off, actually. All he did was multiply the number I gave him by three.

It seemed too simple. Didn't he need to know all of the inner workings of my company to value it?

The answer was no. He knew what multiple of earnings the market was paying for construction businesses—the Market Multiple. In my case, the company sold for three times the net operating income.

The Market Multiple is simply the inverse of the market cap rate:

$$\text{Market Multiple} = \frac{1}{\text{Market Cap Rate}}$$

I don't know why commercial real estate folks like to divide by a fraction (market cap rate) to figure out the value instead of just multiplying by a whole number (Market Multiple) like my business broker did, but that's how it's done. If the business broker had explained to me that the market cap rate for construction companies was 33%, and we would divide my average earnings by 0.33 to derive the market value, my eyes would have glazed over.

Instead of getting lost in percentages, you can choose to value real estate using the same method the broker did to value my company: project the future NOI and then predict what multiple of that NOI the market will pay for it.

Value = NOI × Market Multiple

Here's another way to think about it.

How much is the market willing to pay for a dollar of NOI?

If the market cap rate is 8%, then a dollar of NOI is worth $12.50. Therefore, the Market Multiple is 12.5. If the market cap rate is 5%, then a dollar of NOI is worth $20.00 and the Market Multiple is 20.

If a business normally sells for two, three or even five times its NOI, then why will a piece of real estate sell for ten, fifteen, or even twenty times its NOI? Because it's *perceived* as less risky—and history shows that it actually is.

Throughout this book, I may use a market cap rate or a Market Multiple. Just remember they are the inverse of each other and are interchangeable. Use whichever method is easier for you.

In the Center Drive case, the property was being offered at a cap rate of 5% ($40K NOI ÷ $800K list price) and I ended up buying it at a 5.7% cap rate ($40K NOI ÷ $700K purchase price). The market cap rates were actually much higher than that. This is why other investors passed on it because they were not able to see the upside we could see by doing the market analysis and realizing the rents were really low.

You might be inclined toward properties with good credit tenants that are in high demand. But those properties will have really low cap rates overall, and your ability to generate cash flow and build value in them will be harder. In other words, the perceived risk does not always equate to real risk. And that's where the opportunity lies: buying properties with high-perceived risk while structuring a plan to solve those problems so you can create tremendous value. That's the plan that reduces your real risk.

Absorption Rates are the net change in occupancy within a given market for a given timeframe. Most reports are done quarterly, so the report will show what submarkets are filling more space than becomes vacant, and vice versa. Positive absorption rates equate to high demand, which puts upward pressure on rental rates and downward pressure on cap rates and vacancy rates. The opposite is also true. Negative absorption means more square footage was vacated than was filled. You should read the notes to see if certain areas have a high amount of new construction, because that can impact the numbers too. If the spaces are filled, it increases absorption dramatically, but if they are built and not occupied, the absorption suffers.

You won't use the absorption rate directly in your analysis, but by understanding what's happening in the submarket, you can make adjustments to what's likely to happen to rent, vacancy, and cap rates in the future based on the shifting supply and demand. For example, if the absorption is negative, I might analyze my deal using a rent rate that is slightly lower than the current posted rent rate, and I might use a vacancy and cap rate that is slightly higher.

Now that you understand the four key market metrics, let's discuss how to get them.

There are four ways to conduct your market research:

- Market Reports
- Active Listings
- Sale and Lease Comps
- Broker Interviews

Market Reports

You can get local market reports free from most large brokerages. They publish them to attract investors to their brand in order to win business. These reports usually include rent and vacancy rates and sometimes market cap rates for the metropolitan area that is closest to you.

My favorite reports come from the following companies.

- Cushman and Wakefield
- CBRE
- SVN
- Lee & Associates
- JLL
- Colliers
- NAI Global
- Avison Young

- Transwestern
- Marcus & Millichap
- Kidder Mathews
- Newmark Knight Frank
- RE/MAX Commercial
- KW Commercial
- Savills
- Coldwell Banker

Go pull a market research report right now.

Figure out the net rent rates, vacancy rates, and absorption rates for the submarket this property is located in. Pay attention to the type of rent rate they are reporting—full service, modified gross, or NNN.

If you are not familiar with the different types of lease/rent rates, go read the "Negotiate and Sign Leases" chapter in the Fill step.

Active Listings

It's also good to see what is currently available on the market that is similar to the property you are analyzing. Search competing listings for lease and for sale online by using services such as Craigslist, LoopNet, MLS, and CoStar.

If you are licensed, you may have access to a commercial exchange in your area that non-licensed people can't access. You want to see what units are currently available for lease and what the asking rates are per square foot. You should also get a feel for the listing price per square foot.

Lease and Sale Comps

Comps is short for Comparables. Deals are seldom done at the list price, and you want to search comps for deals that actually got done. I use the MLS, CoStar, and my local commercial exchange to do this, or I have my VP of Acquisitions do a market comp analysis for me to see what rate or price per square foot deals are actually getting done at.

Doing sales comps is the same for commercial and residential with one exception: you need to ensure the financial conditions of the properties match. In the next chapter, I will show you how vacancy can impact value and the number of units can impact who you plan to sell your building to after you fix it up.

For now, here are the traditional methods to determine whether properties are comparable:

- **Style:** Asset class and subclass should match. Construction type should generally match. A poured wall warehouse will be worth slightly more than a block construction warehouse of the same size. A thirty-foot-high warehouse will be worth more than a fifteen-foot-high warehouse with the same square footage.
- **Size:** Remember larger spaces rent for less per square foot in general, so you can't compare a one hundred thousand-square-foot warehouse rate to a ten thousand-square-foot warehouse rate. The smaller the space is, the higher the rate will likely be.

- **Sale or Lease signing date:** The more recent the better. I usually go back a year.
- **Site:** This varies widely by asset class, but location should be close as well. Retail is especially finicky about location, whereas office and industrial are not as critical. You should also see how much land the site has and what it's zoned for.
- **Situation:** Is the property completely vacant or is it fully occupied? Is it fully renovated or not? Take the physical and financial condition into account when selecting comps.

As you look at each comp, ask yourself if it matches your subject property, but don't spend too much time obsessing over this stuff. Compare what you are seeing in the market to the market reports you pulled and see whether they line up or not. If not, you'll be able to figure out why in the next step.

Broker Interviews

The final piece of your market research is what I call "primary research" because you are doing it yourself and not relying on somebody else's research. It's nothing more than having conversations with brokers and appraisers. After you've found some comps, call the brokers who were involved in those deals and ask them some questions:

- What are the **net rent rates** they are seeing deals get done at for this type of space?
- What are the **operating costs per square foot** for your type of product you are targeting?
- What kind of **vacancy rate** are they seeing in this submarket?
- What kind of **cap rates** are they seeing things trade at?
- Are most leases **gross or net leases** for this type of product?
- What kind of **tenants** are looking for these types of spaces?
- How much per square foot are tenants asking for in **tenant improvement allowances** in this market?
- How long are **vacant units** sitting on the market?
- **How can we work together?**

You are not wasting the broker's time—you are killing two birds with one stone. You're getting market research done as well as interviewing them as a potential broker for a nonexclusive right to represent you as a buyer or an exclusive right to represent you in listing your property for lease if you buy it.

If you are calling on active listings, schedule a property tour. Then as you move through this book you will have what you need to make an offer on these properties and consider having that same broker lease the building for you. Throw the carrot out there that you want to pay them a commission. That's how you get them to give you free information. They want to earn your business.

> ### Pro Tip
>
> I recommend starting with brokers who have the CCIM designation. CCIM is the PhD of commercial real estate. Agents with this designation will have a thorough understanding of the market and a minimum of $10M in deals done. Go to the CCIM website and click "Find a Broker." Call them and tell them what you are looking for, and offer to let them keep both sides of the commission if they bring you an off-market deal that they are going to sell before they list it.

This is a critically important part of the process, but it's not an exact science. You will encounter a lot of contradictory information. Never take what you find in the reports, listings, comps, and interviews as gospel. Let me show you why.

How Cap Rates Are Determined

I got a call one day from a researcher asking me a million questions about a property I sold, specifically my income and expense numbers. They were an appraiser using this transaction as a comp for the appraisal of another building, and they wanted to know the NOI of my building at the time of sale so they could derive a market cap rate. This is how it's done: researchers at large real estate, research, and appraisal companies interview property owners after they sell their property and ask what the NOI was at the time of the sale.

The challenge is that there is no standard for how that annual NOI is calculated, nor is there a way to verify the number reported is even accurate, since these aren't publicly traded companies that own the properties so there are no public-facing, audited financials. I could have told that appraiser a number that was way off from reality, and it would have drastically affected his valuation of the property he was appraising.

Do you see the issue here? How can you trust the NOI calculation owner's report at the time of sale? How do you know all the property owners are calculating their NOI the same way? Are they projecting the next twelve months, trailing twelve months, last fiscal year? Or are they taking the most recent month and multiplying by twelve? These are all legit ways to calculate an NOI, I suppose, so you might have four owners looking at the same data and reporting different NOIs at the time of sale. You will likely see a wide variety of cap rates because there is human error in how the NOI data is calculated, reported, and collected.

Pull the market reports, look at what has leased in the past and what is active on the market now, and then talk to at least five brokers. Then come to your own conclusion on what the true rent, vacancy, and market cap rates are in your area.

You now have everything you need to understand your market metrics which you will combine with the data you gathered from the seller documents and the property tour in order to analyze the deal.

Key Takeaways

☐ Market metrics you need to know are the rent rate, vacancy rate, cap rate, and absorption rate.

☐ Use market reports, past and current listings, and broker interviews to figure out what the market rates are.

Action Items

☐ Pull two market reports, review properties for lease in the area, find three online lease and sale comps, and interview five brokers for the property you want to analyze.

☐ Use this information to determine the most probable future rent, vacancy, and cap rates over the next couple years.

FIGURE

Chapter 11

Calculate the MACO

Objective: Determine Your Max Allowable Cash Offer

There are two things you need to do really well in order to become a millionaire investing in commercial real estate.

1. Accurately predict the *future* value of a property.
2. Calculate the costs to get the *current* property to that value.

In this chapter, you'll learn how to use these two skills to determine how much to pay. We call this the Max Allowable Cash Offer, or MACO for short. It's the most you can pay for a property in order to achieve your desired profit margin.

Valuing a property and determining how much to pay for it are two totally different things.

There are three ways to *value* a property, residential or commercial:

1. Cost Reproduction
2. Sales Comparables
3. Income Capitalization

Cost Reproduction Approach

This method suggests a property is worth the cost of land plus what it costs to build new, minus wear and tear.

$$\textbf{Market Value = Land + Construction Costs} - \textbf{Wear and Tear}$$

You won't use this method to value buildings—only to ensure you can price your buildings below the cost of new ones. You need to know if a developer can buy the piece of land across the street from the building you're analyzing and rent it out for cheaper than you. If they can build for less per square foot than you are paying, they can probably rent their new building out for less than your used building as well. This can make leasing difficult. You figure out what the cost to build new is in your area by interviewing developers, builders, and brokers.

Sales Comparables Approach

This method suggests a property is worth what comparable properties just like it have recently sold for. This is how you value houses and vacant rental properties that are best suited for single-tenant users.

$$\textbf{Market Value} = \frac{\textbf{Average Sale Price}}{\textbf{per SF of Comps}} \times \frac{\textbf{SF of Subject}}{\textbf{Property}}$$

Income Capitalization Approach

This method suggests that a property is worth a multiple of its net operating income. We already covered this method as the primary method you will use to project the future value of a multi-tenant commercial property.

$$\text{Market Value} = \frac{\text{NOI}}{\text{Market Cap Rate}}$$

There are two types of buyers who might want to buy your building someday—financial buyers and owner-users. Which one you plan to sell to will impact your business plan and the method you should use to project the future value.

Financial buyers purchase property to make a return on their investment. They will value your building using an income capitalization approach.

Owner-users purchase property for utility—that is, they buy based on what the building can do for their business. They will value your building using a sales comparables approach.

Imagine two identical buildings next door to each other. One is fully occupied with great credit tenants on long-term leases with third-party property management in place, and the other one is vacant. Which one is worth more?

The answer depends on who the buyer is. An owner-user would pay more for the vacant building because they want to move their business in there. Whereas a financial buyer would pay more for the fully occupied building because they wouldn't have to incur the holding costs, tenant build-outs, or leasing fees it would take to stabilize the building.

A building is stabilized when you achieve market-rate occupancy at market-rate rents. As a Value-Add investor, your goal is to buy unstabilized assets and stabilize them.

How long does it take to stabilize a building?

It could take a month; it could take three years. It depends on how messed up the situation is!

As you fix and fill the building, the values change over time.

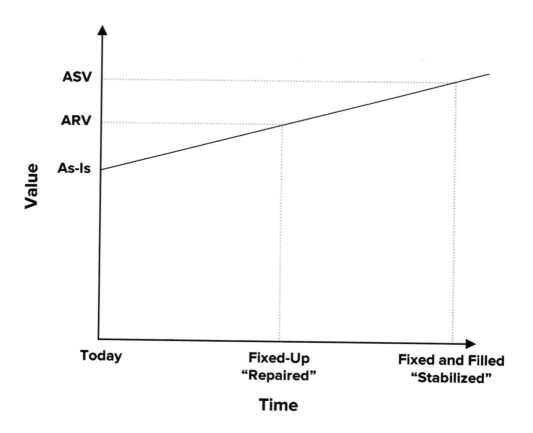

Value Changes as You Stabilize the Property

The **as-is value** is the value of the property as it sits today.

The **as-repaired value** (ARV) is the value of the property after you renovate it, but before you fill the vacancies. It's the value an owner-user would pay who would occupy the building to run their business out of (or a homeowner who would occupy the property in the case of residential). The bigger the renovation, the bigger the difference between the as-is and as-repaired values will be. You use the sales comparables approach to predict this value.

The **as-stabilized value** (ASV) is the value of the property after you fix it up, fill it with tenants, and stabilize the financials. It's the value a financial buyer would pay to buy the stabilized cash flow you created. You would use the income capitalization method to predict this value.

Most books will teach you to take the CURRENT NOI and then divide it by the market cap rate in order to come up with a value that you should pay for the property today (as-is). They argue that if you value it based on the future income, you are overpaying. This approach works great for stabilized properties if you don't care about creating any equity and you are only investing for cash flow.

Only one problem—you aren't targeting stabilized properties and you aren't only investing for cash flow! You want to create equity, so you are *only* targeting properties that are messed up and have depressed NOIs.

You can't apply a cap rate to an unstabilized NOI and derive a meaningful value.

Let me prove it to you.

A vacant building has no income but lots of expenses, so it has a negative NOI. If you apply the market cap rate to that NOI, you would end up with a negative suggested value. Obviously, the building and land are worth something, so that approach is out the door. You could value the building by using the sales comparables approach of what other unstabilized assets like it sold for in the area, but that method won't guarantee you a profit.

The workaround is to project the FUTURE value of the property, then deduct the costs to stabilize the property and your desired profit margin to back into what you can pay for it today.

Remember that you can project two different types of future values—ARV and ASV. You'll pick one of these to use based on your business plan and which type of buyer you plan to sell to in the future.

OPTION 1: SELL TO OWNER-USER

Your plan will be to fix the building up and sell it to an owner-user. This is a great strategy for single-tenant buildings under twenty thousand square feet. You'll project the future value by finding sales comps of fully renovated, vacant, single-tenant buildings and figuring out what price per square foot they traded at. You'll take that price per square foot times the square footage of your building to project an After Repaired Value. Then you will deduct your costs to close, hold it, and fix it up, and your desired profit margin to back into what you can pay for it. Here is the formula you have probably already used.

$$\text{MACO} = \text{ARV} - \text{Costs to Fix/Close/Hold} - \text{Desired Profit}$$

OPTION 2: SELL TO FINANCIAL BUYER

Your plan will be to fix the building up, fill it with tenants, stabilize the financials, and then sell that income stream to a financial buyer. You should project the future value by projecting what the stabilized NOI is, and then apply a market cap rate to that to derive an "As-Stabilized Value." From there, you will deduct your costs to fix, fill, close, and hold the property, and your desired profit margin to back into your MACO.

$$\text{MACO} = \text{ASV} - \text{Costs to Fix/Fill/Close/Hold} - \text{Desired Profit}$$

Pro Tip

If you plan on doing Option 2, you'll still want to pull comps to see what other unstabilized assets were sold for per square foot and compare that to the price per square foot you arrive at using option #2. You do this to make sure if you got into a pinch and had to turn around and sell your property quickly as an ugly, vacant building that you could at least do so for the price you paid.

Our system is designed to target multi-tenant buildings, create value in them, and then either sell them or refinance them and hold them for long-term cash flow.

I don't like single-tenant buildings (like standalone McDonalds) for long-term commercial holds because if the one tenant ever defaults, you are in deep water. It doesn't mean you should never buy single-tenant properties. For single-tenant properties under twenty thousand square feet, fix them up and sell them to an owner-user. For single-tenant buildings over twenty thousand, split them into multiple units so you can diversify your tenant base, then fill those units, and sell the building to a financial buyer.

The MACO worksheet in this chapter is built for option #2—future value based on income approach for exit to a financial buyer. We will cover that first, then I'll show you how to modify the analysis if you plan to exit to an owner-user.

You'll calculate the NOI at two points in time when completing the worksheet:

1. NOI at the time you purchase (as-is NOI)
2. NOI in the future (as-stabilized NOI)

We'll go line by line through a MACO worksheet for the Center Drive property here, so pull out your forms package or pull up your spreadsheet template from the website.[2] By the time you are done reading this chapter, you will be able to analyze *any* property using this worksheet.

FIGURE

2 www.CREInvestingBook.com

#	Calculation	Data Point	As-Is	As Stabilized	÷SF	Where you get it
1		Net (Base) Rent Rate	$2.00	$5.93		
2		Expense Passthrough Rate	$3.50	$2.07		
3	1+2	Gross Rent Rate	$5.50	$8.00		Market Research
4		Building Square footage		20,000		As Reported by Seller, Verified by You
5	3×4	Potential Rental Income		$160,000	$8.00	Use Rate × SF or Itemize by Space in Rent Roll
6		Occupancy Rate		93.00%		Market Research, 100% Minus Vacancy Rate
7		Collection Rate		95.00%		Review of Tenants in the Building
8	5×6×7	Total Operating Income	$110,000	$141,360	$7.07	
9		Taxes	$10,000	$10,000	$0.50	County Website
10		Utilities	$16,500	$500	$0.03	Historic Exp Adjusted for Upgrades/Billing
11		Maintenance	$15,000	$7,000	$0.35	Itemize Out. Use Seller Historic.
12		Management	$0	$7,000	$0.35	Mgmt Company or 4–5% + Asset-Mgmt Fee 1–2%
13		Insurance	$4,500	$3,000	$0.15	Insurance Broker or $0.25÷SF
14		Repairs	$22,500	$9,800	$0.49	5-7%
15		Admin	$1,500	$4,060	$0.20	Flat Fee
16	sum 9-15	Total Operating Expenses	$70,000	$41,360	$2.07	
17	8-16	**Net Operating Income (NOI)**	**$40,000**	**$100,000**	**$5.00**	NOI Went from $2÷SF to $5÷SF
18		Market Cap Rate		8.00%		From Market Research
19	17÷18	"As Stabilized" (Future) Value		$1,250,000	$62.50	
20		Costs to Fix		$35,000	$1.75	Renovation Spreadsheet
21		Costs to Fill		$15,000	$0.75	Leasing Cost Calculator
22		Costs to Hold		$0	$0.00	Cumulative Negative Cash Flow
23		Costs to Close		$25,000	$1.25	Closing Cost Calculator or 3%
24	sum 20-23	Total Costs to Stabilize		$75,000	$3.75	
25	19-24	Break Even Purchase Price		$1,175,000	$58.75	
26		Desired Profit (Margin)	28%	$350,000	$17.50	You Pick
27	25-26	**MACO**		**$825,000**	**$41.25**	

Line 1: Net (Base) Rent Rate

If the building has net leases in place, you fill in the as-is column with the current net (base) rent rates and the as-is column with the market base (net) rent rates you got from your market research. Base rent and net rent are the same thing. You will see that term interchanged quite a bit.

If the building has gross leases in place, you can skip lines 1 and 2.

For example, below you can see if we had net leases and a market net rent rate of $5.93, I would plug that in, add the projected building expenses of $2.07, and solve for the Gross Equivalent Rent Rate. On the right where we have gross leases, I just skipped lines 1 and 2 because I started with the gross rent rate on line 3.

Net Lease versus Gross Lease Approach for Potential Income

Net Lease				Gross Lease		
Sign	**Item**	**Amount**		**Sign**	**Item**	**Amount**
	Base Rent	$5.93				
+	Additional Rent (Exp. Pass-Throughs)	$2.07				
=	Gross Equivalent Rent Rate	$8.00			Gross Rent Rate	$8.00
×	Building RSF	20,000		×	Square Footage	20,000
=	**Potential Gross Income**	**$160,000**		=	**Potential Rental Income**	**$160,000**

FIGURE

Pro Tip

If you have gross leases, you can fill in line 3 but then work backward to line 1 by subtracting the operating expenses to solve for a "net equivalent rent rate." The rate you are calculating isn't a real net rent rate you would see anywhere. You're just using it as a reference to compare to market net rent rates to see how you're doing.

Line 2: Expense Pass-through Rate

Again, you would skip this if you have gross leases.

If you have, or plan to put, net leases into place at the property, you will pass some or all of the operating expenses through to the tenants as "additional rent." We cover how to do this in the Fill and Financials steps.

For now, just take the numbers you have on line 16 and divide them by the square footage on line 4 and plug the result in here. For the as-is column, I took the current expenses of $70,000 and divided it into the building square footage of twenty thousand to come up with the current expenses of $3.50.

I'm projecting the expenses to go down to $41,360 ($2.07 per square foot), so I used the new expense pass-through number in the as-stabilized column.

Line 3: Blended Gross Rent Rate

If you have gross leases in place, this is where you start. Put the blended current rent rate in the as-is column and the blended market rent rate in the as-stabilized column. You'll learn how to blend using a rent roll on line 5, but here is the formula.

Calculating the Blended Net Rent Rate

$$\text{Blended Net Rent Rate} = \frac{\text{Office SF}}{\text{Total SF}} \times \text{Office Rate} + \frac{\text{Warehouse SF}}{\text{Total SF}} \times \text{Warehouse Rate} + \frac{\text{Retail SF}}{\text{Total SF}} \times \text{Retail Rate} + \frac{\text{Apartment SF}}{\text{Total SF}} \times \text{Apartment Rate}$$

If you have net leases in place, simply add lines 1 and 2 together here. That is, you will add the expense pass-through rate to the base rent rate to arrive at a gross equivalent rent rate.

Line 4: Building Square Footage

Use the square footage you calculated, or if you don't have that, the square footage the seller provided to you. This is the square footage for the entire building. Remember, you can do this by using a combination of Google Earth Pro and a laser tape measure.

Line 5: Potential Rental Income

This is the total income you would expect to receive if the building were 100 percent occupied and everyone actually paid their rent.

If the building is all the same type of space, you can just use the gross or gross equivalent rent rate times the total building square footage.

If the building has different types of spaces that would rent at different rates, break the building up and analyze each space separately and then add them back together. You can use a rent roll to do this.

There is no one standard way to write up a rent roll. Keep in mind that you are targeting mismanaged properties, so don't expect the seller to have a nice clean rent roll to give you. If they did and the building was professionally managed, you'd probably have a smaller chance of making a deal at the price you want. So get used to having to make sense of whatever data you can get out of the seller.

Here is the rent roll for Center Drive:

Rent Roll Worksheet for Center Drive

Unit	Tenant	Length (Mos)	RSF	Lease Rent	Actual Rate	Market Rate	Market Rent	Probable Rent
8409	Tenant A	36	2,400	$1,600	$8.00	$10.00	$2,000	$1,600
8411	Tenant B	3	1,220	$900	$8.85	$8.00	$813	$813
8413	Tenant C	5	3,300	$2,200	$8.00	$8.00	$2,200	$2,200
8415	Tenant D	MTM	2,610	$1,250	$5.75	$8.00	$1,740	$1,740
8419	Tenant E	MTM	3,050	$650	$2.56	$8.00	$2,033	$2,033
8421A	Tenant F	MTM	3,420	$1,950	$6.84	$8.00	$2,280	$2,280
8421BF	Tenant G	MTM	1,740	$825	$5.69	$8.00	$1,160	$1,160
8421BR	Vacant		2,260			$8.00	$1,507	$1,507
Total			**20,000**	**$9,375**	**$5.63**	**$8.24**	**$13,733**	**$13,333**
							× 12	× 12

Annual Gross Potential Rent = $164,800 $160,000

Start a new spreadsheet and use the information given by the seller to fill in the current lease information for each space in the building, including the monthly rent and the square footages. With those two, you can solve for the current lease rate.

$$\text{Actual Rate} = \frac{\text{Lease Rent} \times 12}{\text{Rentable Square Footage (RSF)}}$$

We cover rentable versus useable square footage more in the Fund step, but make sure you are using rentable square footage here. You can see that unit 8419 is ridiculously low on rent rate. Turns out the owner was friends with this tenant and gave him a sweetheart deal.

DETERMINE POTENTIAL RENT

Next, compare the lease rent to the market rent rates. The lower of the two is the potential rent. You can see in our rent roll that unit A rents for a higher rate than the rest because it's nicer. I used a market rental rate of $10.00 on that one because it has better access, visibility, and parking.

Sometimes the current lease rent is above market. This can happen when someone has a lease bump every year on their lease, but the market didn't go up at that same rate. If that tenant defaults, you won't be able to rent it back out at the same price. That's why we are making this comparison. In my example, Tenant B is paying over market rent right now. Don't overvalue the property based on this artificially inflated lease income.

Sometimes the current lease rent is below market. You're locked into a lease, so use the lease rent, which is the most probable amount you are going to collect. Of course, if they default or you can renegotiate the terms, you will have some upside if you can get the unit rented at market rent again, but that doesn't come without a cost.

Be careful not to miss renewal options that the tenant may have. The lease might be up in a year, but they might have several options to renew at below-market rates.

Pro Tip

Some savvy owners trick inexperienced buyers by putting leases in place at way above market to get the buyer to think the building is worth a lot more than it really is. I see this all the time on sale-leaseback transactions.

A sale-leaseback transaction is where an individual owns a business *and* a piece of property that the business resides in. They sign a lease with their own business at way above market rates to try to sell the building off to someone for way above market value.

FIGURE

Don't be the sucker who overpays for a property based on leases that are above current market rates if those leases will last more than two years.

Ask yourself, "What will be the most *probable* rent rate in two years when I want to sell or refinance?"

If the leases are month-to-month or have less than twenty-four months and no option to renew, you can use the market rent rate. However, if the leases will still be in place in two years when you go to refinance, use the lower of the current lease rate or the market rate.

In our example, we used the market rent for every unit except Unit 8409 which had longer than two years left on it.

Now that you have the potential gross rent for each space, add them together to get the Potential Gross Rent for the whole building. In our case, the most probable rent was $160,000, which we put into row 5 in the as-stabilized column. It just so happens that this is the exact same number as we got by taking the $8.00 times the twenty thousand. If it wasn't, we would always use the number we arrived at using the more detailed rent roll approach, because that is going to be more accurate.

Line 6: Occupancy Rate

The occupancy rate is the average percentage that the building is occupied throughout the year. You learned how to find the market vacancy rates in the last chapter and convert them to an occupancy rate by taking 100% minus the vacancy rate. For Center Drive, we projected a 7% vacancy rate, so I plugged a 93% occupancy rate or 0.93 into line 6 on the MACO worksheet under the as-stabilized column.

Note that the current occupancy and the as-stabilized occupancy are different. The current occupancy was 100% but the stabilized occupancy was 93%.

Line 7: Collection Rate

The collection rate is the percentage of potential rent you can expect to actually collect. Most people combine this with the occupancy rate, but I like to separate it out so I can adjust it based on the tenant-specific risk that I perceive at the time I analyze the deal.

How do you figure it out?

You pick a number based on the creditworthiness of the specific tenants in the building. There's no science to it. It's a SWAG—sophisticated wild ass guess. I usually end up with a collection rate between 90 and 100%.

I was once asked by a student what collection rate I should use for a single-tenant building. I thought long and hard but couldn't come up with an answer. Later on, I asked one of my CCIM instructors what they use, and he changed my perspective on the "collection rate."

He said, "Well Mike, in the next five years, is there a greater than zero chance that the tenant won't pay their rent?"

I said, "Yes, of course."

He said, "What percentage of likelihood would you give that?"

I answered that it depended on how solid the tenant was—the creditworthiness of the tenant would impact it. A large corporate tenant with good credit would probably have a fairly low likelihood of default, maybe 2–3 percent, whereas a mom-and-pop shop would probably have a much higher likelihood, maybe 10–20 percent.

He said, "Then what you are really figuring out is the percent likelihood that you will collect from the tenant(s) in the building." Make sure you look up who the tenants are. If they are local tenants, I would use 90 percent, and if they are credit tenants like Best Buy or Target, then use 98–100 percent.

Line 8: Total Operating Income

This has other names, like effective rental income, total building income, or gross operating income. Get used to the different terms, but essentially it's the amount of total income you expect to actually collect in a one-year timeframe, without any expenses applied to it. Just take the potential income and multiply it by the occupancy rate and collection rate.

$$\frac{\text{Expected}}{\text{Income}} = \frac{\text{Potential}}{\text{Income}} \times \frac{\text{Occupancy}}{\text{Rate}} \times \frac{\text{Collection}}{\text{Rate}}$$

That covers the income side of the NOI equation. Now let's deduct our operating expenses.

Lines 9–15: Operating Expenses

Your job here is to figure out what the expenses on the property will be, going forward. The best way to do that is to look at the past and then adjust for the future.

I created the acronym TUMMIRA to help you remember the seven types of operating expenses.

1. **T**—Taxes
2. **U**—Utilities
3. **M**—Maintenance
4. **M**—Management
5. **I**—Insurance
6. **R**—Repairs
7. **A**—Admin

It may put you at ease to know that I only use data I get from the seller to help project my utilities and maintenance costs. The rest of the expense categories are projections based on my own research.

Let's go through each of the seven expense categories to see where to find the data and how to manipulate it based on your business plan.

Line 9: Taxes

This is simple: take the number right from the county website and adjust it for the change in assessed value that is likely to occur after you buy it.

For example, if your property is assessed at $700,000 today, and you buy it for $1,000,000, do you think the government will raise your taxes? Yep.

Here's how you adjust:

Let's say the current taxes on that property are $21,000. Figure out what percentage of the assessed value that is. This percentage is called the mill rate. Each city or county has a mill rate. If the property was assessed at $700,000, the mill rate would be 3% of the current assessed value ($21,000 ÷ $700,000).

$$\text{Mill Rate} = \frac{\text{Property Tax Amount}}{\text{Assessed Value}}$$

If the assessed value goes up to $1,000,000, it's reasonable to assume the taxes would be 3 percent of the new value, or $30,000. You'd have a sharp drop in your NOI in year two or three as a result, and you wouldn't be happy if you didn't account for this up front. Ask me how I know! For Center Drive, we were buying the property at the same price it was assessed at, so I kept the taxes the same.

Pro Tip

There are some tricks of the trade to keep your taxes down. Always challenge the assessed value. There are attorneys who specialize in helping you challenge your taxes, and they are quite successful. Search the internet for property tax attorneys, or get referrals from other investors on who they use.

FIGURE

Line 10: Utilities

This is by far the most challenging category of expenses to predict, so take your time.

Analyze the historic utility costs by utility type. Use the numbers from the past as a baseline. Then adjust them downward for energy upgrades and billing practice improvements you will make, or adjust them upwards if your occupancy will go up. Be sure to look at each utility separately: electric, gas, and water.

Get the last two years of actual statements from the seller. If you can't get them from the seller, call the utility companies. They won't give you someone else's utility numbers, so I figured out a workaround. Tell them you have the property under contract and want to get set up on a budget plan. They will quote you an average budget per month going forward, based on the property's historical expenses.

Remember that better utility billing practices and energy upgrades are the best ways to decrease your utility costs and dramatically impact your NOI. In the Fix step, you are going to learn about energy upgrades, and in the Financials step, you are going to learn about how to improve your utility billing practices. If you are going to separate the meters, your utility costs should be close to zero, but account for the costs to separate the meters on line 20 as a cost to fix the building.

Most landlords absorb utility costs because it takes time and money to set up a good system. This impacts their NOI dramatically and devalues their building. Reverse that trend by doing the upgrades, then pass those costs on to the tenants as best you can.

Line 11: Maintenance

Maintenance includes the ongoing vendor services that keep the building operating smoothly. This step is about preventative maintenance, including:

- Internet
- Trash
- Janitorial
- Lawn
- Snow
- Pest Control
- Elevator Inspections

- Asphalt Maintenance
- Roof Maintenance
- HVAC Maintenance
- Fire and Sprinkler
- Security Systems
- Miscellaneous

Itemizing them and reviewing the actual numbers from the seller will always yield more accurate results, so if the seller gives you an itemized detail, feel free to use it. If they don't, just use 5 percent for now. Don't worry if it's off a bit. If the seller accepts your offer, you will get vendor quotes in the Fund step and adjust your numbers accordingly before your contingency ends.

As you build your business, collect and save pricing from vendors so you know the cost in advance. For example, my cleaning company charges me $0.065 per RSF of common area to clean twice per week. I know how much snow removal and roof maintenance cost per year on a square-foot basis. Try to get everything down to a per-square-foot number so you can get more accurate and granular on your analysis for your second and third deals.

> **Pro Tip**
>
> I always ask for a historic expense detail in spreadsheet format. I can run pivot tables to summarize the data. If you don't know what a pivot table is and aren't a spreadsheet addict like I am, don't worry. You don't need to know how to do this stuff to make a million bucks investing in commercial real estate, but there are advanced techniques like this to make your job easier.

Line 12: Management

Putting third-party property management into place is a great way to make your income stream more sustainable and transferable. We usually pay a fee of 4–5% for commercial tenants and 5–7% for multifamily properties. This does not include leasing fees.

Leasing fees are expensed if you do one-year leases like you would see on apartments, but since commercial leases are usually more than one year, the leasing fees are typically put on the balance sheet and amortized over the life of the lease. Capitalize them either way and include them in the "Fill Costs" on line 21.

The management fee is usually based on gross revenue, but not always. Interview a couple of property management companies to find out. Even if you manage it yourself, you want to know market management fees, so you know what to pay yourself.

Most sellers won't have a market rate management fee in their proforma or historical expense numbers, so disregard their numbers and use the rates you should expect to pay a third-party company going forward.

It's also important to note that your role will be the asset manager that oversees the property manager, and you will also charge a fee of 1–2% of total rental income too. Make sure you factor that in here as well. You don't really make money on this. This is "turn the lights on" kind of money that just covers your overhead.

Line 13: Insurance

Property insurance is how you protect your asset if something goes wrong. There are tons of different types of policies and deductibles, so don't put too much weight on what the seller was paying as a good predictor of the future.

Get an estimate from a broker if you can, but if you don't have time for that, just use $0.25 per square foot. After you get your first estimate, divide the actual quote into the square footage for the building, and update your analysis sheet to use that price per square foot going forward.

> ### Pro Tip
>
> Get a full replacement cost value policy, not an actual cash value policy. I don't recommend buying actual cash value policies, or you will be very disappointed if you ever have to file a claim. With an actual cash value policy, you cannot recover the depreciated value of your improvements that were damaged, whereas in a replacement cost policy, you can.

Line 14: Repairs

Repairs are small unforeseen costs you incur to repair the property, which should not be confused with large repairs that you will capitalize and include on line 20: costs to fix. Repairs are things like the toilet clogging. A kid throwing a rock through a window. Having to redo the paint and carpet in a unit to get it lease ready. A rooftop unit breaking down. A lightbulb going out. You get the idea.

Remember that *proactive* measures to maintain the building, like swapping out furnace filters, repainting the trim, doing the lawn and snow removal, and other items like that are maintenance items. Conversely, repairs are unforeseen items, so you can't really accurately predict them. This is why it doesn't really matter what the seller spent on repairs in the past—you are making sure to fix all of these problems on your initial remodel so you won't have these expenses impacting your NOI going forward.

Figure in 5 percent and you should be pretty solid. If it goes over that in real life, you will hold some cash back from distributions to the partners to replenish your reserve for repairs.

Line 15: Admin

This includes tax preparation, attorney's fees, bank service charges, office supplies, software costs, and other admin items that you incur to operate your business. I usually figure a few grand per property per year. If you're off, it won't matter much. This is the least important item; don't spend much time here.

Line 16: Total Operating Expenses

Add up lines 9–15 and you have your total operating expenses. I like to divide this total into the total square footage of the building to see what my operating expenses are per square foot.

Compare this against what property managers and other brokers tell you other buildings run. You will start to get a feel for it over time. For example, in my area, I know that total Ops (operating costs) run around $3.00-$4.00 PSF (per square foot) for warehouse and $6.00-$8.00 PSF for suburban office.

Pro Tip

In the case of Center Drive, we projected operating costs at $41,360, or $2.07 per square foot which is low for the entire market. When I realized this, I took a deeper look and realized the taxes were really low in this city. When expenses are really low, you can do gross leases at market rates and make a higher margin. When expenses are high, you can do net leases at market rates and pass through the higher expenses to the tenants.

Line 17: Net Operating Income

The NOI is the Operating Income minus the Operating Expenses.

NOI = Operating Income – Operating Expenses

Compare the current NOI with the stabilized NOI. Do you see a large difference?

If your stabilized NOI is at least 20 percent higher than the current NOI, then you have a Value-Add deal. If the NOI you are projecting is almost the same as the current NOI, you are working with a stabilized property. For Center Drive, our NOI was projected to go from $40K to $100K. That's a 150 percent jump, so it definitely qualifies!

Remember, trust *your* NOI numbers, not theirs (and certainly not their broker's!).

> **Pro Tip**
>
> If you find yourself adjusting the numbers over and over trying to make them work, stop it. Move on. Make an offer based on what you calculated. Your first answer is usually the best answer, just like they taught you for taking multiple-choice tests in school.

On line 3 of the worksheet, I showed you how to "gross-up" a net lease to get the "gross equivalent rate." Then we deducted your expenses from there to get NOI. This is the appropriate method if you want supreme accuracy.

However, in some cases, you want to analyze a net lease deal faster. I have a little shortcut for that. Let's say you have a building where all the tenants are on triple net leases. The net rent rate on the lease is really the **potential** net rent per square foot.

If you multiply that by the square footage of the building and apply a collection and vacancy rate to it, you could effectively predict your NOI—except you will likely absorb some expenses for things you cannot pass through to the tenants like capital improvement costs (CapEx), or costs for vacancies like leasing fees, advertising, and utilities.

You can apply an expense pass-through rate to account for those items quickly. Here is the shortcut formula:

$$\text{Stabilized NOI} = \text{SF} \times \frac{\text{Net Rent}}{\text{Rate}} \times \frac{\text{Collection}}{\text{Rate}} \times \frac{\text{Vacancy}}{\text{Rate}} \times \frac{\text{Expense Pass-}}{\text{Through Rate}}$$

Center Drive had gross leases, but let's say I decided to do absolute net leases for all the units instead. The square footage is twenty thousand square feet, and the net rent rate was $6 per square foot. I got that by looking at what the net rent rates in the area were. Our occupancy rate was 93%, collection rate was 95% and let's say I expected to pass 95 percent of the expenses through to the tenants (and absorb 5 percent).

$$\text{NOI} = \frac{20{,}000}{\text{SF}} \times \frac{\$6.00 \text{ Net}}{\text{Rent Rate}} \times \frac{93\%}{\text{Occupancy}} \times \frac{95\%}{\text{Collection}} \times \frac{95\%}{\text{Expense}} = \$100{,}719$$
$$\times \text{Occupancy} \times \text{Collection} \times \text{Pass-Through}$$
$$\text{Rate} \quad \text{Rate} \quad \text{Rate}$$

So your potential NOI was $6 per square foot per year but the effective NOI was around $5 per square foot per year because we accounted for vacancy, credit loss, and expense absorption.

We quickly came up with almost the same NOI number as we did with the full MACO analysis without going through the exercise of figuring out what the expenses were. We just used the net rent rate and worked down from there. Lots of market reports have market net rent rates, and buildings you will look at have net leases in place. You can use this method to quickly analyze these net lease deals on the fly.

You're welcome.

Pro Tip

If you ever hear the phrase "above the line" or "below the line," they are simply referring to whether the item is included in the NOI calculation or not. Reserves are generally factored into the NOI for multifamily properties but not for office, industrial, and retail properties.

Line 18: Market Cap Rate

You should have this from your research earlier. What cap rate do you think a financial buyer will value this asset at after you stabilize it? Adjust the market cap rates for any deal-specific risk or any changes you think may happen in the market.

Do you have really long leases with credit tenants? If so, you can probably use a lower cap rate (higher multiple). If you have all month-to-month, mom-and-pop shops, you should probably use a higher cap rate (lower multiple).

If you have no clue what cap rate to use, go back and read the "Conduct Market Research" chapter again. If you have multiple space types, be sure to blend your cap rate using this formula.

Calculating the Blended Cap Rate

$$\text{Blended Cap Rate} = \frac{\text{Office SF}}{\text{Total SF}} \times \frac{\text{Office Cap Rate}}{} + \frac{\text{Warehouse SF}}{\text{Total SF}} \times \text{Warehouse Cap Rate} + \frac{\text{Retail SF}}{\text{Total SF}} \times \frac{\text{Retail Cap Rate}}{} + \frac{\text{Apartment SF}}{\text{Total SF}} \times \text{Apartment Cap Rate}$$

Line 19: As-Stabilized Value (ASV)

The ASV is the as-stabilized value. This is what you are predicting the property will sell to a financial buyer for when you are done executing your business plan (or appraise at if you decide to refinance instead of sell). It's the stabilized NOI divided by the market cap rate (or stabilized NOI times Market Multiple).

$$ASV = \frac{\text{Stabilized NOI}}{\text{Market Cap Rate}}$$

In our example, we are predicting the Center Drive property would appraise at or sell at a price of $1,250,000.

Line 20: Costs to Fix

Plug in your construction budget from your renovation cost worksheet here. You will learn how to complete this worksheet in the Fix step. These are your capital improvement costs on the major things you want to fix on the building.

I've dedicated two whole chapters in the Fix step to show you how to estimate these for a preliminary budget, and how to collect bids later on to confirm these numbers and finalize your construction budget. If you want to learn how to estimate them right now, go read the "Estimate Repair Costs" chapter in the Fix step. Don't forget to include a contingency for unforeseen circumstances (10–20 percent) in this number.

Line 21: Costs to Fill

This is where you plug in your advertising and leasing commissions—the fees you will incur to get to 100 percent occupancy. The calculation is different for each asset type, but it's typically somewhere between 5-8% of the cumulative rent obligation on the leases you sign.

The cumulative rent obligation is the total amount of rent the tenant will pay over the entire term of the lease. For example, a sixty-month lease at $1,000 per month with no rent bumps is a $60,000 cumulative rent obligation. If there is a 3% per year rent bump, then the cumulative rent obligation will be slightly higher because the rent increases each year. Expect the leasing commission on that to be somewhere in the range of $3,000–$4,800. In the Fill step, you will learn how to figure out what the commission rates are in your area.

If two brokers are involved, the fee you pay goes up by 50–75 percent. I know what you're thinking: *I'll just lease it out myself and save the commission.* That's exactly what I thought. I figured out pretty quickly how dumb that was. It takes much longer to lease it yourself, and time is money in this game. Don't be an idiot like I was and not hire a professional broker to do this for you.

If you are doing enough deals and you can hire an agent to work as a dedicated leasing agent, by all means, rock it out! But don't be the person who thinks they made a bunch of money on a commercial flip, but really just bought themselves a construction management and leasing job.

You'll use the real percentages people in your market will charge you, but here is the actual calculator I have in my spreadsheet:

Leasing Cost Worksheet

Period	# Months	Rent	MOs × Rent	Comm. Rate	Commission
1	12.00	$11,733.33	$140,800.00	7.00%	$9,856.00
2	12.00	$12,085.33	$145,024.00	6.00%	$8,701.44
3	12.00	$12,447.89	$149,374.72	5.00%	$7,468.74
4	0.00	$12,821.33	$0.00	4.00%	$0.00
5	0.00	$13,205.97	$0.00	3.00%	$0.00
6	0.00	$13,602.15	$0.00	2.00%	$0.00
7	0.00	$14,010.21	$0.00	2.00%	$0.00
8	0.00	$14,430.52	$0.00	2.00%	$0.00
9	0.00	$14,863.44	$0.00	2.00%	$0.00
10	0.00	$15,309.34	$0.00	2.00%	$0.00
Total Rent Obligation		**$435,198.72**			
Leasing Commission with 1 Agent					**$26,026.18**
Leasing Commission with 2 Agents				× 150%	**$39,039.26**

I usually plan for a sliding scale commission schedule. If a broker is representing both sides of the transaction (tenant and landlord), then I take 150–175 percent of that schedule. Again, the commission rates vary widely across markets and agents, and ultimately, the rate is dictated by the market, the broker, and the client.

I've seen office agents charge $1.00 per square foot per year with one agent and $1.50 if two agents are involved. Apartments are usually a month's rent per year of the lease. For warehouse, I typically see a scale of 7 percent of the first year rent, 6 percent of the second year, 5 percent of the third year, 4 percent of the fourth year, and 3 percent of the fifth-plus years, like I've shown in the calculator example above. Retail can be $1.00 per square foot or a flat 3–5 percent for really large, long-term leases.

It's whatever the parties agree to. There is no standard method. In fact, it's illegal to have a standard method—the department of commerce sees that as price fixing.

In Minnesota, we get paid all the commission up front. In other markets, the agents get paid over the course of the lease. If the landlord doesn't get paid, the agent doesn't get paid. I wish that's how it was in our market, but it's not the norm. Focus on finding the right brokers and not haggling them too much on leasing fees. Don't get a cheap heart surgeon, and don't price shop brokers too hard.

Interview leasing agents and figure out what you can expect for your market prior to starting your journey, or you won't be able to calculate this accurately. Ask questions about how leasing commissions are calculated, and start developing relationships with agents that you may want to hire when it's time.

Line 22: Costs to Hold

You may or may not have holding costs. If your building has break-even or positive cash flow to the partnership on day one, then put a zero in for this line. If the annual debt service is bigger than the NOI, then you will have negative cash flow.

Calculate what you expect the cumulative negative cash flow to be during the stabilization period, not including partner distributions. Here is a diagram that illustrates what your cash flow position might look like if the building has an NOI smaller than the annual debt service:

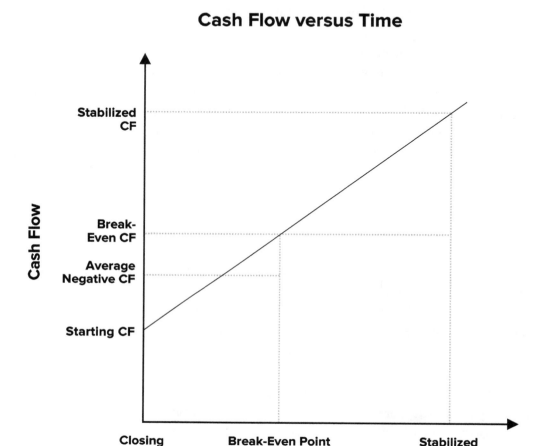

In this case, the starting cash flow is negative and slowly increases as you fill vacancies until you reach your break-even cash flow. This model assumes a straight-line lease-up when in reality, it's more of a hyperbolic curve because your activity is minimal in the beginning and ramps up as you approach completion of the construction. Don't try to get all calculus on me here, or you'll spend too much time worrying about numbers that don't make a big difference.

Just take your starting negative cash flow times the number of months you think it will take to get cash flow positive, and then divide by two to get the average.

For example, let's say you're evaluating a property with a super high vacancy where the NOI is negative $2,000 per month. That is, your income is $2,000 less than your operating costs every single month. And let's say your construction loan payments are $3,000 per month. So you actually need $5,000 per month to operate the property and pay the mortgage.

Now let's say you think it will take twelve months to get cash flow positive. You would estimate your holding costs like this:

$$\text{Holding Costs} = \frac{\textbf{Negative Monthly Cash Flow} \times \textbf{\# Months to Stabilize}}{2}$$

Holding costs, in this case, were twelve months at $5,000 per month divided by two, to get $30,000. That's what you would plug in on line 22. For Center Drive, I was cash flow positive, so I plugged in zero.

Line 23: Costs to Close

Closing costs are the costs you incur when you buy the property, including:

- Real estate broker fee
- Acquisition fee
- Funding fees: origination fee, doc prep fee
- Soft costs: appraisal, phase I, survey, legal
- Title insurance fees: premiums and closing fees
- Government fees: mortgage registry tax and recording fees

Typically, the seller will pay your broker if you have a broker representing you on the buy-side. If you don't have a broker representing you and the property is listed, have the listing agent credit that commission to you at closing unless they brought you the deal off market, in which case you let them keep it.

You can set up a spreadsheet to do the math for you, or you can get lazy and just use 3–5 percent. I like to have the spreadsheet calculate an exact number for me so there is no guesswork.

Closing Cost Worksheet – When Buying – Center Drive

Item	Qty	Rate	Total
Broker Fee (Paid by Seller)	$825,000	0%	$0
Acquisition Fee	$825,000	1%	$8,250
Lender Required Fees			
Origination Fee	$570,000	0.75%	$4,275
Appraisal	1	$2,500	$2,500
Phase I	1	$2,200	$2,200
Survey	1	$1,500	$1,500
Legal	1	$1,250	$1,250
Title Company Fees			
Owner's Title Insurance	$825,000	0.0846%	$698
Lender's Title Insurance	$551,250	0.2388%	$1,316
Closing Fee			$250
Exam Fee			$550
Recording Fee			$30
Government Fees			
Mortgage Registry Tax	$825,000	0.24%	$1,980
Recording Fees	2	$46	$92
Total Transactions Costs		**3.02%**	**$24,892**

Include any brokerage fees you owe a broker that aren't being paid by the seller, as well as an acquisition fee to yourself if you want. It's customary to get 1–2 percent of the purchase price for putting the deal together.

Line 24: Total Costs to Stabilize

Add up the four types of costs on lines 20–23. These are your total costs to stabilize the property. This is the cost of executing your business plan to create value in the building. If you've done your job well, you should be increasing the value substantially more than it costs to increase that value. In our example, it cost $75,000 to stabilize the building, but we increased the value by $550,000.

Line 25: Break-Even Purchase Price

This is your break-even price—meaning that if you pay this price, you would break even as a *partnership*. It's important to understand that the partnership can make money, but not make enough money for you to get paid. In the Fund step, I will show you why.

It's easy to calculate this. Simply take your ASV on line 19 and subtract your Total Costs to Stabilize on line 24.

It's super useful to know this number because if the seller comes back with a different price, you can simply subtract their new price from this break-even purchase price to figure out how much profit you would make.

For example, on Center Drive, if they had countered my offer at $750,000, I could have easily figured out that I would have still made $425,000 at that price ($1,175,000–$750,000).

Line 26: Desired Profit Margin

You can choose how much profit you aim to make on the deal given what you know about the problems, the market, and all of the risk factors we discussed in the first half of this book. The size of the transaction can make a big difference in how much you can demand.

I like to make a minimum of $250,000 or 15 percent of the as-stabilized value, and I often shoot for 20–30 percent of the ASV to begin with. For Center Drive, I used

$350,000, which came out to be 28 percent of the as-stabilized value. I ended up doing even better than that as you'll see in a minute.

Line 27: MACO

Congratulations! You made it.

The MACO is the maximum amount you can pay for a property in order to achieve a desired profit margin, assuming the seller walks with all cash at closing.

We call this a "cash" offer because that's what the seller gets without financing any of your deal. Don't worry; you don't have to dig up bags of money from your backyard—you can still raise 100 percent of the capital from debt and equity partners. We cover exactly how to do that in the Fund step.

In our case, the MACO is $825,000. We got that by taking our ASV of $1,250,000 and deducting our costs of $75,000 and our desired profit margin of $350,000.

MACO = ASV – Total Costs to Stabilize – Desired Profit Margin

This is the most important formula in this book, so consider getting it tattooed on the back of your hand. (I'm only partially kidding.)

Pro Tip

Calculate the MACO per square foot and do a couple sniff tests to this number, making sure it isn't out of line with market comps per square foot and the cost to build new per square foot. Our MACO per square foot is $41.25. Fully renovated multi-tenant buildings like this were trading at $75.00–$80.00 per square foot and they cost $100.00 per square foot to build new, so I knew I was sitting good at this price. This is a good way to double-check your numbers before you make your offer.

Max Allowable Investment

In the last chapter, you learned that if a market cap rate is 8%, a dollar of NOI is worth $12.50 to a financial buyer. In this chapter, you see that we valued the $100,000 stabilized NOI at $1,250,000, but we couldn't pay that because we had to account for our costs to stabilize and for our desired profit margin.

Since we desired to make $350,000, we had to keep our costs at $900,000. We call this $900,000 number our max allowable investment or MAI for short. The MAI is the total we can *invest* in the property to achieve our desired profit, and it includes the purchase price AND the costs to stabilize. In this scenario, our cost-to-value ratio was 72% ($900,000 ÷ $1,250,000; that is, our max allowable investment or all-in number was 72% of the ASV, which left us with a margin of 28% or $350,000.

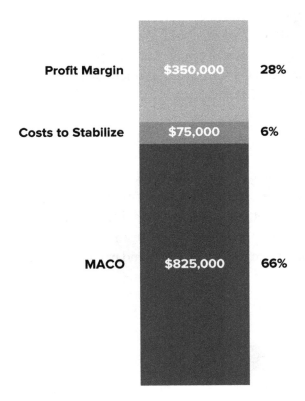

ASV Composition

Profit Margin	$350,000	28%
Costs to Stabilize	$75,000	6%
MACO	$825,000	66%

Magic Multiple

The cost-to-value ratio for your deal is something you pick, and it's simply what percent of the ASV you want to keep your costs at.

You can use a cost-to-value ratio to convert the Market Multiple to what I call the Magic Multiple. The Magic Multiple is simply the Market Multiple adjusted for the desired cost to value ratio. In our example, the Magic Multiple was 9.0 (12.5 × 72%).

Magic Multiple = Market Multiple × Desired CTV Ratio

So where the market would pay $12.50 for each dollar of NOI, we desired to keep our costs at 72 percent of that and only pay $9.00 so we could make a 28 percent profit margin.

The Magic Multiple is super slick because you can use it to quickly figure out your maximum allowable investment for any NOI. Basically, you can skip a few steps. For example, on Center Drive, I could simply take the projected stabilized NOI of $100K and multiply it by nine to get the max investment of $900K and then subtract my costs of $75K to get my MACO of $825K.

But wait—there's more!

You could go a step further and combine this with the shortcut I showed you earlier for getting NOI using net lease rates without itemizing expenses. By combining the Magic Multiple with this net rent approach to solving for NOI, you can actually determine the max investment per square foot for any property in any market for a given rent rate, occupancy rate, collection rate, and cap rate combination. Let me show you how to do it.

First, here is the formula.

MAI per SF Formula

$$\frac{\text{MAI}}{\text{SF}} = \frac{\text{NOI}}{\text{SF}} \times \textbf{Magic Multiple}$$

Net Rent Rate ×
Occupancy Rate ×
Collection Rate ×
Expense Pass-Through Rate

Market Multiple ×
Desired CTV Ratio

So the most you can be all-in on a property per square foot can be found by simply taking your NOI per square foot times your Magic Multiple. For example, on Center Drive, our market net rent rate (equivalent) was $6, occupancy was 93%, collection was 95% and cap rate was 8%. We figured on an expense pass-through rate of 95% to account for expenses we would absorb. Our Magic Multiple is nine. Put them together in the formula:

Max Allowable Investment per SF = ($6.00 × 93% × 95% × 95%) × 9 = $45.00

This means you can be all-in at $45 per square foot for any properties matching this same criteria. If I was looking at another building like Center Drive that was one hundred thousand square feet and needed $500,000 in costs to stabilize, I could evaluate it quickly.

MAI = $45.00 × 100,000 = $4,500,000

I would subtract the $500,000 from that to back into my MACO of $4,000,000.

This property is way bigger though, so what if we think the rental rate will be lower than Center Drive?

You can use this technique to assemble a Market Matrix or a table that summarizes the market data and helps you calculate the max investment per square foot you can make in any property across a variety of metric combinations.

Here is an example:

How to Calculate Max Allowable Investment per Square Foot

Line #	Sign	Metric	Warehouse	Office	Retail
1		NNN Rent Rate	$5.00	$6.50	$7.00
2	×	Occupancy Rate	93%	93%	93%
3	×	Collection Rate	95%	95%	95%
4	×	Expense Pass-Through Rate	95%	95%	95%
5	=	NOI ÷ SF	$4.20	$5.46	$5.88
6		Desired CTV Ratio	75%	75%	75%
7	÷	Market Cap Rate	9.00%	8.50%	7.00%
8	=	Magic Multiple	8.33	8.82	10.71
9	ln 5 × ln 8	Max Investment per SF	$34.97	$48.14	$62.95

You can download this tool on our website or recreate it within a spreadsheet by using the formulas on the left side. Then simply plug the numbers you got from market research into it to figure out roughly how much you can invest per square foot for each type of property. This will help you know if a deal is a good deal or a bad deal right away.

In my example, you are looking at an area where NNN rents for warehouses are $5.00 per square foot, vacancy rates are 7%, and delinquency rates are 5%. If your desired CTV ratio is 75% and the market cap rate is 9%, then your Magic Multiple for warehouses is 8.33 and the max investment per square foot is $34.97.

The NNN rent rate is the potential net rent. You might see it referred to as "net rent." You adjust that for vacancy and credit loss to get your actual expected NOI per square foot. If the market demands a 9 percent return for this product (or a Market Multiple of 11.11), and you want to pay 75 percent of what the market will pay, then you can invest up to $34.97 per square foot to achieve that 25 percent gross profit margin. For office space, you know you can spend $48.14 per square foot, and for retail, you can spend $62.95 per square foot.

Your time is valuable. Use this tool to pre-filter deals before you start looking at what's listed. If you are looking at a warehouse listed at $75 per square foot, you know quickly that it's double what you can pay in cash. You are a financial buyer who can pay a multiple of the NOI per square foot that the market will bear, and because you want to create equity, that multiple is lower than the Market Multiple. If it's a great deal, you will probably have to do a creative seller financing deal to get anywhere close to that number—or you can just spend your time finding better deals to look at instead of trying to make a bad deal work.

For Center Drive, the MACO was $825,000 for me to make $350,000. I made an offer at $600,000 and it got rejected. Ninety days later, we revived the deal and got it done at $700,000.

Figuring Out What to Pay for Exit to Owner-User

Remember earlier I said I would also show you how to project an ARV and exit to an owner-user instead of a financial buyer? Here's how you do it.

You should use this method to analyze vacant buildings that are best suited for a single tenant. This approach is the exact same way you analyze how much you can pay for a house you want to flip. Pull sales comps for fully renovated buildings that sold to owner-users to project the future value, then build in your desired margin and deduct your costs to back into what you can pay.

In this case, you still have fix costs, closing costs, and holding costs, but you won't have fill costs. This is the same as the MAO formula for house flips.

MACO = ARV – Costs to Fix/Hold/Close – Desired Profit

If we have a ten thousand-square-foot single-tenant warehouse building and we want to renovate it and sell it to a business owner, I would see what other pretty buildings like that sold for per square foot.

Comparable Sales Approach Example

Property	Sale Price	SF	Price ÷ SF
Comp A	$1,050,000	10,000	$105
Comp B	$950,000	11,000	$86
Comp C	$775,000	8,500	$91
		Average	**$94**

In this case, the average price per square foot for the comps is $94. Now let's analyze how much we can pay if we want to make the same $350,000 margin. Let's assume our costs are $60,000 now since we don't have to lease it.

$$\text{MACO} = (\$94 \times 10{,}000) - \$60{,}000 - \$350{,}000 = \$530{,}000$$

In this case, we would pay $530,000 and put $60,000 into it. We would be all in at $590,000, and the property would sell on the open market for $940,000. I'm sure by now you're wondering about the costs to sell. I take them out of the $350,000 profit to keep it simple, so I would really net more like $300,000 after paying 5% for closing costs and commissions on the sell-side.

If the seller counteroffered me at $700,000, which is way above my MACO, I would figure out my break-even price to see how much I would make at that price. My break-even price is $940,000 minus the $60,000 in costs, or $880,000. So if I accepted the offer at $700,000, I would have a gross profit of $180,000 and a net profit of around $130,000 after closing costs. You can see why it's important to know what your break-even price is so you can make an informed decision instead of just drawing a line in the sand that you aren't willing to cross.

MACO Worksheet Summary

This is how to analyze any property to figure out exactly how much you can pay for it. It is a critical skill, so let's summarize it again just to make sure you got it.

You don't apply a cap rate to the current NOI to figure out what to offer. You figure out the current NOI to evaluate as-is cash flow and account for any negative cash flow as a cost to hold the property in your analysis.

To figure out what to pay, project the future NOI and estimate how much you can sell that NOI for someday in the future. From there, subtract the costs to stabilize and desired profit margin to back into what you can pay for the property today—your MACO.

To figure out your NOI, you calculated the potential gross income using a rent roll. Then you applied an occupancy and collection rate to the potential rent to convert it to actual rent. From there, you deducted the seven operating expenses (TUMMIRA) to arrive at your NOI.

You accomplished all of this using the MACO worksheet.

If you plan to sell to an owner-user instead of a financial buyer, you do the same process, but you use sales comps to project the future value instead of an income approach, and you leave out the cost to fill as a cost to stabilize.

Now that you know how much you want to pay for the building, you are going to learn how to draft, present, negotiate, and get your offer accepted.

Key Reader Takeaways

- ☐ Use a rent roll and market research to project your income.
- ☐ Blend historic expenses with research and common sense to estimate future expenses.
- ☐ Translate your stabilized NOI to an as-stabilized value (ASV) using a market cap rate.
- ☐ Deduct your costs to fix, fill, hold, and close on the property from your ASV to determine your break-even price. This is the top end of your negotiating range.
- ☐ Deduct your desired margin to arrive at your MACO. This is the starting point of your negotiating range.
- ☐ Charge yourself an acquisition fee.

Action Items

- ☐ Decide if you will flip the building to an owner-user or fill it with tenants and sell it to a financial buyer.
- ☐ Figure out your Magic Multiple.
- ☐ Create a market matrix for different rent rate, vacancy rate, and cap rate combinations and see what the max investment per square foot is that you will pay for those scenarios.
- ☐ Complete a MACO worksheet for the property you toured using the appropriate method.
- ☐ Write down your break-even price and MACO.

Chapter 12

Determine Creative Offers

Objective: Come Up with Two Other Offers That Are at Higher Prices but Include Seller Financing

After crunching the numbers on Center Drive, I got excited when I uncovered that the existing rents were significantly below the market rents. I ran into my partner's office and shouted, "We have to make an offer right now and lock this thing up! This building has tremendous potential. The effective rent rate today is not what the market rent rate is and…"

He stopped me dead in my tracks. "STOP. Listen to me, and you listen good—"

He proceeded to tell me a story about two bulls—a father and a son—who had come over the hillside and looked down on a field full of cows.

The young bull screamed at his dad in excitement and said, "Dad, let's RUN down there and get one of them!"

Dad-Bull, said, "Whoa, son, not so fast. Let's WALK down there SLOWLY and get them all!"

My partner was teaching me Negotiations 101, and I didn't even know it.

Never fall in love with a deal, and always be reluctant and willing to walk away. Do not be too excited, or the seller will take advantage of that, and you will end up over-paying. Remember the cat and mouse game you played with your spouse when you first met them? If you play hard to get, they will want you even more, but if you're easy to get, they don't want you anymore.

I left his office feeling kind of depressed, but I did write up the offer for $600,000 like he asked me to. I presented the offer. They rejected it.

He told me, "That's okay. My first offer gets rejected on almost every deal I do. Follow-up is the key." And it was. I followed up ninety days later and got the deal done at $700,000, which was $475,000 less than my break-even purchase price.

In the last chapter, you determined your Max Allowable Cash Offer—the most you could pay for a property to achieve your desired profit without the seller helping to finance the purchase.

In this chapter, I'm going to teach you about different seller financing structures and show you how to pay *more* than the MACO if you can get the seller to finance part of the deal. Then you'll compile and present the different offers to see if the seller cares more about price or terms. Just remember to be flexible on your terms to get a deal done, as long as it meets your minimum margin requirements (mine again, are 15% of the ASV or $250,000, whichever is greater).

Benefit of Seller Financing

Let me run you through a common real-world scenario. You just calculated your MACO and presented it. The seller is sticking to their (much higher) price. You try to employ some PhD-level negotiating tactics, but it falls flat. You both come to the conclusion you are too far off, hang the hat up, and leave the conversation feeling frustrated.

The typical zero-sum negotiation is about arguing over who gets what pieces of the pie. It is a win-lose proposition. If you get more pieces of the pie, the seller gets less. The creative negotiation is about how you guys can increase the size of the pie altogether so that each party doesn't just get what they *need*; they also get what they *want*.

Meeting Needs and Wants with Creative Offers

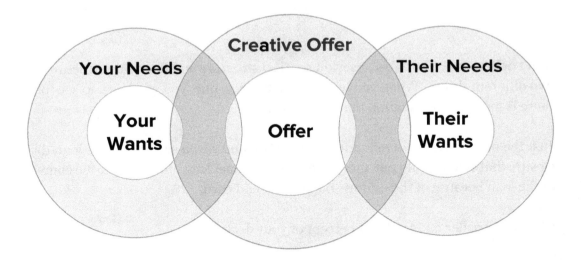

I'm going to teach you how to give them the price tag they want if they will give you the terms you need. Unlocking this secret will extend your negotiating price range by up to 50 percent (although you want to cap it at 30 percent), and you will win 30–50 percent more deals if you present multiple offers at different price points.

Here is a diagram showing how your negotiating price range is extended when you can reduce your overall cost of capital by getting seller financing.

Negotiating Ranges for Cash and Creative Offers

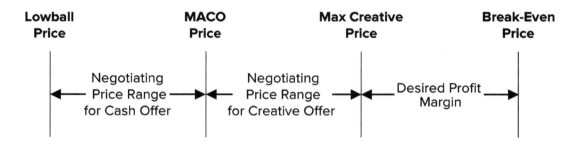

You can pay up to $1.5M for a $1M property and close with a smile on your face.

Don't believe me? That's because you see deal structure and financing structure as two different things. When you learn to see them as one, you will learn to see that there is more to the equation than just price.

Just the other day, I was refinancing my house and saw a section on the loan disclosure that said I would pay 150 percent of the actual loan amount over the course of the loan because of the interest the bank would earn.

What if the seller financed 100 percent of your deal?

Couldn't you pay them 1.5 times your MACO and still achieve the same cash flow for the entire duration of the loan period? That's just giving the interest to the seller instead of the bank. Similarly, if the seller reduced the amount of capital you have to raise from equity partners by financing some of the deal, couldn't you share with them some of the profits you would pay your limited partners in the form of a higher price?

Furthermore, if you pay a higher price and a below-market interest rate to the seller, they save taxes because the principal portion of the payments is only taxed at the capital gains rate—and they pay those taxes over time, which keeps them in a lower tax bracket every year.

In most creative offer scenarios, the seller will actually make more money than they would if they sold for all cash. They'll get a higher price and an above-checking-account interest rate on the financing they provide, and they'll pay a lower effective tax rate on the gains. Plus, they'll also enjoy an income stream they no longer have to work for.

This methodology (paying a higher price in lieu of the seller reducing your cost of funds) is the basis for creative seller-financing offers. Everyone thinks cash is the best offer until you show them a different way. They won't be convinced unless you are, so let me show you why this actually is better for the seller.

BEYOND THE CASH

The reality is that the seller doesn't want all cash. They want what the cash can do for them. Here are four things cash can do for them.

1. Allow them to buy something
2. Provide income for retirement
3. Give them peace of mind
4. Create a legacy for their heirs

Remember that all human decisions are based on one of two things: avoiding pain or seeking pleasure. Figure out what their pain points are and what pleasure they seek. This is why I taught you to ask so many probing questions during the tour to try and uncover their hot button. Sometimes they open up to you and sometimes they don't. That's why you give them multiple options to choose from, so they can decide for themselves even when you can't uncover their real motives.

An offer includes two key elements: price and terms.

FIGURE

The old trick is to tell the seller, "You pick the price, and I will pick the terms, or you pick the terms, and I will pick the price." If they draw a line in the sand for a price that is higher than your MACO, then you have to get seller financing, reduce your desired profit margin, or walk. If they name the terms, like receiving all cash, then you will name your MACO price.

Here are my favorite deal structures:

1. Cash Offer
2. Seller Carryback for 20%
3. Contract for Deed at 80% or 90%
4. Master Lease with Option to Purchase

The main goal of a contract for deed, seller carryback, or master lease with option to purchase is to decrease either the amount of equity or the rate on the equity, thus reducing your cost of funds. This will allow you to pay more for the building and achieve the same cash flow. Your ability to get deals done will increase dramatically if you can foster this creative approach to finding solutions that work for you *and* the seller.

Here is a visualization of how the capital stack changes with each of these offer types.

Capital Stacks for Various Offer Types

LTC	Cash	Seller Carry	CD @ 90%	CD @ 80%	Master Lease
100%	LP Capital	LP Capital	LP Capital	LP Capital	Master Lease
90%	LP Capital	Seller Carryback		LP Capital	Master Lease
80%	LP Capital	Seller Carryback			Master Lease
70%	Bank Debt	Bank Debt	Contract for Deed	Contract for Deed	Master Lease

A capital stack is nothing more than the way the debt and equity capital are stacked to fund the deal. There are an unlimited number of options for how the capital can be stacked. You are going to be focusing on deals from $500K to $2M to begin, so it won't require a lot of equity. As you scale your business up and start doing deals that are $5M, $10M, or even $100M, you will need to have much more complex capital stacks to bring in funding from other sources.

Let's do a quick recap on each of the deal structures to be sure you understand how they work and why we use them.

A Cash Offer is really a cash equivalent offer. You will likely finance 70 percent of the total capital you need with a bank loan and raise the down payment from limited partners by forming a partnership.

A Seller Carryback is where you buy the property, but the seller gives you a second mortgage behind the new bank loan. Usually, you can pay them a very nice interest rate on this second loan and still have it be far less than you would otherwise pay equity partners to come in on your deal. Plus, you keep a much higher percent ownership in your deal. The IRS favors sellers that do a seller carryback, and they also get taxed over time much like the contract for deed scenario, plus they have a note guaranteed by you and a mortgage on the property should you ever default.

A Contract for Deed is where you contract with the seller to make payments to them for a certain period of time and then make a lump sum payment at the end, at which point they will deliver you the deed to the property; hence its name, contract for deed. Many states call this a land contract. Same thing. The major benefits of a contract for deed include faster due diligence, lower closing costs, flexibility on rate and term, and being able to get a much higher loan-to-value. Sometimes it's only having to put 10 or 20 percent down instead of 25 to 30 percent that a bank would require. The seller doesn't pay the tax liability on their entire capital gain up front; they pay it over time as they receive the contract payments. They also earn interest on their funds. If you ever default, the seller simply cancels the contract which is far easier than foreclosing on the property.

A Master Lease with Option to Purchase is where you just sign a lease for the entire property. It's called a master lease because they assign all of the rights in all of the current leases to you, and you make one absolute net lease payment to them each month. They get to keep the entire depreciation since they still own the property. If you default on the lease, they just evict you. These scenarios work great on properties where the seller wants a premium on price, and you convince them to give you some time to clean up the property to increase the value so you can afford to give them that price. You don't want to have a lot of cash in the deal. If the property has a stable income, but it's still depressed, you can offer to make lease payments for the amount they are already netting, secured by a $50,000 down payment or something of that nature. Then they can be relieved of the joys of management. As you stabilize the building and create value, you get to enjoy the spread between the NOI you are getting and the net rents you are paying them until you exercise your option, which you will do when the value far exceeds your option price. I like to build in a few months of free rent on the front to sweeten the deal, and I like to guarantee a certain amount of renovation will be done during that time period to make them feel more comfortable. I also like to have 30 percent of my monthly rent payments get applied to my option price, which effectively reduces my strike price that I can exercise the option at.

Now that you understand the scenarios, let me show you how to figure out what terms you need to get in order to pay a premium on price.

Pro Tip

Balloon and amortization are two different things. The amortization is the period over which the loan would be paid in full, whereas a balloon is the period after which you will be forced to pay off the loan in full. The balloon period is often referred to as the "term."

USING THE MACO PRICE MULTIPLIER TABLES

Below, you will find four tables. Two of them are contract-for-deed scenarios, one is a seller carryback scenario, and one is a master lease with the option to purchase. I created these tables by solving for the MACO you can pay in order to have the annual cost of funds and the total balance due on your debt and equity obligations (at the time the seller financing balloons) be the same as the cash scenario.

To accomplish that, I used a ridiculously complicated formula and a spreadsheet that would make you sick to your stomach. You can get the calculator with all of the formulas and a training video on how to use it in our course. Feel free to check it out at www.commercialinvestingmastery.com/course.

What you need to know is that each of these scenarios reduces your weighted average cost of funds because you are replacing expensive equity with cheaper seller financing. In turn, you can pay more for the property and still achieve the same cash flow. The longer the seller lets you benefit from this cheaper financing, the more you can pay. That's why you will see the multiplier go up as the balloon period increases. In the case of the option, you will see it's an option period instead of a balloon because you are just leasing the property with an option to buy.

Contract for Deed Price Multiplier Table
25-Year Amortization, 90% CD

Rate Over (Under) the Debt Rate

Balloon	−2%	−1.50%	−1%	−0.50%	0%	+0.5%	+1%	+1.5%	+2%
5	115%	113%	111%	110%	108%	106%	104%	103%	101%
10	127%	124%	120%	117%	114%	111%	108%	105%	102%
15			128%	123%	119%	115%	111%	107%	104%
20				128%	123%	118%	114%	109%	105%

Contract for Deed Price Multiplier Table
25-Year Amortization, 80% CD

Rate Over (Under) the Debt Rate

Balloon	−2%	−1.50%	−1%	−0.50%	0%	+0.5%	+1%	+1.5%	+2%
5	109%	107%	106%	105%	103%	102%	101%	99%	98%
10	115%	113%	111%	108%	106%	104%	101%	99%	97%
15	121%	117%	114%	111%	108%	105%	102%	99%	96%
20	124%	120%	117%	113%	110%	106%	103%	100%	97%

Seller Carryback Price Multiplier Table
Interest Only, 20% Seller Carryback

Rate Over (Under) the Debt Rate

Balloon	0%	+1%	+2%	+3%	+4%	+5%	+6%	+7%	+8%
5	108%	107%	106%	105%	105%	104%	103%	102%	102%
10	115%	113%	111%	110%	108%	107%	105%	104%	103%
15	120%	117%	115%	113%	111%	109%	107%	106%	104%
20	124%	121%	118%	116%	113%	111%	109%	107%	105%

FIGURE

Lease with Option Price Multiplier Table
100% Financing

% of Annual Cost of Funds Made as Net Rent Payment

Option Period	80%	85%	90%	95%	100%	105%	110%	115%	120%
2	110%	108%	106%	104%	102%	100%	98%	96%	95%
3	112%	110%	108%	106%	103%	101%	99%	97%	96%
5	115%	113%	111%	109%	107%	105%	103%	101%	99%
10	120%	117%	115%	112%	110%	108%	106%	103%	100%

FIGURE

Let me walk you through each table and show you how to use it to convert your MACO price to a seller financing price.

There are two ways to use these tables:

1. Seller picks a price, and you have to figure out the terms you need in order to pay that price.
2. You pick the terms from the table and calculate what price you can pay at those terms.

I started this chapter by giving you a very real scenario where the seller is stuck on a price that exceeds your MACO. Our MACO for Center Drive is $825,000. Let's say the seller was stuck on $900,000 as a price and wouldn't budge. What I would do is present my cash price at $825,000 along with a couple scenarios at their price of $900,000.

To figure out what terms we need in order to give them their price, we need to figure out what multiple their price is as a percent of our MACO.

$$\text{MACO Price Multiple} = \frac{\text{Creative Price}}{\text{MACO Price}}$$

In this case, the answer is 109% ($900,000 ÷ $825,000). That is, their price is 109% of my MACO price. So I could find a scenario in any of the four tables close to 109%, and that's the terms I would need to get. I've highlighted scenarios that get you close to their price in gray. (Note that my cost of debt is 4.5% for all of these assumptions as the debt rate.)

For example, in the first table, if they gave you a contract for deed at 90% of the purchase price, you would only have to raise 10% in capital from limited partners. If they gave you an interest rate the same as you could get at a bank, on a twenty-five-year amortization with a five-year balloon, you could pay 108% of the MACO. There is a little flexibility here, so it's not necessary to calculate the creative price down to the dollar. Feel free to round up to a number that presents well. The result is that 108% of our MACO is $891,000, but $900,000 sounds better, so go with that. The goal is to have at least one offer at the price they are sticking to. I'll show you why in the next chapter.

From the second table, you could do a CD at 80% of the purchase price requiring you to raise 20% of the capital from your partners, at a rate 1% lower than you would get at your bank with a ten-year balloon.

From the third table, you could pay them their price if they did a 20% seller carryback at the same rate your bank would give you with a five-year balloon or at a rate 5% higher than your bank would give you on a fifteen-year term.

From the fourth table, you could propose a master lease with an option to purchase with a monthly payment equal to 80% of what your annual cost of funds would be if you financed the deal under a cash scenario. The deal would be structured with a two-year option to purchase at 110% of your MACO. We will calculate your cost of funds in a minute.

Those are the ways you can fix a price and back into the terms you need. Alternatively, you can fix the terms by simply choosing a scenario in any of the tables and calculating the price you can pay under that scenario.

These tables are a game changer because they allow you to quickly figure out what terms you need to get in order to pay them their price. Notice that none of the tables have a MACO price multiplier that exceeds 128 percent. You don't want to have your price be higher than your break-even purchase price. It's one thing to get seller financing long term and make it a cash flow play more than an equity play, but you still want to have some equity in the property beyond your total investment. Double-check to make sure that your new creative price isn't higher than your break-even purchase price. If it is, select new terms that reduce the creative price.

HOW TO CALCULATE YOUR ANNUAL COST OF FUNDS

You calculate your annual cost of funds as follows.

$$\textbf{Annual Cost of Funds} = \textbf{WACCC} \times \textbf{Total Capital}$$

Here is a table showing you how to do this.

WACCC Calculation for Center Drive

Line #	Calculation	Metric	Amount
1	Get from Lender	Debt Rate	4.50%
2	Get from Lender	Debt Amortization (Yrs)	25
			↓
3	Loan Calculator	Debt Constant	6.670%
4	Sources and Uses	Debt Ratio	71.13%
5	You Pick	Seller Carry Rate	
6	You Pick	Seller Carry Ratio	
7	You Pick	Equity Rate	8.00%
8	100%-4-6	Equity Ratio	28.87%
9	(3×4)+(5×6)+(7×8)	**WACCC %**	**7.054%**

The WACCC is your weighted average cost of capital constant, which is just the weighted cost of your funding shown as a percentage. You get it by adding up the weighted cost of capital for each piece of the capital stack. I show you how to do that in the chart above. You'll see I used a debt ratio of slightly under my 75% loan-to-cost because we are not financing the repairs, so we actually have to raise 28.87% in equity. In the next chapter, I show you how to figure this out using a sources and uses worksheet.

If you raised \$1M and your WACCC was 10%, then it would cost you \$100,000 per year to service your debt and equity (which includes principal). In our scenario, our MACO was \$825,000, and our costs to stabilize were \$75,000, so we needed to raise \$900,000 in capital. As you can see in the table, the weighted cost of capital in our cash scenario is 7.054%, so our annual cost of funds would be \$63,486 (\$900,000 × 7.054%). You have \$100,000 in NOI and you burn up \$63,486 of it servicing your debt and equity partners. The partnership will have \$36,514 per year in cash flow once the building is stabilized. You will get a cut on that.

Please note that if you calculate the WACCC and the annual cost of funds under any of the other scenarios, you will get a similar annual cost of funds because that's the method I used to create the tables in the first place.

It's good to calculate your WACCC for your baseline financing scenario and know what it is because you can compare this to your cost cap rate to figure out if you will cash flow as the general partner. If the WACCC is lower than the cost cap rate, then you will get paid as a general partner.

A cost cap rate is the stabilized NOI divided by the total investment.

$$\text{Cost Cap Rate} = \frac{\text{Stabilized NOI}}{\text{Total Investment}}$$

It's similar to a market cap rate but with one major change: the denominator is the total investment as opposed to value. If you know any two parts of the formula, you can solve for the third. For example, for Center Drive, you already know the stabilized NOI is \$100,000 and the total investment for our Center Drive scenario is \$900,000 if our MACO offer was accepted.

Let's solve for our cost cap rate.

$$\text{Cost Cap Rate} = \frac{\$100,000}{\$900,000} = 11.11\%$$

Here's an infographic showing you how this all comes together nicely.

Cash Flow and Equity Upside to the General Partner

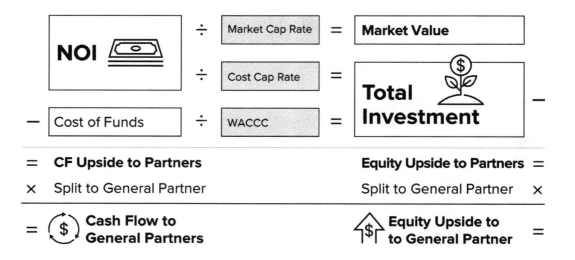

You use the market cap rate to translate NOI to market value. You use the cost cap rate to translate NOI to total investment. You use the WACCC to translate the total investment to your annual cost of funds.

The delta between market value and total investment is your equity upside to the partnership. The delta between the NOI and the annual cost of funds is the cash flow upside to the partners. You will get your split of this upside on the cash flow and the equity, and we cover how to determine that split and structure the partnership in the next step, Fund.

You made a massive leap forward in your understanding in this chapter. Now you understand how market cap rate, cost cap rate, and the WACCC all play an important role in determining your equity and cash flow. Here are the final rates and the corresponding multiples for the Center Drive property, assuming we paid the MACO. We will recalculate these later using the real purchase price on the sources and uses worksheet. Remember, the multiples and the rates are just inverses of each other.

The 3 Key Multiples/Rates

Market Value	Break-Even CF to Sponsor	Total Investment
Market Cap Rate 8.00%	WACCC 7.054%	Cost Cap Rate 11.11%
Market Multiple 12.5	Sponsor Multiple 14.176	Magic Multiple 9

FIGURE

You'll see a new term here called the Sponsor Multiple. That's just the inverse of the WACCC and it's the multiple of NOI you can invest in the property for you to break even on cash flow during the holding years. If you invest more than that, you won't get paid as the deal sponsor during the holding years.

You unlocked the secret to a creative deal structure using seller financing and understand the moving pieces of the pie that create cash flow for the partnership. You now have a set of MACO price multiplier tables you can use to figure out what terms you need in order to give the seller their price. Or you can simply select some terms and make up a couple different price points if you can't get the seller to name a specific price.

Remember that equity is expensive but doesn't have guaranteed payments. Debt is cheap but does have guaranteed payments. The idea is to get cheaper overall financing by finding ways to reduce the amount of equity you have to raise without overleveraging yourself and creating more risk. Now select a few scenarios and write your terms/prices down. In the next chapter, we are going to present your deal and get this property under contract.

Key Reader Takeaways

☐ Price or terms: let the seller pick one.

☐ Always present multiple offers.

☐ Use seller financing to reduce your WACCC, which allows you to pay a higher price and achieve the same cash flow.

☐ If cost cap rate > WACCC, you will get paid during the holding years as the deal sponsor.

☐ If cost cap rate > market cap rate, you will get paid at disposition as the deal sponsor.

Action Items

☐ Pick a few scenarios from the MACO price multiplier tables and calculate the corresponding prices.

☐ Calculate your WACCC.

☐ Calculate your cost cap rate for the deal you are analyzing and see how it compares to the market cap rate and your weighted average cost of capital constant.

Chapter 13

Present Your Offers

Objective: Present Three Offers and Get a Signed Purchase Contract

FIGURE

In the last two chapters, you figured out your cash and creative offer prices. Now it's time to get the numbers into a presentable format and get your deal inked.

The first step is to summarize the price, down payment, and monthly payment to seller for each creative scenario. I use a spreadsheet to calculate these for me, but you can do it using a loan calculator on your phone too if you wish. You'll want to do this for each piece of the capital stack under each scenario by calculating the annual payments and then dividing by twelve to get the monthly payment.

Write them (or type them) out on a simple offer sheet like this. Always put the highest offer price first and work your way down to the lowest offer price, which is usually the cash scenario.

Offer Term Sheet

☐ Option 1: Master Lease

- Option Price $1,000,000
- 10-Year Absolute Net Master Lease
- Tenant to Make $35K in Repairs to Building Minimum
- Monthly Net Rent $4,250 via Direct Deposit
- 6 Months Free Rent
- Close in 45 Days

☐ Option 2: Contract for Deed

- Purchase Price $935,000
- 25-Year Amortization, 5-Year Balloon
- 10% Down at Closing, $93,500
- Monthly Payments $4,000 @ 3%
- Close in 60 Days

☐ Option 3: Seller Carry

- Purchase Price $907,500
- 10-Year Balloon
- $181,500 Seller Carryback @ 7.5%
- Monthly Payments of $1,134.38
- Close in 90–120 Days

☐ Option 4: Cash Equivalent

- Purchase Price $825,000
- 100% in Cash at Closing
- Close in 90–120 Days

_____

Seller Signature

Here's how I got the numbers.

I used the master lease scenario at 80% of the cost of funds($63,486 × 80% = $50,788.80 annually, or $4,232.40 monthly). The ten-year-option multiplier was 120% which comes out to be $990,000. I rounded the purchase price and monthly payment up slightly and compensated with free rent. I also guaranteed them I would make the repairs necessary as I had planned to do anyway.

For the contract for deed scenario, I used the 90% table "−1.50%" scenario with a five-year balloon. The multiplier is 113% which came out to be 932,250 ($935,000 with rounding). Then I took 90% of the $935,000 ($841,500) and calculated the loan payment at 3% interest (4.5% debt rate minus 1.5%), twenty-five-year amortization to get the monthly payment of $3,990.49 which I rounded up to $4,000 even.

For the seller carryback, I used the multiplier for the scenario at bank rate plus 3% with a ten-year balloon to get the price of $907,500 ($825,000 × 110%). Then I took 20% of that price to calculate the seller carryback amount of $181,500. I'm doing interest only, at 7.5% (4.5% debt rate + 3% increase), and my monthly payments are $1,134.38. I decided not to round this one.

PRESENTING THE OFFER

Once you have your offer summary sheet created, here's how you present it.

At the presentation meeting, build rapport, confirm their price and hot button (reason for selling), and then say, "Other than price or terms, is there any reason we wouldn't be able to put together a deal today?"

If they say yes, figure out why. If they say no, then slide your offer summary sheet across the table to them (or pull it up in the middle of a video call).

> **Pro Tip**
>
> Try to avoid sending offers in writing without being there to present them. If you absolutely can't get around it, make sure you take the time to explain your offers in a cover letter.

"Mister Seller, I've taken the liberty of structuring a few different offers that all work for me. Why don't I show them to you and then you can tell me which one will work best for *you*."

Then here's how I would go on to present each of the four offers.

OFFER #1: MASTER LEASE WITH OPTION

I understand you don't know me that well, and I want to prove myself to you. So my first offer is not a purchase at all. There is zero risk in it for you. I would propose a ten-year master lease with the option to purchase the property for $1M anytime during the ten-year period. I would pay you rent in the amount of $4,250 every month.

You would assign us all of the headaches, responsibilities, and leases at closing, and we would take over all rent collections, repairs, and capital improvements. You will never have to deal with leasing, collections, management, or maintenance on this property ever again. We would also begin paying 100 percent of all expenses, including taxes, utilities, maintenance, management, insurance, repairs, and administrative costs. Our contract will require us to do at least $35,000 in repairs to fix up the property within the first six months.

Because I will be investing so much money into the property in that time, and since the building isn't cash flowing that great, we are asking for six months of free rent until we can get the cash flow going.

The main benefits of this offer are freeing up your time, getting someone to manage the property for free, and getting a guaranteed net rent from us in one lump sum every month after that time is up. The best part is that since you are not selling the property, you would not have a recognizable capital gain from sale, and you get to keep taking the depreciation write-offs to offset your rental income.

Our reward for the hard work we would put into your property is that once we increase the NOI of the property, we would enjoy a spread between the rent we are collecting and the rent we are paying you. We are able to give you an above-market price under this scenario because you are giving us time to clean the property up and share the upside with you by way of a higher price.

We could close a deal like this in the next thirty to forty-five days.

OFFER #2: CONTRACT FOR DEED

The second offer is $935,000 on a contract for deed. I will hand you 10% of that in cash at closing, $93,500, and make ACH deposits to you every month in the amount of $4,000, which includes 3% interest for sixty consecutive months, at the end of which I will pay you off in full. I only need sixty days total to close, and once we close, we will cover 100% of the expenses. You won't have to pay a penny for anything.

The main benefits of this offer are a solid price, no headaches, and lower taxes because you pay them over time as you receive the money from me, and a nice passive income stream to enjoy.

I know you don't know me that well, so you're probably wondering what happens if I miss a payment to you. That's the best part of this for you. If we ever default, you keep our down payment, cancel the contract, and get your property back along with all the improvements in as little as sixty days. This should give you enough comfort that I'm going to see this through to completion and that this is a very safe deal for you.

OFFER #3: SELLER CARRYBACK

Now as you know, Mister Seller, equity is expensive and the banks make me come up with 30% down. I can pay you more if you can help me reduce my down payment. The third offer is $907,500 payable as 80% cash to you at closing and a second mortgage from you behind the bank for 20%, or $181,500. I would make monthly payments to you in the amount of $1,134.38 at an interest rate of 7.5% until I pay you off no later than ten years out. You would be secured by a lien against the property, and I would be personally guaranteeing the note.

I would still be putting down 10% so you know you're secure, and I would need the same timeframe to obtain financing as before. The main benefits to you with this offer are a little bit of a premium on price, substantially reducing your capital gain because you don't take it all at closing, and a very nice residual income stream at a super aggressive interest rate that lasts for ten years. If you want it to last longer, we can do that for you. With this scenario, we could close this within sixty days.

OFFER #4: CASH

The last offer is $825,000 all cash to you at closing. I will get a bank loan, and we can close after we get the clear to close from the lender. I probably need around sixty days contingency and sixty days to close.

CLOSE

"Is there one of these that would work for you?"

Then S.T.O.P.

Read their facial expressions as they read over your offers again.

He who speaketh first, loseth!

This can get super awkward, but let it marinate. Do not say a word. When they finally speak, they will either have selected an offer and you have a deal, or they will give you an objection.

Handling Objections

First, read the book *Never Split the Difference*. If you want to be a superstar negotiator, knowing their objections up front will help you begin overcoming them earlier in the process.

Some people wait until the close to get all the objections on the table. By then, it's too late. You should be asking deep probing questions during the tour to get them all on the table. That is the whole purpose of the trial close at the end of the tour—so you aren't caught with your pants down at this stage.

Objections will come up. You won't be able to overcome all of them on the spot. For those, your goal is to schedule a follow-up action that will help to overcome them. Others are not really objections at all. It's just their subconscious paralyzing them from making a decision because they have fear. You can overcome their fear with this process:

- Agree
- Identify
- Validate
- Propose
- Close again

AGREE

"Appreciate" and "Understand" are my two favorite words. Be genuine. Don't just pretend to listen. Actually listen and seek to understand. If you say, "I can appreciate that," can you really appreciate it? If you can, you will come across as more genuine. Say it while nodding your head up and down. Then pause for a full second or two before continuing.

IDENTIFY

"Let me be sure I understand what you are saying," then repeat what they said but in different words. Doing this lets them know you actually comprehend what they are telling you.

If they say, "I need to talk to my partner," you failed because that should have come up in the trial close during the tour part and the partner or key advisor should already be at this table. However, they may just say something like, "I need to think about it." Here, you might just stare at them for twenty seconds in silence before saying this in a very calm, quiet manner, "Sure. What part do you need to think about?" They will eventually tell you, if you keep asking the same question in different ways—" Sure. What piece of information is missing to help you make your decision?"

VALIDATE

If they confirm your identification of the problem, then it's time to validate their feelings. For example, if they want to make sure they will net enough cash to buy the RV of their dreams, you can say, "I know how you feel. I would want to make sure I was getting what I want before signing too."

PROPOSE

Next comes an "if...then..." statement. For example, "So **if** you do run the numbers and determine you can make it work, **then** which scenario are you leaning toward?"

You're trying to get conditional approval by removing the condition they are using as their reason for not saying yes. If they say, "I have to talk to my advisors," then you can say, "So if your advisors approve the transaction, then the deal works for you?" They may say yes, maybe, or no. In any case, you're closer to isolating the problem.

CLOSE AGAIN

Pull back. Create a scarcity mentality. "Well John, I'm out making offers every day—and I would love to do this deal with you, but we only have so much equity raised right now. Do you need a day or so to make a decision, and we can schedule a time to check in by phone?"

Negotiation is an art form, and the gauge of your success is a signed purchase contract.

FOLLOW UP

Expect a *no* when you present your offer—or at least some kind of objection you can't get past. Almost every single one of my deals was a *no* or *maybe* that turned to a *yes* later. Do not come out of your offer presentation feeling defeated.

Resiliency and persistence are critical if you want to be successful in commercial real estate.

As with setting a tour, a *no* to an offer you made often means not right now, not the way you presented it, or not until I get more information. Anything you can do to facilitate the additional information and follow-up is key to getting more deals done.

On Center Drive, I called the broker ninety days after our $600K offer was rejected and asked her what it would take to put a deal together. Her dad's condition had taken a turn for the worse and their motivation level increased. We ended up getting that property under contract for $700K, and my MACO was $825K.

> **Pro Tip**
>
> I used to use a letter of intent (LOI) to present my offers. One time, I spent $15K in attorney's fees drafting the purchase agreement (PA) after a property owner signed the LOI, only to have the guy get talked out of the deal on the very last weekend by his family. I was out the money because the LOI is non-binding. Now I do one of these three things to protect myself: One, make them responsible for the legal fees if they back out. Two, skip the LOI altogether and write the offer up using the commercial version of the Realtor® board-approved purchase agreement forms. Three, just have their attorney draft the PA.

You learned to write out a term sheet and present it to the seller, starting with the highest price point and working your way down. You learned how to answer objections and follow up until you get a firm no or an exciting yes.

You'll do this over and over again until you get your first deal under contract.

Once that happens: Congratulations. Now the real work begins! In the next step, we cover how to structure away the risk in the deal by double-checking all of your underlying assumptions about income, expenses, and costs to stabilize. Then you will secure your debt and equity funding and close this bad chicken!

Key Reader Takeaways

- ☐ Start with the highest offer first when presenting.
- ☐ Stay silent after you ask the closing question, even if it's awkwardly silent.
- ☐ Follow-up is the key. Expect a no and expect to have to follow up to keep pursuing the deal. Their motivation may change over time.

Action Items

- ☐ Figure out the payments and organize your terms into a term sheet for the various offer scenarios you picked. Try to limit this to three to four offers.
- ☐ Write a cover letter or present your offers verbally, either in person or by video call.
- ☐ Get a purchase agreement signed, or figure out where you are off and schedule a follow-up.
- ☐ Go back and do more activity to look at more deals.

FIGURE

Step 3
Fund

You have a deal under contract! Now it's time to raise funds from your debt and equity partners. The Fund step is the third step of the seven steps and is all about structuring away as much risk as possible, raising the money, and getting the deal closed.

You'll need to be resilient when raising your debt and equity. Be prepared to hear no. A lot. When it happens, just listen, learn, and don't be afraid to change your business plan based on the feedback you are getting. Unless you come to the conclusion that your deal is not a winner, never give up.

You'll also have to dig deep into the numbers with the intention of finding a reason to cancel the deal. Don't make the mistake of falling in love with your deal or mentally cashing the check. You may create a blind spot for yourself and not see evidence that you made some bad assumptions in your initial MACO analysis. I learned this the hard way!

Here are the parts to getting your deal funded:

- Conduct Due Diligence
- Structure the Partnership

- Raise the Capital
- Secure the Debt
- Close the Deal

These steps are not necessarily done in sequential order. Most likely, you will be working on all of these steps at the same time, and probably starting the process to find investors and lenders before you even identify properties to make offers on.

Let's dive into each part in more detail.

Chapter 14

Conduct Due Diligence

Objective: Clear Your Contingency, Renegotiate, or Cancel Your Deal

There was a noticeable aching in my upper back. My shoulders felt like one hundred-pound bags were sitting on them. My stomach was growling, but I didn't have an appetite. I tried to shovel a piece of food into my mouth here and there so as not to raise any alarms with my wife, but it didn't work. About halfway into the dinner, she looked at me and said, "Honey, is everything okay? You haven't said a word all dinner!"

She called me out. I guess I better tell her.

"I think I made a big mistake. I signed a purchase agreement for a big commercial property today, and I am afraid I have no clue what I'm doing!"

I was literally paralyzed by fear. This experience is still very vivid in my memory because it was deeply emotional. My limiting beliefs and self-doubt began creating scenarios where I lost everything for our family, my wife divorced me, and I died cold and alone.

At a time when I should have been excited, I was more scared than I had ever been about a deal. That's because I didn't have a plan.

The underwriting action plan I'm going to lay out here lets you systematically structure away as much risk as is humanly possible so you can be confident in moving forward on your deal, cancelling it straight up, or asking the seller to come back to the table to renegotiate. I get very excited now when I have properties under contract, because I know I have a plan to reduce or eliminate most of the risk.

There are two parts to underwriting:

1. Collecting the due diligence documents from the seller.
2. Performing a list of tasks in a systematic way.

When you made your offer, you made some assumptions. Now it's time to test those assumptions, from financial and non-financial sides. The financial side is simply recalculating your MACO after you get your discovery done. Then you can make a decision to:

- Proceed with the contract as-is
- Renegotiate the contract
- Cancel the contract

The non-financial side is understanding the building, tenants, and market as a whole, so you can see the big picture. Your job is to start developing your business plan, which outlines the specific steps you will take to improve the NOI and the NOI multiple that the property will ultimately sell for.

Underwriting simply means to do your due diligence. The terms are synonymous.

It is your job to structure away as much risk as possible in this stage for your family, your partners, and your lender. Be thorough. Go in with eyes wide open. Never stop seeking advice that challenges your assumptions. Proactively seek feedback, digest what you need from it, and move forward. Don't let other people's opinions hold you back from executing your plan, but always leave room in your plan for improvement, flexibility, and adaptation. Become a mad scientist who constantly challenges his or her own hypothesis.

Update and keep notes on these items as you progress through the underwriting process.

You will put up earnest money when they accept your purchase agreement. I usually offer 1 percent of the purchase price, but you can do whatever amount you want. Time is of the essence. If you need to cancel your agreement, do it before your contingency expires, or you'll lose that money. Take a look at the overall timeline again as presented in the introduction.

Here are the action steps you can take to complete a very thorough due diligence in a systematic way to make sure you know exactly what you are buying:

- Review the Seller Documents
- Interview the Property Manager
- Interview the Tenants
- Interview the Vendors
- Inspect the Property
- Visit City Hall
- Measure the Interior of the Building
- Redo Market Research
- Survey
- Appraisal
- Title Commitment
- Collect Your Bids
- Update the MACO Analysis
- Make a Decision

Review the Seller Documents

The main purpose of the seller documents review is to verify the rent roll and historic expenses for the building, figure out how it operates, and uncover problems you were not previously aware of.

In the appendix, I've included a due diligence documents list you should have the seller provide. I recommend including it as part of your purchase agreement, so it is crystal clear what they are required to provide. Add any special documents that are deal-specific and eliminate any documents you don't want. Take the extra time to customize this and reference it in your PA so they are legally obligated to provide it.

Pro Tip

We give the seller fifteen calendar days to provide the seller documents, but we set the contingency deadline at forty-five days from the day they **actually** deliver the final document. This ensures they work swiftly to provide them in a timely manner, and it also automatically extends our contingency for every day they are delayed in delivering any missing documents. We also have them deliver the documents in an online folder like a Dropbox or Google Drive folder, so they are easy to review and organize.

Once you've collected the documents from the seller, take the time to *actually* read them. Let's go through some of the specific documents we review and what to look for in them.

LEASES

The leases are the most important to see. **Who pays what, when, and how?** Are there rent bumps? Are there options to purchase the building? Do they have the right to renew or cancel their lease? Are there any obligations the landlord has under the lease, like tenant improvements or credits that need to be credited to you at closing? How much is the security deposit? Does the tenant have to provide annual financials and insurance for their space? Do you have those items from the seller in your package?

PROFIT & LOSS DETAIL

If the seller uses an accounting software, request a general ledger report for the past three years in spreadsheet format (.xls or .csv). They can export these easily from QuickBooks or any type of software. That's all you need!

You can run a pivot table summary to see expenses by category for each year and review the actual expenses to see what they have been spending money on. Is one of the tenants consistently late on rent? Are there repairs being done every year for the roof or parking lot? Maybe it's time to replace them. Are there personal charges the seller included on there to be added back to the NOI? Does the rental income match the rent roll?

Adjust your final MACO worksheet with any changes to income or expense projections you may want to make.

OWNER STATEMENTS

We get signed statements from the owner for various things. I like them to describe the building operations—who does the janitorial work, mows the lawn, and plows the snow? How are the different meters billed out to the tenants? You can also interview the seller, write the statement out, and then have them sign it.

Get them to sign off on any known code violations, open issues with the city, descriptions of deferred maintenance, and descriptions of any insurance claims or lawsuits pending or completed in the last five years.

BANK STATEMENT REVIEW

Match the income and expenses from the bank statements to the income and expenses from the financial set they gave you. It's easy to manipulate a profit and loss statement, but hard to manipulate a bank statement. Make a spreadsheet with each month and the total deposits and checks written for each of those twelve months.

Use a formula to add up the whole year and compare that to the P&L. Figure out where the gaps are and make a list of questions for the seller. Maybe the expenses are a lot higher than they are saying they are in the P&L, or maybe the income isn't what they are stating it is.

UTILITY BILLS

Get two years of actual statements. Sellers rarely have these, so have them call and request the utility company to send them. Review all of the utility bills. Do they match your budget? How much can you save on electrical with LED upgrades? Can you shave gas bills down by installing a new heating system? How many meters are there, and who is paying them?

This is a big one, so spend time here and update your business plan and MACO worksheet with your findings. This will impact your utility expenses and costs to fix line items.

Interview the Property Manager

Start by interviewing the current owner's property manager and asking them to tour the building and show you everything they know. If the owner is the property manager, then you are doing this step with them.

Make notes. Create diagrams. Do whatever you need to do in order to extract their knowledge and get it in written format to pass on to the new property management company.

I like to have my new property manager at all of the interviews I'm doing during due diligence, which is one of the main benefits of selecting a property manager early on. If you don't have a management company in place yet, don't worry. This gets easier on the second or third deal.

Interview the Tenants

The main purpose of the tenant interviews is to uncover problems the tenant or building may have. They are in the building far more often than the owner and the property manager. Who best to tell you about the hidden problems!

The seller doesn't want you talking to the tenants because the tenants are going to give you the real story. Make it part of the purchase agreement that you will have the right to interview the tenants *without* the seller present.

I mail a welcome letter with a questionnaire. Then I request that we schedule a call or walkthrough. Are they happy where they are at? If their lease were up right now, would they renew? Why or why not? Do they want more or less space? Are there issues or repairs they are aware of or have requested to be done? Are there disputes with the landlord? Has the seller made any promises they haven't kept?

Interview the Vendors

Make sure you get a written vendor list from the seller and review it along with any contracts that may survive the sale. Call the existing vendors, introduce yourself as the potential buyer, and request a proposal. Here are some questions to ask:

- How are things going at the building?
- Any issues you are aware of you would want to see fixed?
- Any tenants they have trouble with or things they think we should know?
- Do they want to continue servicing the building?

Get them to send you new quotes for services in your company's name so you don't inherit an old contract. Let them know you have vendors you already use, but you would love to consider them to continue doing the service. This will keep them honest with their pricing.

Inspect the Property

The main purpose of the inspection is to uncover items you need to repair that you may be unaware of. You have a list of concerns from the property manager, seller, tenants, and vendors on potential issues with the building. Make sure your property inspector knows about those items.

Who cares if some paint is chipping—you want to know if the skeleton is in good shape or if it has an unseen cancer. Take a deep dive into the roof, mechanicals, electrical, asphalt, and structure.

Your inspector should use an inspection checklist. Follow them while they do this and ask questions. Figure out which walls are load-bearing and which ones are not. Have them figure out the gas, water, and electric meter setup. Walk every single nook and cranny. Are there any tenants on the rent roll whose units look vacant or no one is ever there? Make a note of the condition of tenant spaces. Trust me; they will happen to not have the keys for the closet with all the mold in it or where the foundation is cracked. Don't accept anything less than 100 percent access. Let them know that if you miss any units, you'll need to come back and see them.

Most good inspectors can summarize all of their findings into a table that shows all the big-ticket items and what they should cost to replace, how old they are, and what you should set aside for reserves each year. Have them create a capital reserves budget. Update your renovation budget with this information and how much you are setting aside for reserves.

Visit City Hall

The main purpose of the visit to city hall is to ensure you can use the building how you plan to use it and make sure they don't have open issues. Go visit the various city departments to do primary research on the building. Here are the departments I visit and the information I gather from each department.

BUILDING DEPARTMENT

The building department is a great place to understand what's been done to the building and what will be required for you to make the improvements you intend to make. Here are the questions I ask:

Are there any open building violations/permits? What permits have been pulled? How does that list match up with the scope and timing of the items the seller reported to you? If they said they replaced the roof five years ago but there is no permit, you might want to note that and question the seller further.

Were any permits pulled and not closed out that become your problem after closing? Make a list of them and require the seller to have them closed out before your real estate closing or ask that they escrow funds until they are closed. Don't inherit that headache without being compensated to do so.

What is the process for getting a permit? Get the city's permit fees and permitting process and grab an application.

What are the ADA requirements or other things you need to know in advance so you can budget for them? In many states, the city requires you to put 20 percent of your construction budget toward ADA upgrades in commercial buildings. I learned this the hard way. They usually have a pecking order for how the money needs to be spent, like access, elevators, upgraded bathrooms, ADA signage, doors, and so forth. Ask the city what they require, and learn how to be in compliance. Then make sure you have this in your budget.

Finally, if you have one, make sure your elevator has had a recent inspection and is in compliance.

FIRE DEPARTMENT

Sprinkler compliance. The fire department sometimes requires you to "upgrade" a building if you do a remodel and pull a permit. Don't ever assume that you can skip it just because the building has operated for one hundred years without it. The fire department likes to use any opportunity they can to get you to upgrade your building to increase the safety of the tenants. Tell them what you plan to do and see if it would trigger any fire or life safety upgrades.

ZONING DEPARTMENT

Get the zoning packet for your property. This tells you what you can use the building for. Read it. Make sure all of your tenants have certificates of occupancy or that their use of the space is a permitted use, or if not, that they have conditional use permits. Most buildings I buy have at least one tenant not in compliance. Don't raise the white flag down at the city just yet. Be careful how you ask your questions. You don't want to create issues for yourself down the road, but you do want to be able to decide to accept the risk or ask for a price concession.

Measure the Interior of the Building

You measured the building from the outside to get the overall dimensions, but you based your entire income projection on a square footage you were given for each tenant on the rent roll. Now it's time to verify the interior dimensions by measuring each unit within the building. A space measurement study is a study to determine the useable and rentable square footage of each unit in the building. You can find out if certain tenants are overpaying or underpaying by comparing the square footage on their lease to the rentable square footage of their unit.

It is critical that you understand the difference between useable and rentable square footages. Almost every single property I've ever looked at had very poor space measurement studies done, and the rentable square footages of the units were not accurate. If all of your leases are based on the rentable square footages, this can either be a big problem or a big opportunity. Use the results of the space measurement study to update your rent roll. Remember that you sign leases using rentable square footage, not useable square footage. Rentable square footage is the actual square footage plus their share of the common areas.

USEABLE SQUARE FOOTAGE

Useable square footage is the actual square footage of the tenant spaces within a building, including the walls surrounding their space. When measuring, you measure to the exterior surface on exterior walls and to the drywall on the common area side of an interior common area wall. On walls shared between two units, measure to the middle of the wall that separates them. We call this a demising wall.

RENTABLE SQUARE FOOTAGE

Rentable square footage is the useable square footage *plus* the unit's proportionate share of the common areas (if there is a common area).

Rentable Square Footage = Useable Square Footage × Common Area Factor

You always use rentable square footage on your advertising for vacant spaces, tenant leases, and discussions with tenants. That's why it's so critical that the building gets professionally measured to figure out the USF and RSF of each unit. This process is called doing a "space measurement study" and can be done by most architectural firms. Budget for it.

For buildings with common areas, you basically allocate the common areas back to each tenant based on their share of the building, like this:

How to Calculate Rentable Square Footage (RSF) from Useable Square Footage (USF)

Unit	Useable Square Footage (USF)	Common Area Factor (CAF)	Rentable Square Footage (RSF)
Common Area	300	0.000	0
A	900	1.0833	975
B	1,500	1.0833	1,625
C	600	1.0833	650
D	600	1.0833	650
Total	3,900		3,900

Here is how you translate the useable square footage for each unit to the rentable square footages:

- Step 1: Calculate the total USF. Add up the useable square footage first. We add the square footages for units A, B, C, and D, and it adds up to three thousand six hundred useable square feet.
- Step 2: Calculate the total RSF. We add the three hundred square feet for the common areas to get the total rentable square footage of the building. In this case, the total RSF is three thousand nine hundred square feet.
- Step 3: Calculate the CAF. Now you can calculate the common area factor. Basically, it's the multiplier that converts the total useable square footage to the total rentable square footage. In our example, it would be $3900 \div 3600 = 1.083$.

$$\textbf{Common Area Factor} = \frac{\textbf{RSF}}{\textbf{USF}}$$

- Step 4: Calculate the RSF of each unit. Multiply the useable square footage of each unit by the common area factor to translate it to the rentable square footage for that unit.

Pro Tip

We do a 3D tour of the building using a Matterport Camera and download the 3D model data to a file. This file can be uploaded into CAD to make exact floor plans and calculate the useable and rentable square footage of each unit, all without ever having stepped foot on the property. This saves tens of thousands of dollars. Then you will also have a 3D model and can move around walls and change space structures.

Redo Market Research

Verify that the rent rates, vacancy rates, and cap rates you used in your analysis at the time of the offer still stand. The best way to do this is to do comps and solicit broker proposals to lease the property.

LEASE COMPS

Pull actual comps for leases signed, and call the brokers involved and ask questions. Don't just look at stuff online. Pick up the phone and you will learn far more. You need to be 100 percent confident in what you can lease these spaces for, so just keep checking and calling until you get to that point. Go look at listings for sale and lease in the area and call the brokers to see what types of lease rates they are getting deals done at.

BROKER LISTING PROPOSALS

Walk a few brokers through the property and ask them these questions:

How much would they charge to list it? Who would they market it to? How would they market it to them? What price do they think it's worth today? What net rent rate do they think they can get for it? What kind of tenant improvement budget should you set aside? How long do they think it would take to lease? Have a formal proposal sent over and begin thinking about selecting a broker. We will cover this process in more detail in the Fill step.

Survey

Order an ALTA survey to satisfy your lender. I usually wait to do this until I've cleared all my financial due diligence to limit my exposure in case I have to cancel. Review the survey and make sure there are no encroachments, which are things that other people have that extend onto your property or items on your property that extend onto theirs. What's the actual size of the parcel? Is any of it wetland?

Appraisal

Read the appraisal you get on the property. This may come after your contingency expires, but you should still do it. It will have some really awesome information on the leasing market in your area and will have comps. You paid for it, and it's a very good resource as the final way to double-check your numbers. Compare it to what you concluded on both rounds of market research (at the time you analyzed the deal and during due diligence here). Pay special attention to the cap rates they used.

Title Commitment

The last thing to do is see if the title company has any exceptions on their title commitment that you would inherit if you don't object to them. These are problems that are known, and they are not insuring against them. Have your attorney review the title commitment and send a title objection letter for anything that they think may become an issue for you. Title insurance doesn't cover you for everything, so make sure you read Schedule B on the title commitment to understand what the exceptions to the policy are.

Collect Your Bids

You will solicit bids and use them to confirm your renovation costs you made on your renovation cost worksheet that went onto your costs to fix line item on your MACO. We cover how to do this in detail in the "Gather Firm Bids" chapter in the Fix step. That part needs to be done here as part of due diligence before you make your final decision.

Update the MACO Analysis

Now recalculate your MACO with all the new information. Is it significantly different than the first MACO you calculated when you made the offer? What equity multiple will you achieve? What is the project cash flow and the sponsor cash flow?

You will learn how to calculate equity multiple, project cash flow, and sponsor cash flow in the next chapter.

Make a Decision

Now that you have the final numbers, it's time to make a decision.

If your MACO didn't change much, and you are hitting your equity and cash flow goals, then just move forward. If you uncovered something that would make the deal undesirable to do at any price, then cancel.

The world of commercial real estate is small. Don't try to chip away at the seller if you don't need to. Some books out there teach a strategy where you lock up properties at a price you never intend to close at. You might be wondering if this is a good or bad strategy. Listen closely:

Don't get a reputation for renegotiating all of your deals.

We call this "re-trading" the deal, and if, when, and how you do it matters a lot. Never enter into a deal with no intention of closing at the price you agree to.

I'm not saying don't renegotiate your deal. What I'm saying is you should *only* do it if you found something that changed your MACO significantly (more than 5 percent). There are certain things that will change your MACO that are good to cite and there are certain things that are not.

REASONS TO CITE FOR RENEGOTIATING

- Underlying issues with the building that are not easily visible
- Roof or mechanical equipment needs replacement
- Rent roll didn't match actual leases
- Expenses disclosed up front didn't match actual expenses
- Issues with tenants you found through due diligence
- Building is smaller than the seller said it was

I try to use one or more reasons from the first list if I ask for a discount because these are things that the seller disclosed (or failed to disclose) but you later found out weren't necessarily accurate.

REASONS NOT TO CITE FOR RENEGOTIATING

- Issues with the building that are easily visible, like carpet, paint, and parking lot
- You underestimated a cost to replace something
- You used the wrong rent rates, vacancy rate, or market cap rates in your initial analysis.

I would try to avoid presenting evidence like "The roof cost more than I anticipated," or "We realized we will have to replace the carpet, paint the building, and repair the parking lot." These are all things you could have reasonably determined on your visual inspection during the property tour and accounted for up front.

It's your job to measure the building and accurately estimate the repairs up front. If you blow it on what you think the roof costs, don't beat yourself up. This is bound to happen. Get better next time. Adjust your numbers, but try to keep that to yourself to keep your reputation tip-top.

> **Have a clear reason for asking for a discount, and be willing to actually cancel the deal if they say no to your new terms.**

Don't underestimate the power the broker has over their client in helping decide which offer to go with or whether to accept your new terms or not. If you re-trade without a reason, every broker in town will advise their clients not to accept your offers because you don't intend to actually close at that price. If you ask for a discount and they say no and you close anyway, they will tell other brokers you just chip away at people for the sake of chipping away.

Deals will come and go, but your reputation lasts forever.

I'm winning opportunities at lower prices because I have a reputation for closing at the price I agree to unless some major unforeseen cost prevents me from doing so.

When I do renegotiate, I usually approach the seller (or their broker if they are represented), and lay out the evidence, then say I can't make the numbers work anymore.

For example, if they tell you the roof is fine and the core sample finds that the roof needs to be replaced right away, you can show them the results of the roof report and ask them to help subsidize the cost of the roof.

Another example would be if their proforma on their marketing materials show expenses at $4 per square foot, but after you complete all of your due diligence, you determine the actual expenses are $5 per square foot. You can show them that you made your offer based on the expenses being $4 per square foot against the breakdown showing that the expenses are actually $5 per square foot and that you would need to adjust your price to achieve the same cash flow.

Remember not to ask for concessions on things that any reasonable buyer should have reasonably determined would need to be done from a simple visual inspection.

I have found people to be receptive and logical if I show them that I uncovered a cost or expense that any other buyer would want an adjustment for. Create a story and get good at telling that story to help them see that the only logical decision is to give you what you are asking for as opposed to starting over again with a new buyer.

If they agree to your new terms, get a signed amendment to the purchase agreement. If they don't, send a cancellation.

Pro Tip

We present our offers with a cover letter that spells out a list of the assumptions the seller or their agent gave us so we can easily reference them later if they turn out to be off or untrue altogether.

Always be willing to walk. I have fallen in love with deals before. It happens. I walked away from a hotel development deal after having spent over $20K and six months of my time in due diligence. It turned out to be the best decision I've ever made. I would have lost hundreds of thousands—if not millions—had I moved forward. Hindsight is 20/20.

Sometimes walking away from a bad deal is the right thing to do, even if you have thousands into the deal. Be careful when spending due diligence money, and do it wisely to limit your exposure. That's why I wait to order the appraisal and survey until I've verified my final MACO and renegotiated if I need to or waived my contingency.

> **Decipher the difference between walking because you are scared and walking because the numbers don't work anymore.**

If you find yourself altering your assumptions to force the numbers to work, then you should probably re-trade or walk. If the numbers work and you have triple-checked them, but you're afraid to move forward out of fear, get bold and close! This is the part where you jump out of the plane on your skydiving adventure. I promise that once you get to the ground, you are going to look back and say, "That wasn't that scary after all!"

Now that you have made a decision on your deal, let's talk about how to structure the partnership and raise the equity. This is the most exciting part of the process—where the kids get separated from the grown-ups. If you've been crushing it in residential, this next chapter is probably going to be the most valuable chapter in the whole book.

Key Reader Takeaways

☐ Make the seller documents a requirement in the PA and set the contingency timeline based on the day they actually deliver them.

☐ Use a checklist to perform a series of systematic due diligence tasks.

☐ Update your MACO worksheet as you gather information.

☐ Decide on a go, no-go, or re-trade.

☐ If you re-trade, present a clear and compelling story with third-party evidence to back up your ask, and avoid using reasons that make you look like you didn't do your homework up front.

☐ Be willing to actually cancel the deal and leave your due diligence money on the table.

Action Items

☐ Send your seller the required documents list if it wasn't already included as part of your purchase agreement.

☐ Perform all of the due diligence tasks.

☐ Gather firm bids.

☐ Update your MACO worksheet and make a conclusion.

☐ Re-trade your deal, but only if you need to.

Chapter 15

Structure the Partnership

Objective: Structure a Partnership to Fund the Down Payment

You understand the value of using bank debt to leverage your money, so why aren't you using equity partners to leverage it even further? In this chapter, I'm going to pull back the curtain on all of the secrets the mega-rich have been hiding from you on how to raise equity capital in order to fund massive deals.

You don't know what you don't know, so most of these concepts will be brand new for you. But private equity firms and the filthy rich have been using these tactics for centuries to structure partnerships to do big things, buy big companies, and solve major problems. I'm going to show you how you can use them to scale up your business and join the top 1 percent. Here are some of the crucial items that you need to understand to make that happen:

- Joint Venture vs. Fund Structure
- Legal Structure
- Membership Units
- Sources and Uses Worksheet
- Ownership Interest
- Distributions
- Cash Flow Worksheet
- Sales Proceeds Worksheet
- Equity Multiple
- Internal Rate of Return
- Net Present Value

Joint Venture vs. Fund Structure

At closing, you'll get 1–2 percent of the purchase price as an acquisition fee. You can reinvest that acquisition fee in the deal as your "skin in the game," or contribute capital from your IRA, savings, checking, or other sources of liquid funds you might have. You don't have to put up any capital at all, but if you do, you'll get other investors to place their funds in with yours, and you'll leverage all of that equity with a bank loan. But to do any of that, you need to structure a partnership. There are two ways to do this—a joint venture or a fund.

A joint venture, or JV, is where two or more investors come together as partners to form an entity and buy a property. Usually, you will elect one of them to be the manager who will have more responsibility than the others, and some or all of the members will bring capital to the deal. A JV does not require a private placement memorandum. In most cases, all of the members of the LLC have voting rights and a say in how things are done.

You are truly starting a business, and having multiple partners can create a risk that the partners someday disagree on how things should be done. Usually, everyone signs on the loan and guarantees the debt personally to share in the risk and the rewards.

Alternatively, you can structure a fund to buy one or more properties, though most people do a single asset fund when starting out—that is, the fund only owns one property. It's best to structure your fund after you have a property under contract instead of trying to do what's called a blind fund, where you raise the money before you have a deal on the table.

The fund is started and operated by a deal sponsor (that's you!) who does all the work and raises all the money from limited partners. The sponsor may or may not bring money into the deal, but they usually personally guarantee the loan. The limited partners generally do not sign on debt unless they own more than 20 percent of the entity, and they usually have no voting rights.

A fund requires a private placement memorandum because you are actually selling equity in a company, which falls under the securities act. You will need a securities attorney to advise you on the different regulations regarding the securities laws and which exemptions to use for your specific offering. Focus on your deal structure, your business plan, and your efforts to raise the capital, and let the expert attorney handle the offering documents.

Here is a summary of what you just learned.

Joint Venture versus Fund Structure

Category	Joint Venture	Fund
Definition	A Partnership that Is Formed between Two or More Active Partners for a Specific Property.	A Structure Where General Partners Are Active, Do the Work, and Raise Capital from Passive, Limited Partners.
Partners	All Partners Are Active.	General Partners Are Active and Limited Partners Are Passive.
Debt	All Partners with 20% or More Ownership Sign on Debt.	All Active or Passive Partners with 20% or More Ownership Sign on Debt. Be Careful Not to Have Any One Limited Partner Own 20% or More.
Liability	Liability Generally Falls on All Partners.	Liability Generally Falls Only on The Active Partners. The Limited Partners' Liability Is Usually Limited to Their Initial Contribution.

Which one should you do for your first deal? It depends. Do you want silent partners and complete control over everything? If so, do a fund. It will cost you more but may be worth it.

If you want to just partner with a couple people who have cash and split the workload with them, then form a joint venture and figure out the roles for each partner. I often see people raising money from limited partners who have no say in the deal but use a joint venture structure to avoid having to do a PPM that a fund requires.

If you dress a wolf in lamb's clothes, it can still eat you. Being cheap often ends up being expensive if you get sued for cutting a corner.

Legal Structure

I frequently get asked what legal structure to use, and I always tell people to seek advice from a competent tax advisor. This is not a book on high-level tax strategy, and none of that matters if you don't have a deal anyway.

I can't tell you how to structure your deals, but I can tell you how I structure mine. I use a new LLC for each property we buy, and to keep it simple, I name the LLC the address of the property name with the LLC at the end.

Each LLC gets filed with the Secretary of State, then I get an EIN and state tax ID on the IRS and state websites. Then I take the articles of formation and EIN number down to the bank to get the LLC/property its own operating checking account.

I set all this up during due diligence, oftentimes before I've finalized the partnership agreement. That's because I have to start paying due diligence costs and I want to track those in my accounting system. Sometimes a deal falls apart, and I have to close the account and the company. I'm okay with that. If the deal does go through, I add my internal property manager and any active partners with check-writing authority on the bank account once I'm ready for them to fund or manage the account.

Membership Units

Most likely, you are going to form an LLC whether you're doing a joint venture or a fund. LLCs are not corporations, so they don't have stock or shares. They have what's called membership units. You will usually structure the entity to have two or more classes of membership units, and you can call them whatever you want. Sometimes I call them Class A and Class B Units, and sometimes I call them GP Units (for general partner units) or LP Units (for limited partner units). It doesn't matter what naming conventions you use—what matters is what rights the units give the holders of those units. In most cases for funds, I only give voting rights to the GP Units, but if this were a joint venture, everyone would likely have voting rights. To figure out how many units of each type you would actually issue, you first need to figure out how much equity you will need. To do that, you need a sources and uses.

Sources and Uses Worksheet

Let's use the Center Drive deal as an example. We got a term sheet from the lender that said they would give us 75 percent loan-to-cost or 70 percent loan-to-value, whichever was less. Our MACO was $825K and we got it under contract at $700K cash to the seller at closing. We planned to put 25 percent down.

How much equity did we need to raise?

If you guessed $175K...you are wrong!

To figure out how much equity we needed to raise, we need to create a sources and uses worksheet. A sources and uses worksheet summarizes all of the different ways you will use your capital and then shows all the different sources that capital will come from.

Up until this point, we have been working off the MACO price which was a "potential" purchase price. Now that you have a real purchase price, you need to use that number instead of the MACO going forward for the rest of the process. Make sure you are also pulling the costs to stabilize in from your final numbers on your revised MACO worksheet, not your original one.

Here is a sources and uses worksheet for our Center Drive property:

Sources and Uses Worksheet – Shown with Actual Purchase Price

Uses	%	$	
Actual Purchase Price	90.32%	$700,000	Use Maco Price to Start, Then Replace Later with Actual Purchase Price
Costs to Fix	4.52%	$35,000	From the Renovation Cost Worksheet
Costs to Fill	1.94%	$15,000	From the Leasing Cost Worksheet
Costs to Hold	0.00%	$0	Cumulative Negative Cash Flow, in this Case Zero
Costs to Close	3.23%	$25,000	From Closing Costs Worksheet Rounded to Nearest Thousand
Total Uses of Capital	**100.00%**	**$775,000**	

Sources	LTC	%	$	Am. (Yrs)	Rate	Constant	Cost of Funds Annual	Cost of Funds Monthly	WACCC
Bank Debt*	75%	71.13%	$551,250	25	4.50%	6.67%	$36,768	$3,064	
Investor Equity		28.87%	$223,750		8.00%	8.00%	$17,900	$1,492	
Total Sources of Capital		**100%**	**$775,000**				**$54,668**	**$4,556**	**7.054%**

Equity Assumptions		
Total Equity Capital		**$223,750**
Outside Investors	90%	$201,375
You	10%	$22,375

Take a minute to study this chart. You can learn a lot about this stage of the deal from just understanding all of the moving parts in this section.

The percent column shows the percent of the sources or uses. You'll notice the sources and uses are both $775,000. They should always match. Notice also that the loan-to-cost was 75%, but since the lender only finances the purchase price and repairs of $35,000, they base the 75% on the $735,000 number—which gives you a loan of $551,250. That loan amount is 71.13% of the total sources of capital, so you are actually raising 28.87% of the total capital in equity.

Our WACCC is 7.054% which is the blended overall cost of money across the entire capital stack. We used the same capital costs as estimated before. If those changed during due diligence, we would use the final real numbers for what things would cost. I'm keeping them the same here to keep it simple for this exercise.

We are also showing that we need to raise $223,750 in equity. In my example, I chose to put up 10 percent of that or $22,375. You are raising the other 90 percent

FUND

from limited partners in a fund structure. Our monthly payments to the bank will be $3,064 and our preferred return of 8 percent to capital partners will be $17,900 per year (you are getting 10 percent of this, or $1,790 per year). We cover what a preferred return is in a minute. Ignore any small rounding errors when you're doing your numbers.

Ownership Interest

Now that you know how much money you need to raise to fund your whole capital stack, let's summarize the offering you will have.

Membership Units for Center Drive

Membership Units Before Refinance

Unit Type	# of Units	Price per Unit	Type of Interest	Ownership	Pref/Unit	Annual Pref
LP Units	223,750	$1.00	Equity Interest	70%	$0.08	$17,900
GP Units	95,893	$0.00	Profits Interest	30%	–	–

Membership Units After Refinance

Unit Type	# of Units	Price per Unit	Type of Interest	Ownership	Pref/Unit	Annual Pref
LP Units	223,750	$1.00	Equity Interest	20%	–	–
GP Units	895,000	$0.00	Profits Interest	80%	–	–

Study this chart for a minute. You will see that we are raising 223,750 LP Units because I want to issue one LP Unit per dollar of capital I need. I chose to set the unit price at $1 per unit. You can set the unit price at whatever price you want. There are two ways to treat the capital you put into the deal yourself: You can put it in as LP capital and treat it the same as everyone else, or you can put it in as GP capital. I highly recommend the first option, and that's how I showed it in this example. In this case, you would own 22,375 of the LP Units, and the 95,893 of GP Units would be split between you and any active partners you brought in to help raise the capital, execute the business plan, or sign on the debt.

How did I come up with 95,893? That is the number of units you need to issue the general partner to force the ownership percentages to equal 70/30. Why do I want the ownership to equal 70/30? Because I want the ownership to match the expected distributions, which will follow the splits on the waterfall as you will learn about later.

Here's the math and the steps:

$$\text{GP Units to Issue} = \frac{\text{LP Units}}{\text{Desired LP Ownership Percent}} - \text{LP Units}$$

- Step 1: The first thing you do is calculate the total units you need to issue by dividing the number of LP Units by the desired percent of ownership you want the LP Units to be. In this case, it's 223,750 divided by 70% to determine that you need a total of 319,643 membership units.
- Step 2: To figure out the GP Units, simply subtract the LP Units from that number: 319,643 −223,750 = 95,893. Now the GP Units are exactly 30% of the total units, and the LP Units are exactly 70% of the total units.

Ownership is typically based on the percent of total units. Taxable income is typically passed through to the members based on ownership percentage. In our example, the GP Unit holders would get 30 percent of the taxable gains each year.

> **Here's something you need to understand: ownership percentage and cash distribution percentage will seldom match.**

Ownership percentages are how profit and loss are awarded on paper for tax purposes and it really doesn't affect how much people actually get paid.

Distributions are how cash flow is distributed, which *is* how people actually get paid.

For example, you could have a very profitable year but choose not to distribute any cash to anyone. Maybe you are saving up for a big roof project you have coming up. At the end of the year, your profit will be passed through to the owners on a K-1 tax form based on their ownership percent. In this case, the GP would pay taxes on 30 percent of the profit. They may have been distributed zero cash to pay the tax liability on that income though, if you held all of the cash back as reserves to pay for the roof next year.

I chose 30 percent ownership for the GP in this scenario because that was the GP split on the top tier of the waterfall that determines distribution splits.

The goal is simple—to match the ownership to distributions the best you can.

It is not an exact science because the ownership is a defined split that doesn't change, whereas the cash split is a multi-tier system that *does* change based on performance.

As the general partner, you will pick a distribution model which determines the way cash is distributed, and then you do your best to try and align the ownership percentage splits to match the way the cash is being split.

Distributions

How you distribute the cash depends on the pecking order you agree to in the operating agreement for the LLC. This distribution model is often referred to as the "waterfall" because there are multiple tiers in place.

Here's how it works: the cash flows down the waterfall until it runs out.

There are two types of cash flows to distribute:

1. Cash flow during holding years
2. Cash flow at refinance or sale

CASH FLOW DURING HOLDING YEARS

This is how I usually structure my waterfall to distribute cash during the holding years of the investment, as in, this is the order people get paid. I pay each tier until the money runs out.

1. Mortgage payments to the bank
2. Any junior liens, mezz debt, or seller carryback
3. Preferred return to the LP partners (including any accrued preferred returns)
4. (Optional) Paydown of LP membership unit capital accounts
5. Tier 1 Upside: Up to 10 percent annual cash-on-cash return, 70 percent to LP Units, 30 percent to GP Units
6. Tier 2 Upside: Up to 15 percent annual cash-on-cash return, 50 percent to LP Units, 50 percent to GP Units
7. Tier 3 Upside: Up to 20 percent annual cash-on-cash return, 30 percent to LP Units, 70 percent to GP Units
8. Tier 4 Upside: Beyond 20 percent annual cash-on-cash return, 100 percent to GP Units

Here is a diagram table and graphic to help you see this in two different formats.

How Tiers Are Calculated within a Waterfall Structure

Waterfall Structure	Cash-on-Cash Returns		Tier Limits/Amounts			Cash Flow Split		Max Paid per Tier	
	From	To	Low Limit	Top Limit	Tier $	GP%	LP%	GP $	LP $
Preferred Return	0.00%	8.00%	$0	$17,900	$17,900	0.0%	100.0%	$0	$17,900
Tier 1 Upside	8.00%	10.00%	$17,900	$22,375	$4,475	30.0%	70.0%	$1,343	$3,133
Tier 2 Upside	10.00%	15.00%	$22,375	$33,563	$11,188	50.0%	50.0%	$5,594	$5,594
Tier 3 Upside	15.00%	20.00%	$33,563	$44,750	$11,188	70.0%	30.0%	$7,831	$3,356
Tier 4 Upside	20.00%	+	$44,750	+	+	100%	0.0%	+	

Example Waterfall Structure During Holding Years

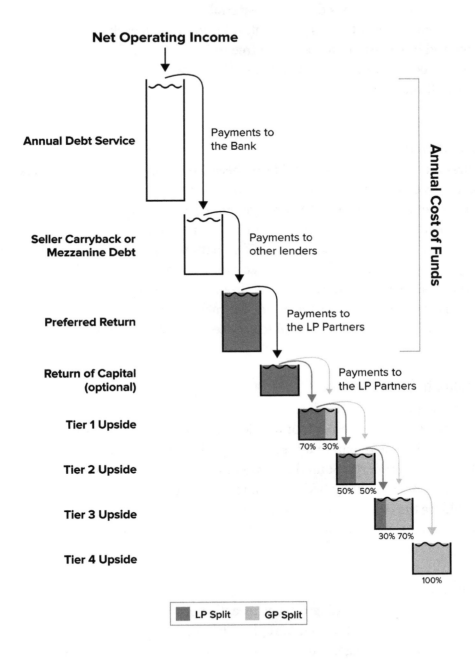

Net Operating Income

Annual Debt Service

Payments to the Bank

Seller Carryback or Mezzanine Debt

Payments to other lenders

Preferred Return

Payments to the LP Partners

Return of Capital (optional)

Payments to the LP Partners

Tier 1 Upside

70% 30%

Tier 2 Upside

50% 50%

Tier 3 Upside

30% 70%

Tier 4 Upside

100%

Annual Cost of Funds

LP Split   GP Split

Don't fall out of your chair quite yet—I'm going to explain this! The cash flow from operations, the NOI, flows down the waterfall satisfying each tier until it runs out. This can have as many tiers as you want. Let's go through each tier to make sure you understand it. Have patience and feel free to read this over a few times to really let it sink in, because what you just looked at is the secret sauce to splitting the profit with your limited partners.

Payments to the Bank

The first mortgage always gets paid first because having the lender foreclose is the worst-case scenario for you. However, in most Value-Add deals, your NOI is not enough to cover operating expenses AND pay the mortgage on day one. Typically, you are using reserves in your checking account to cover the gap to pay for operating costs, renovations, leasing fees, and debt service. That's why it's so critical to take the time to get your sources and uses right to make sure you have enough holding cost reserves to cover these cash needs during the stabilization period. If you run out of capital, you will need to sell more units, which is not desirable, so try to raise those funds up front to get by until you have enough NOI to service your debt and equity obligations.

Payments to Other Lenders

If you have junior liens or other business loans, those get paid next. This can be a line of credit, mezzanine debt, or a seller carryback mortgage. Mezzanine debt is essentially a business loan that is secured by a UCC filing against the entity instead of a lien on the property. Sometimes you have a gap in your financing, and you can raise additional capital by taking out a loan against the company or the property. This reduces the equity you have to give up, but it increases your risk because if you miss a payment, these lenders can call the loan due and take your asset.

Replenish Reserves

This doesn't show on the diagram because it's not really a cost, but sometimes you need to steal cash from the NOI to replenish your reserves. Once you have enough NOI to pay your mortgage, you will replenish your reserves before paying any of the accrued returns because you don't want to run out of money again in the next cycle.

Preferred Return

If you have satisfied all of your debt obligations, then you pay a preferred return to the holders of the LP Units. We call this a preferred return, because you are giving a preference to the LP Units and paying them first. Remember, the people who put up the cash hold the LP Units. You can think of their capital as a kind of "loan" against the company that they earn interest on except it's not a guaranteed payment. They earn this interest either way, but they may not get paid until the LLC has enough cash to do so, in which case it just accrues on their capital account.

A capital account is an equity account you create for the LLC in your accounting software to track how much the LLC owes each member. Think of it like the principal balance on your equity. If someone contributed $100,000 and were owed an 8% preferred return but didn't get paid for the whole year, their balance at the end of the year on the books would be $108,000. For the following year, you could choose to let them earn 8% on the original $100,000 (non-compounding) or the full $108,000 (compounding).

In our Center Drive case study, our preferred return was 8% annually. Eight percent of $223,750 is $17,900. That $17,900 goes to the LP Units' pro-rata their share of ownership. Since you set the unit price at $1.00, the dividend per unit is $0.08 per unit per year ($1.00 × 8%). Since you own 10% of those units, you personally would get $1,790 per year. I usually distribute quarterly, so I would pay $0.02 per unit per quarter.

Upside

Once you've satisfied your obligation to pay a preferred return on the LP Units, the rest is what we call upside. This is when you start getting paid for the GP Units.

You only get paid out of returns you bring the investors, and you have to deliver a minimum return (the pref) before you start getting paid. You might hear the pref referred to as the "hurdle rate" because it's the hurdle you have to get over in order to start getting paid as the deal sponsor. If you don't bring the returns, you don't get paid. The idea is simple: you get paid a higher proportionate share of the earnings as you deliver better results.

As you bring better and bigger returns, you get a larger share as you drop into each subsequent tier. These operate exactly like federal tax brackets do. The LP Units are the taxpayer and The GP Units (you) are the government. The government takes a higher proportionate share of the earnings as the taxpayers make more money and drop into higher tax brackets. We call the "tax" the GP Units take the "promote."

You have complete control over this structure, but it needs to be enticing for the type of investor you will target. In the next chapter, I will teach you how to modify this structure based on whether you are targeting small individual investors or large corporate investors.

Let's work from left to right. First, you pick the cash-on-cash thresholds for each tax bracket, so to speak. The first bracket is the preferred return at 8%. How did I get that number? I picked it based on what I know I can raise the funds at. You may have to start with a number, but be open to negotiations with the investors as this evolves.

The tier limits are calculated by taking the cash-on-cash thresholds for each tier and multiplying them by the total capital. The total tier dollar is the incremental dollar amount which is found by subtracting the low limit from the top limit. Let's go through how the cash is split between the GP and LP once you've paid all the debt:

- Every dollar goes to the LP Units until you have distributed the first $17,900.
- The next $4,475 is split—30% of each dollar to the GP Units and 70% of each dollar to the LP Units until you distribute all $4,475 or run out of money.
- The next $11,188 would be split—50% to the GP and 50% to the LP Units— until the tier is satisfied or you run out of money.
- The next $11,188 would be split—70% to the GP and 30% to the LP Units— until the tier is satisfied or you run out of money.
- The remaining cash all goes to the holders of the GP Units.

The chart shows the max amount the GP Unit holders and LP Unit holders would get under each tier if and only if it was fully satisfied. Of course, if the cash runs out within that tier, then the amount paid would be less.

This is just one example of how to structure a waterfall based on cash-on-cash tiers. You can make this as simple or as complicated as you want.

For example, you could pay a 10 percent preferred return to the LP Units and split every dollar after that 50/50 in a single-tier upside. I've actually done deals this way. It's easy to explain to someone that I will pay them 10 percent on their money first and then we will split the upside down the middle.

If you plan to raise your capital from smaller investors like friends and family, you might want to stick to a single-tier structure. However, once you start raising money from more sophisticated investors, they will likely want to see a multi-tier structure that incentivizes you to drive the overall returns up.

If you don't have great credit, you might bring in a partner to help you raise the capital and split the GP Units with them. Otherwise, you will own all of them if you qualify on your own. In our scenario, you own 100% of the GP Units and 10% of the LP Units.

Now let's cover how to distribute cash if you sell or refinance.

CASH FLOW AT REFINANCE OR SALE

These tiers would work much the same way, with a couple of slight differences. Here is my most common structure:

1. Pay off mortgage (original mortgage)
2. Pay off other debt
3. Pay current and any accrued preferred returns to the LP Units
4. Pay down the capital accounts to zero (give everyone their money back)
5. (Optional) Buy back LP Units (refinance only)
6. Upside split based on Tier 3 (30% to LP Units, 70% to GP Units)

Here's how it looks visually.

Example Waterfall Structure at Sale or Refinance

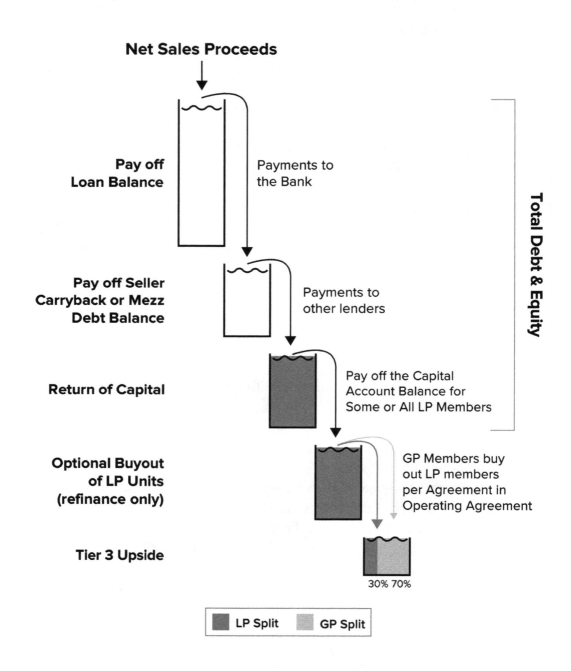

The net proceeds from the sale or refinance trickle down the waterfall, satisfying each tier until the money runs out. There are a couple key differences between the distribution model for holding period cash flows and the distribution model for liquidation event cash flows (sale or refinance).

The main difference is you have to pay off the principal balances before you calculate the upside, and usually the upside split favors the deal sponsor.

If you sell, you will return their capital and then split the upside based on the waterfall agreement you have in place. In my example, the GP would get 70% of the upside and the LP members as a whole would get 30% of the upside.

If you refinance, you have two options: you can either buy out the limited partners or just return their capital and leave them in. There is a difference between returning the capital and buying back the membership units.

Pro Tip

It's customary for the deal sponsor to get paid a disposition fee or loan guarantee as part of the closing costs, and that would come out before the "net proceeds" are calculated. You should get paid for all the extra time you put into getting the property ready for sale or signing on a larger loan with a personal guarantee.

Pay Off Capital Accounts

Remember that a capital account is the equity account you track for the investor that includes the amount of capital they contributed plus any accrued preferred returns minus any return of capital you have made from the holding period cash flows:

$$\text{Capital Account Balance} = \begin{array}{c}\text{Capital} \\ \text{Contributed}\end{array} + \begin{array}{c}\text{Preferred Returns} \\ \text{Earned but Not} \\ \text{Paid (Accrued)}\end{array} - \begin{array}{c}\text{Return of Capital} \\ \text{Made During} \\ \text{Holding Years}\end{array}$$

If you pay off the balance in the capital accounts, the investors still own their respective units and are entitled to their share of the upside going forward. The splits can change after you return the capital, at your option. Typically, you'd want to eliminate the multiple tiers and just use one of the top tiers for the split going forward. Or you could create a new split as agreed because the LP members have zero risk and are doing zero work, so should not receive as much of the upside.

In our example, if we refinanced and paid everyone's capital accounts down to zero, the NOI would be used to pay the new debt, and then it could be split 70% to the GP and 30% to the LPs. Or alternatively, you could choose a new split after you return the capital, like 90% to the GP and 10% to the LP.

Buy Them Out

If you buy their membership units back, you would give them their capital account balance *plus* an additional amount for their share of the increased value based on what you all agreed to up front for how the membership units would be valued. In this case, the LP members would be paid off and then disappear from the equation altogether.

I usually set my operating agreements so I can buy out the LP Units at any time if I provide an IRR of 20 percent. I cover how to do this in the "Refinance" chapter. We will cover what IRR is in a minute. First, let's project the cash flow for five years out on the cash flow worksheet.

Cash Flow Worksheet

Keep in mind that the projections on the MACO worksheet and the projections on the cash flow worksheet will be different because now we are dealing with real numbers. The MACO worksheet only runs the most likely stabilized cash flow for year one, whereas the cash flow worksheet and the sources and uses run the actual scenario based on the price you got the property under contract at and the revised numbers from your due diligence.

Follow along on the cash flow worksheet for this part.

Cash Flow Worksheet for Center Drive

Item	Sign	Key Data Point	Year –1	Year 1	Year 2	Year 3	Year 4	Year 5
1		BGRR	$5.50	$5.50	$8.00	$8.24	$8.49	$8.74
2	×	Building Total Square Footage	20,000	20,000	20,000	20,000	20,000	20,000
3	=	Potential Gross Rent	$110,000	$110,000	$160,000	$164,800	$169,744	$174,836
4	×	Occupancy Rate	100.0%	100.0%	93.0%	93.0%	93.0%	93.0%
5	×	Collection Rate	100.0%	100.0%	95.0%	98.0%	98.0%	98.0%
6	=	**Effective Rental Income**	**$110,000**	**$110,000**	**$141,360**	**$150,199**	**$154,705**	**$159,346**
7	–	Taxes	$10,000	$10,000	$10,000	$10,200	$10,404	$10,404
8	–	Utilities	$16,500	$6,500	$500	$510	$520	$531
9	–	Maintenance	$15,000	$10,000	$7,000	$7,140	$7,283	$7,428
10	–	Management (Property + Asset)	$0	$7,000	$7,000	$9,763	$10,056	$10,357
11	–	Insurance	$4,500	$5,000	$3,000	$3,000	$3,000	$3,000
12	–	Repairs	$22,500	$7,700	$9,800	$10,514	$10,829	$11,154
13	–	Admin	$1,500	$2,700	$4,060	$4,060	$4,060	$4,060
14	=	**Net Operating Income (NOI)**	**$40,000**	**$61,100**	**$100,000**	**$105,012**	**$108,553**	**$112,411**
		Cash Flow from Operations						
15	–	Bank Debt Payments		$36,768	$36,768	$36,768	$36,768	$36,768
16	–	Seller Financing Payments						
17	–	Mezz Debt Payments						
18	=	**Partnership Cash Flow**		**$24,332**	**$63,232**	**$68,244**	**$71,784**	**$75,643**
		Distributable Cash Flow						
19	–	Reserve Replenishment		$3,300	$4,241	$4,506	$4,641	$4,780
20	=	**Distributable Partnership Cash Flow**		**$21,032**	**$58,991**	**$63,738**	**$67,143**	**$70,862**
		Tier Calculations						
21		Preferred Return	$17,900	$17,900	$17,900	$17,900	$17,900	$17,900
22	+	Tier 1 Upside	$4,475	$3,132	$4,475	$4,475	$4,475	$4,475
23	+	Tier 2 Upside	$11,188	$0	$11,188	$11,188	$11,188	$11,188
24	+	Tier 3 Upside	$11,188	$0	$11,188	$11,188	$11,188	$11,188
25	+	Tier 4 Upside	+	$0	$14,241	$18,988	$22,393	$26,112
26	=	**Total Partnership Cash Flow**		**$21,032**	**$58,991**	**$63,738**	**$67,143**	**$70,862**
		LP Waterfall Tier Splits						
27		LP Preferred Return		$17,900	$17,900	$17,900	$17,900	$17,900
28		Tier 1 Upside		$2,192	$3,133	$3,133	$3,133	$3,133
29		Tier 2 Upside		$0	$5,594	$5,594	$5,594	$5,594
30		Tier 3 Upside		$0	$3,356	$3,356	$3,356	$3,356
31		Tier 4 Upside		$0	$0	$0	$0	$0
32		**Total LP Cash Flow**		**$20,092**	**$29,983**	**$29,983**	**$29,983**	**$29,983**
		GP Waterfall Tier Splits						
33		GP Tier 1 Upside		$940	$1,343	$1,343	$1,343	$1,343
34		GP Tier 2 Upside		$0	$5,594	$5,594	$5,594	$5,594
35		GP Tier 3 Upside		$0	$7,831	$7,831	$7,831	$7,831
36		GP Tier 4 Upside		$0	$14,241	$18,988	$22,393	$26,112
37		**Total GP Cash Flow**		**$940**	**$29,008**	**$33,755**	**$37,161**	**$40,880**
		Reserve Calculations						
38		Beginning Reserve Balance		$50,000	$3,300	$7,541	$12,047	$16,688
39	–	Capital Improvements		$35,000				
40	–	Leasing Commissions		$15,000				
41	–	Unforeseen Capital Costs						
42	–	Reserve Replenishment		$3,300	$4,241	$4,506	$4,641	$4,780
43	=	**Ending Reserve Balance**		**$3,300**	**$7,541**	**$12,047**	**$16,688**	**$21,468**

Project cash flow is also called partnership cash flow. Project cash flow and GP cash flow are two different things. Project cash flow is what the partnership gets, whereas the GP cash flow is your split on the partnership cash flow. Your project can cash flow but not pay you anything if you don't earn enough cash to pay your partners a preferred return on their capital.

The project cash flow is easy to calculate:

Project (Partnership) Cash Flow = NOI – Annual Debt Service (All Debt)

For Center Drive, our NOI was roughly $100,000 in year two. The annual debt service (mortgage payment times twelve) was $36,768. Therefore, the partnership would cash flow $63,232 once the property is stabilized.

Out of that money, you have to pay a preferred return, so the sponsor cash flow is calculated a little differently.

You would pay 8% of the capital raised first—which is 8% of the $223,750, or $17,900. The remaining cash flow would be the upside that you split based on the waterfall structure.

CASH FLOW SUMMARY AND IRR

Here is a summary of the overall project cash flows, LP cash flows, and the GP cash flows for each year including the proceeds from the sale each would get. These came from the cash flow worksheet and the sales proceeds worksheet I'll show you in a second. Remember, you own some or all of the GP Units depending on if you brought in a partner. In our example, you put up 10 percent of the capital, so you also own 10 percent of the LP Units.

Cash Flow Summary & IRR Worksheet

Project IRR

Year	CF Operation	Return of Capital	Distributable Upside		Total CF
0	−$223,750			=	−$223,750
1	$21,032			=	$21,032
2	$58,991			=	$58,991
3	$63,738			=	$63,738
4	$67,143			=	$67,143
5	$70,862	+ $223,750	+ $560,973	=	$855,585

	SPBT =	$784,723	IRR	43.12%

Total Return	$1,066,488
Equity Multiple	3.82

Limited Partners IRR (your position is 10% of this)

Year	CF Operation	Return of Capital	Distributable Upside		Total CF
0	−$223,750			=	−$223,750
1	$20,092			=	$20,092
2	$29,983			=	$29,983
3	$29,983			=	$29,983
4	$29,983			=	$29,983
5	$29,983	+ $223,750	+ $168,292	=	$422,024

	IRR	21.88%

Total Return	$532,064
Equity Multiple	1.89

Your GP Units

Year	CF Operation	GP Split of Upside		Total CF
0	$0		=	$0
1	$940		=	$940
2	$29,008		=	$29,008
3	$33,755		=	$33,755
4	$37,161		=	$37,161
5	$40,880	+ $392,681	=	$433,561

	IRR	N/A

Total Return	$534,424
Equity Multiple	N/A

Negative numbers are cash going out and positive numbers are cash coming in. Year zero is the day you close on the property. If you had *zero* cash in this deal, you'd get paid $940 in year one, $29,008 in year two, $33,755 in year three, $37,161 in year four, and $433,561 in year five as the general partner. Since you also owned 10 percent of the LP Units here, you would get 10 percent of the LP cash flows as well.

You can see in year one at Center Drive, we barely made enough cash to pay the preferred return, so we didn't get paid much as the deal sponsor. You can also see that the GP got 70 percent of the sales proceeds because the partners agreed to split the upside at sale: 70% to the General Partner and 30% to the Limited Partners.

Sales Proceeds Worksheet

You have to know how much you are going to net at sale in order to figure out what the final cash flow for everybody is going to be. Let's start by figuring out how much you expect to net at the sale of the property.

Sales Proceeds Before Tax Calculator

Sign	Item	%	$
	Disposition Year NOI		$112,411
÷	Disposition Cap Rate		8.34%
=	**Disposition Price**		**$1,348,355**
−	Closing Costs	5.88%	$79,316
=	**Net Proceeds from Sale**		**$1,269,039**
−	Bank Debt Balance	35.9%	$484,316
−	Seller Financing Balance	0.0%	$0
−	Contract for Deed Balance	0.0%	$0
−	Mezz Debt Balance	0.0%	$0
−	Seller Carry Balance	0.0%	$0
=	**Sales Proceeds Before Tax (SPBT)**	**58.2%**	**$784,723**
−	Capital Account Balance	16.6%	$223,750
−	GP Capital Account Balance		$0
=	**Distributable Profit**	**41.6%**	**$560,973**
→	**GP Split @ 70%**	**29.1%**	**$392,681**
→	**LP Split @ 30%**	**12.5%**	**$168,292**

We projected the sale price by taking year five NOI and applying a market cap rate to it. If you did your leases correctly, your rent would escalate 3% each year, which drives the NOI up each year. Therefore, your disposition price should be slightly larger than the ASV that you projected in your initial MACO worksheet.

Next are the closing costs:

Closing Costs Calculator – When Selling – Center Drive

Sign	Item	Qty	Rate	Total
	Broker Fee (Listing Side to You if You List It)	$1,348,355	5.00%	$67,418
+	Disposition Fee to Deal Sponsor (You)	$1,348,355	0.50%	$6,742
	Lender Required Fees			
+	Prepayment Penalty	$484,317	0%	$0
	Title Company Fees			
+	Closing Fee			$450
+	Recording Fee			$30
+	Deed Tax	$1,348,355	0.34%	$4,584
+	Recording Fees	2	$46	$92
=	**Total Transactions Costs**		5.88%	$79,316

Here, you earned the 0.50% disposition fee that we had in the distribution language in your operating agreement. You can see the LLC walked with $784,723 after it paid off the bank and closing costs. The first $223,750 of that would go back to the LPs, and then the rest would be split per the waterfall. It would be split roughly 70/30, with 70 percent of the $560,973 upside going to you (the sponsor), which comes out to be $392,681. I didn't put in any prepay penalties, but those can be hefty if you sell early.

Let's look at the metrics of how our deal turned out.

Equity Multiple

Equity multiple is simple to calculate.

$$\text{Equity Multiple} = \frac{\text{Sale Proceeds}}{\text{Initial Capital}}$$

You can run this for the project as a whole and for your position as a GP. Of course, if you don't put in any cash yourself, your personal equity multiple is infinite. I generally run the project equity multiple and shoot for a multiple of two. To get that, you need to create the same amount of value as you and your partners contribute in capital. In our example, we raised $223,750 in capital, and we pulled $784,721 out. The equity multiple was 3.5. For every dollar we put in, we got 3.5 dollars out.

Internal Rate of Return

Some investors use IRR for the waterfall calculations. I recommend using cash-on-cash returns to set the tier limits as opposed to IRR, but since a lot of commercial folks talk about IRR, we should probably cover it. If you never took a finance class, then I'm going to apologize in advance here, but this is a good thing to learn.

The internal rate of return is the rate of return on your cash for as long as that cash is in the investment. It's the overall yield you get on the investment. Yield and IRR are interchangeable terms.

You also need to understand the time value of money and discount rates to understand IRR.

If you invested a dollar today at 10 percent interest, it would be worth $1.10 in a year, right? So let's do that in reverse. If you had $1.10 coming to you in a year, what is that $1.10 worth today at a 10 percent discount rate? The answer is $1.00. We literally just worked backward, like this:

Time Value of Money

Type	Rate	Today	1 Year
Interest Rate	10%	$1.00 ———————→	$1.10
Discount Rate	10%	$1.00 ←———————	$1.10

A "discount rate" is just the interest rate that you use to discount future cash flows back to today's dollars.

The IRR is the discount rate that would make the net present value (NPV) of all future cash flows equal zero. It is essentially the annualized interest rate you earned on your investment, just like the 10% in our example.

At Center Drive, the partnership earned 43.12% IRR and the limited partners earned 21.88% IRR. How did I get that? I simply used the IRR function in Microsoft Excel! You can solve for IRR in an Excel spreadsheet by simply using the =IRR function and selecting a column of cash flows. Make sure your initial cash outlay is negative or you will get an error.

The computer solves for IRR by trying different discount rates until the net present value is zero. It uses an iterative process that would take you forever to do on a piece of paper. Here is proof that using a discount rate of 42.21% to discount the project cash flows back gives an NPV of zero:

FUND

IRR Proof

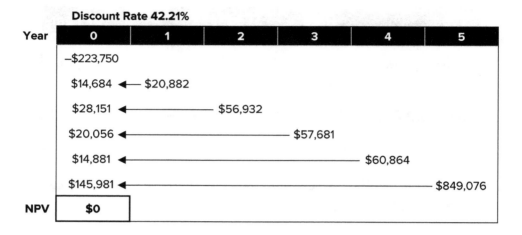

The present value of a cash flow is the future value discounted back at the discount rate.

$$\text{Present Value} = \frac{\text{Future Value}}{(1+\text{Discount Rate})^{\text{Years}}}$$

You multiply to the power of the number of years. For example, the year four cash flow is $60,864, and the present value of that is $14,881. If I invested $14,881 dollars today at 42.21% interest per year, it would be worth $60,864 in four years.

$$\$14,881 = \frac{\$60,864}{(1.4221)^4}$$

This is how the computer calculates IRR, but you will just type the cash flows into the spreadsheet and use the IRR function built into Excel to show the expected yield for the investment to your investors.

The LP IRR will always be lower than the project IRR because they are giving you some of the cash flow for delivering those returns. Remember, you are the taxman charging a tax on the money they make. You can't calculate an annual yield on the GP position because you structured your deal so your cash came in as LP capital, so the GP Units technically have no cash in the deal.

Net Present Value

How much more can you pay to make the IRR equal 20 percent? Simple. You could discount all of those cash flows back using a 20 percent discount rate to figure out the net present value, like this:

Calculating Net Present Value Using a Desired Yield

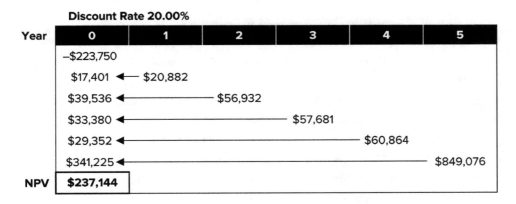

The net present value is +$237,144, which means you could have put out an additional $237,144 in cash up front to earn a 20% yield.

That concludes our finance class.

If you need to go back through and read that section again, do so. This baseline understanding of time value of money will serve you well over the course of your investing career. Understanding how it works behind the scenes is the key. If you can grasp these concepts about how to split the profit using tiers that operate like tax brackets, then you are on a jet plane to your destination.

Now let's dive into how to actually find the limited partners to invest with you and how to pitch them the deal.

Key Reader Takeaways

- ☐ Use a joint venture if you just have one or two partners.
- ☐ Use a single asset fund if you want several silent money partners who only put up cash.
- ☐ You need a private placement memorandum and securities exemptions to do a fund, but not for a joint venture. Consult a tax and legal professional.
- ☐ A sources and uses worksheet shows where all of your cash comes from and how you will use that cash.
- ☐ Ownership percentage only matters for taxes. Distribution models matter for who gets paid what, when, and how.
- ☐ IRR is the overall yield you get on your capital while it's in the investment. Equity multiple is the amount you grow the capital you raise.
- ☐ Common sponsor fees.
    - ☐ Asset management fee is 1–2% annually on rent income.
    - ☐ Acquisition fee is 1–2% of purchase price.
    - ☐ Disposition or refinance fee is 0.5–1% of the sale price.
    - ☐ 20-70% of the upside after preferred return.
- ☐ The common distribution model is a waterfall model, where the waterfall operates like tax brackets. The general partners get more tax as they deliver more earnings to the limited partners.

Action Items

- ☐ Study IRR and equity multiple.
- ☐ Try filling out a cash flow worksheet, a sources and uses worksheet, and a sales proceeds worksheet.
- ☐ Structure the waterfall for your first deal.

Chapter 16

Raise the Capital

Objective: Get Signed Subscription Agreements and a Signed Operating Agreement

There is a gorgeous woman sitting at the bar by herself. You notice several men glancing at her as they chat among themselves. Who will have the courage to approach her? She notices everyone looking at her and knows she has the position of power.

When it comes to investing, you are the hot chick at the bar, not the dude who is drooling over her! You have to put yourself in the position of power and let people come to you.

You don't *need* them. They need you. Get your mind right!

You offer exclusive private partnerships with double-digit returns secured by a real piece of property, and 99 percent of Americans don't even know these types of limited partnerships exist, let alone have the opportunity to invest in one. Especially with a hard-working sponsor who has a killer strategy and a rock solid system like you do now.

As soon as you start "selling" them anything, you lose your luster. Exclusivity increases desire. When you tell people you have a very exclusive list of investors, it puts you in a position of power. If you chase down investors seeming desperate, then nobody wants you. Chase the cat and it runs away. It's a privilege to invest with you.

You have to believe it first, or they won't.

I hope you get shut down on your first request for money. In fact, I hope you get shut down several times. Not only from the banks who make loans, but from money partners. I hope they tell you no, so your resilience can be tested, and you can learn how to get to yes.

Facing Fears: Part 2

Make no mistake: Most people with money want to invest it in real estate but either don't have the *time* or the *experience* needed to actually make it happen. They desire truly passive investments so they can focus their time elsewhere. That's where you come in. They are looking for someone who knows their stuff, and that they can trust. That's it. Show them you have a plan (you do; I'm giving it to you here), and show them they can trust you—if they can. If they can't, just stop now, because you will not make it far.

People with money will never invest with you if they don't trust you. They won't trust you if they don't like you. And they won't like you if you always talk about your needs.

Always speak in terms of other people's interests, and only provide information that is relevant to them and this opportunity. Make it about answering questions, not about selling the investment.

I raised $525,000 on my first development from ten normal, everyday people. Most of them had IRA accounts that they were unhappy with. Sound familiar? Do you know anyone who has $10,000 or $50,000 or maybe even $100,000 in some 401(k) or IRA account, and they have no clue what they even own?

Did you know you can have them roll that money into a self-directed plan and invest it with you in your project? Maybe you do, but you don't want to risk your friends and family's money trying to learn on your first deal.

That is your problem. The issue isn't that other people don't trust you with their money, it's that **YOU** don't trust you with their money!

You are just like the guy who doubted himself about approaching the hottie at the bar.

A coach asked me this one day before I bought my first property. He said, "Mike, are you going to buy a piece of real estate?"

"Yes."

"Are you only going to do good deals?"

"Yes."

"So without a doubt, you are going to make money on it?"

"Yes, or else I wouldn't do it!"

"Well, if it's a good deal and you are going to put your own money into it, why would you want some random person to enjoy the benefits of this opportunity over your family and friends?"

After thinking about it, I did want the people I knew and loved the most to share in the profit of my deals, and I realized that my fear was rooted in a lack of knowledge.

After that, I gained the confidence I needed to raise the money from my friends and family. I had them roll their IRA money into self-directed IRAs and solo 401(k) accounts. The project turned out to be a wild success, and everybody won!

You have a blessing. You are the shiny object. You have what other people want. So now that you have your head right, let's talk about who to target and how to pitch them.

Using Equity Partners

Here are some ways you can raise equity capital outside of seller financing. It's a spectrum. On one end is friends and family, where you have to do a lot of legwork and take on a lot of investors in small chunks, but you generally control the terms of your partnership. On the other end is partnering with a fund where they are the only investor, but they control the terms, and they get most of the equity.

Spectrum of People to Raise Money From

Friend & Family	High Net Worth	Family Offices	Fund Managers
Small Investments			Large Investments
Large # of Investors			1 Investor
Pay 8-12% IRR			Pay 20-25% IRR
Keep Majority of Equity			Give up Majority of Equity
First Deal			Experienced Investors

Let's go through each one:

- Friends, family, and professional network
- High-net-worth individuals
- Family offices
- Fund managers

FRIENDS, FAMILY AND PROFESSIONAL NETWORK

These are small investors—usually $25K–$100K each. That means you have to grind hard to get your deal done.

Who do you know with IRA or 401(k) money earning garbage returns on it with zero control over where the money goes? I bet you could raise half a million or more on your first deal just from that current network. This is the cheapest money because you can dictate very favorable terms for yourself and still give them access to opportunities they would never have otherwise. You will normally pay a 7–8% preferred return plus 25% of the upside.

HIGH-NET-WORTH INDIVIDUALS

These are millionaires who are successful in business and may even own a business. Where do they hang out? At the lake and the golf course. If you want to network with them, those are the places to do it. They want secure dividends and are okay with a lower return in exchange for reduced risk. They are looking for better risk-adjusted returns than what they could get in the stock market, and they want write-offs to shelter their ordinary income. Your competition is their financial advisor. You will be able to get money fairly cheap, but finding them and locking them down is harder. You will normally pay 7–10% preferred return plus 50% of the upside.

FAMILY OFFICES

This is a high-net-worth individual who has hired someone to manage their investments for them. You can actually buy a list of them online. A family office is essentially a team of people (office) to manage family wealth. It can be one person or a whole team of advisors, like a CPA, attorney, investment advisor, and so forth. They will have lots of money and you can do multiple deals. You will normally pay 8–12% preferred return plus 50–70% of the upside. Many of them require you to return all of their capital first before you start taking distributions, which means you can't eat off the upside, but you will still get paid asset management, acquisition, leasing, property management, and construction management fees if you do any of those roles in the partnership.

FUND

PRIVATE EQUITY

This is Wall Street money from fund managers. You can do unlimited deals once you're in, but you are basically getting a small promote for your hard work. They more or less own the property and dictate the terms of the deal. They require a proven track record. Once you get established, they are a great way to scale up and start doing bigger deals. If you start crushing it and are having a hard time raising capital quickly, then a fund may be worth looking into.

If you can raise the money elsewhere, then don't get into bed with the devil! You will pay a 10–12% preferred return plus 80–90% of the upside, and they most likely will not sign on debt with you. You will take all the risk for very little of the reward.

Using General Partners

If you prefer, you can partner with someone who already has a proven track record for raising money. Let them do the entire raise of capital, and you give them 30–35 percent ownership in the general partnership for raising the money. This can be a great way to get approved for a bank loan if you don't have great credit and need a general partner who will personally guarantee the debt with you. You can also pay them a "guaranty fee" of 0.5–2% of the purchase price at closing in lieu of a higher percentage ownership.

Some general partners will want more if they are actively involved in the deal beyond raising the capital too, like 35–50 percent ownership. I recommend you keep at least 51 percent of the voting units if you partner with somebody else. I think partnering with someone who has a track record on your first deal makes a tremendous amount of sense. I did, and it served me well.

My friend Todd Dexheimer gave me the idea to do a tiered offering, which incentivized people to invest more money with me on each deal. He was right because most people will invest whatever the minimum is. Make sure you keep your minimum high—I do $100K minimum now. Sure, I lose some people who are at $25K, but some people who would have done the minimum $25K amount now do the minimum $100K amount. You can always write your deal so you can make an exception to the rule too, which kind of gives you the best of both worlds. You have a higher minimum, but you can break the rules if you want.

How to Pitch

Do you find your investors or the deal first? The answer is both. You should be networking to start building a database of "potential" investors as you start prospecting for deals. Then once you have an actual deal, you have a list of people to "pitch" your deal to. You will create a "pitch deck" and present it in a webinar to explain your deal to them and answer all of their questions.

Let me give you some pointers on how to do this effectively.

INITIAL CONSULTATION

I have two sets of investor meetings and a PowerPoint for each one. We call these pitch decks. The first is for investors when I'm just adding them to my Rolodex. In this first meeting, I ask a lot of open-ended questions to understand where they are investing now, what their interest in real estate is, and what their expectations for returns and timeline are.

I say, "We have lots of investors and they all have different risk and investing profiles. Tell me what's important to you, so I can note your file and be in a better position to only bring you deals that I think will be a good fit for you." It's Sales 101. Build rapport, then do a deep discovery, then when the time is right, flip on your PowerPoint and answer their questions. We include a template of these in our online course.

The PowerPoint should cover the strategy you formed in the first half of this book along with the seven-step investing system we have in the second half of this book. Show them how you are using this proven system to create value in properties which multiplies their capital quickly and also achieves long-term cash flow. You're really just trying to get them excited to invest with you and show them you have a system. Close with this statement, "Would you like me to bring you my next deal for you to look at?"

DEAL-SPECIFIC CONSULTATION

The second is the deal-specific meeting with a deal-specific PowerPoint. I have had great luck doing a group video call for this one with a lot of potential investors on one call. You can prepare really well this way, and you don't have to repeat the same presentation over and over. Do a webinar, not a group video call. This ensures they can't see each other so no one can pick off your investors, and it respects everyone's privacy.

In that presentation, I do a slide with an overview of the deal. I include equity multiple, cash-on-cash return, and a sample $100K investment cash flow sheet that shows them the returns right out of the gate like this:

Sample $100k Investment for a Limited Partner

Year	CF Operation	Return of Capital	Upside at Sale	Total CF	C÷C
0	−$100,000			−$100,000	
1	$8,980			$8,980	9.0%
2	$13,400			$13,400	13.4%
3	$13,400			$13,400	13.4%
4	$13,400			$13,400	13.4%
5	$13,400	+ $100,000	+ $75,214	$188,614	13.4%
	Equity Multiple			1.89	
	IRR			**21.88%**	

Then cover who you are and what problem you will solve on the property to create value.

Keep your presentation simple. Don't have a lot of words on the screen. You don't want them reading—you want them listening to you. Include the site plan, floor plan, and description of work to be completed. Run them through the rent roll. Include pictures, videos, and Matterport 3D if you have it. Run them through the as-is and as-stabilized values on your MACO worksheet.

Don't spend an hour going through the entire cash flow sheet. If you do that, you are doing it wrong.

End by summarizing what the big problem is on the property that allowed you to get it for so cheap and what specific steps you will do to solve that problem, such as fixing it up, filling the vacancies, and overseeing a property management company to drive the financial performance up.

Then ask for their soft commitment. That's them raising their hand to get more information. You will send them the private placement memorandum and a subscription agreement. Then you follow up to answer any questions and get a signed subscription agreement and have them wire the money to your new operating checking account.

Boom. That's how you do it.

FUND

Pro Tip

Get a Non-Circumvent signed. Always. I learned the hard way and trusted people by a handshake. I got burned. Don't ever present your deal to anyone without one. Someone I trusted with a deal I had under contract ended up having one of his team members make an offer while I had it under contract, and the seller refused to negotiate with me. They ended up buying it immediately after I canceled the deal. This was a learning lesson for me. So my advice to you is to make sure you get a good Non-Circumvent signed and have it distributed. This is a legal document you will want your attorney to review to make sure it's legit; otherwise, it's pointless.

Resilience is the key to success in the Fund part. Don't ever give up on raising capital if your deal is a good deal. Just remember it's about finding the right people and presenting the deal in the right way.

I recommend starting off with smaller investors and doing the dirty work to raise the funds. You'll hear a bunch of nos, but then you'll keep going until you get some yeses, and you will keep more equity along the way. In the next chapter, we cover how to leverage the equity you just raised with bank financing to finish funding your deal.

Key Reader Takeaways

- ☐ If you raise money from friends and family and your professional network, you can generally get more favorable terms.
- ☐ Do an initial meeting to generate interest and a deal-specific meeting to secure their interest and answer all of their questions.
- ☐ Get them to sign a subscription agreement for a fund or an operating agreement for a joint venture.

Action Items

- ☐ Make a list of everyone you know who may have at least $25K. Call them all and start setting meetings to do an initial consultation.
- ☐ Build your investor list methodically. Always ask for three referrals.
- ☐ Create a world-class webinar to pitch your deal.
- ☐ Pitch your deal.
- ☐ Follow up with investors to get commitments.

Chapter 17

Secure the Debt

Objective: Secure Loan Approval Letter

I hope you get denied by ten banks, just like I did.

On my first large deal, I got crushed by banks. But getting denied can be one of the best things that ever happens to you—it makes you try harder to refine your deal. Never give up. Doug Marshall told me this when he came on our podcast: "You have to adopt a win-or-learn mentality instead of a win-or-lose mentality." That is so true. Instead of getting mad at the banks, I figured out WHY they had denied me and changed my pitch. In fact, I even changed my project plan. Originally, I was just going to restore the offices, but the lenders and investors kept telling me they thought apartments would be a better fit and that I should do a conversion. I listened, and I'm glad I did.

My plan kept getting better and better, and I kept pitching until one day at church, I got introduced to a new lender. They were financing a new church campus for us, and I sent him the deal link with everything nice and organized. Twenty days later, they closed on the deal for us.

Never give up. Your approval is right around the corner.

I still get denied on most of my deals at least once. It is just part of the game, so get used to someone telling you no. Let it bounce right off you and instill in you a desire to learn why they denied your deal. Sometimes it's you; sometimes it's your project; sometimes it's the bank and their interests not aligning with your project. Learn, then move on to the next lender. When you start asking the right questions instead of being offended, you can learn a lot.

Types of Lenders

Here are some of the different types of lenders you will see out there:

- Private Lenders
- Community Banks
- Credit Unions
- National Lenders
- Institutional Lenders

PRIVATE LENDERS

A private lender is anyone with money who wants to lend it to you. Your best bet for a private lender is the seller! Get them to finance some or all of the deal so you can give them a premium on price and a better return than the bank would give them on a CD or money market account.

Private lenders are easy to work with but hard to find, and they often charge really high rates. Most of them do hard money loans to rehabbers and charge 2% on the front end and 10–12% interest. If you finance your whole deal at hard money rates, you are not going to do well.

COMMUNITY BANKS

Most of my deals are done through community banks and credit unions. Figure out who the top community lenders are in your area.

Oftentimes community lenders will look at the overall loan situation and underwrite based on projected future performance as opposed to historical performance.

Locally chartered banks will have much more flexibility because they care about your deposit relationship with them. Be prepared to have them ask you to move your checking accounts over too.

CREDIT UNIONS

Credit unions are kind of like community banks, but they distribute the profit back to their members, so they often get more aggressive on winning business. Sometimes they want nothing to do with your deal. They tend to be less consistent than community banks, but I like floating my deals by credit unions to see what they have to say and hope to catch them at a time when they are dying to get some money put to work.

NATIONAL LENDERS

Large nationally chartered banks like Wells Fargo, US Bank, Bank of America, etc. prefer stabilized assets. They are "historical" lenders, meaning they qualify the deal based on historical financials. This is bad news for you and your Value-Add project.

If your project has a negative cash flow on day one like most Value-Add deals do, you will have trouble getting a loan from a larger national bank or institutional lender. Trying to get loans from these places on the front end is usually a bad idea. Ask me how I know this.

The loan officers will try to convince you to apply, stating they are flexible on terms, but my experience has been that it's usually a big waste of time. It's best you wait to pitch your deal to them when it comes time to refinance once you have stabilized the asset.

INSTITUTIONAL LENDERS

Institutional lenders are large organizations, like hedge funds, pension funds, and life insurance companies, that lend their money out as part of their overall investment strategy. They offer longer terms, usually ten years fixed instead of five years fixed. The main drawback is they usually include a yield maintenance clause in their loans, so if you ever sell or refinance, you could have a ridiculous prepayment.

I recently acquired a property and assumed the existing institutional loan for $2.6M because his prepayment penalty was over $500K. He couldn't sell to anyone else because no one was as dumb as me to step into a loan like that. I solved the seller's prepayment issue, got a great price, and since I plan to hold it for the full term anyway, I won't pay the prepayment penalty.

What a Bank Is Looking For

Now that you know what different types of banks are out there and which are best for the upfront loan versus the back-end loan, let's dissect the brain of a chief credit officer who actually sits on the committee that approves these loans.

They are generally looking at three things—I use the acronym ICE:

- **I**—Income
- **C**—Credit
- **E**—Equity

INCOME

Income of the partners and the income of the property are taken into consideration. That includes a number of factors. Let's take a look.

Global Cash Flow

They want to see the general partners' global cash flow. Global cash flow is a term they use to look at the entire picture of your income.

If you were to stop getting rent on this property, do you have other sources of income to make the payment to them? If you do, great. If you don't, you may need to bring in a general partner who will also sign on debt with you and you split the GP Units with them.

It depends on the deal and the lender, and this is why you shouldn't necessarily wait until you have pitched the whole deal to your equity partners to start your discussions with the lender. They should happen simultaneously.

Debt Service Coverage Ratio

The deal income matters too. If it's covering its own debt service on day one, that's a good thing. Lenders use a term called Debt Service Coverage Ratio (DSCR) which is simply the net operating income divided by the annual debt service.

With the Center Drive property, the going-in NOI was $40,000 per year and the going-in debt service was $36,768. Therefore, the DSCR = $40,000 ÷ $36,768 = 1.08.

Large lenders like to see 1.20–1.25, but smaller lenders are okay with 1.08 if the final DSCR, once the property is stabilized, is at least 1.20–1.25.

Once I stabilized Center Drive, I refinanced with a new loan where the annual debt service was roughly $50,000. The DSCR after I stabilized the asset was 2.0 ($100,000 NOI ÷ $50,000 ADS).

DSCR is the number one indicator of long-term loan default risk, which is the biggest risk you take in real estate investing. When you focus on Value-Add deals, you may end up with a poor DSCR on the front end, but you will have a very solid DSCR on the back end once the asset is stabilized, which equates to much lower long-term risk.

Remember to look at the numbers on the cash flow worksheet when calculating your DSCR, not the MACO worksheet. MACO was only comprised of the *potential* numbers so you could figure out what you can pay, whereas the cash flow worksheet is done after you get the property under contract and includes your revised *final* numbers.

CREDIT

Credit of the general partners matters. The bank wants to know if you are credit-worthy. If you have bad credit, write up a letter of explanation as to why, and have that as part of your loan package. If your credit is garbage, you should probably consider partnering with another general partner to do your deals who has good credit and give them part of the deal.

There are tons of books out there that lead you to believe credit doesn't matter on commercial loans and that they only look at the deal, not the person. That's a load of baloney. Work on restoring your credit immediately if you have bad credit, but don't let bad credit prevent you from achieving success buying your first property.

EQUITY

This includes the down payment and net worth. They look at how much equity you are putting into this deal and how much equity you have outside of this deal. They also look at liquidity. How much of your net worth is tied up in non-liquid assets like real estate, CDs, and cars versus how much is in liquid assets like cash, stocks, and bonds.

Basically, if the deal goes south, can they sue you and collect any loss they might incur from your other assets easily, or can you liquidate to pay the debt service if the tenants default?

How to Get Fast Approval

I recommend putting together a package in an online folder.

Assemble a list of local community banks and send them a bcc with the link to your deal documents. Ask that they review and let you know if they have interest. Then you can follow up with a call in a few days if you haven't heard anything. This saves you both time.

Make it easy for the loan officer to pitch the deal to the committee—organization is the key. Don't have a discussion with a lender over the phone and just start throwing numbers around. That is a waste of your time and a great way to get caught saying something you don't want to say.

Be methodical, almost surgical, when submitting your loan request packages to the lenders. This shows you know what you're doing. You already created a folder system in your due diligence step. Now you are choosing the information from there you want to share with your lender.

Here is a sample list of the folder hierarchy I commonly create for the lender:

- Appraisal
- Bids
- Sworn Statement
- Loan Request Overview
- Pictures/Media
- Plat/Survey
- Drawings/Floorplans
- Environmental
- MACO Worksheet
- General Partner Financials
- Leases
- Rent Roll
- Market Reports
- Management Agreement
- Purchase Agreement
- Subscription and Operating Agreements
- Tenant and Vendor Contact Sheets
- Title Work
- Vendor Contracts
- Written Seller Statements
- Zoning

FUND

If you assemble your package in one shareable link, you will get great results quickly.

Three Approvals

There are three parts to getting bank financing:

- Term Sheet
- Committee Approval
- Clear To Close

TERM SHEET

The first goal is to get a "term sheet." This will spell out the terms they are willing to lend to you on. This is not a binding commitment to lend but will be very helpful for you in underwriting your deal. I recommend getting the term sheet right away.

Their numbers aren't locked in stone, and neither are yours. Get a general idea of what lenders are willing to do. I would get a term sheet from a few lenders and compare them if you can.

The lender will want to know who your partners are. Tell them you are still working on it. Lining them up before submitting is ideal, but it rarely happens that way in the real world. That's okay. You don't have to wait until you have all the equity raised to begin applying for debt, but if you have a general idea of who your partners will be, you can be more effective in your loan application process. Just let them know the general structure you want to do (fund or JV) and submit your information. Don't worry. You can change this later if you need to.

On the right is a term sheet with some redacted confidential information.

COMMITTEE APPROVAL

Once you select a lender to move forward with, you usually have to write them a check for the cost of the appraisal and the Phase I environmental investigation. You can see in the letter to the right, they want $7K to get the deal started. Once they get that, they will start the underwriting and submit your loan application to committee.

This is where the people who actually make the decision review your deal. Your loan officer and their analyst will take your package and use it to make their credit committee presentation. That's why giving them as much information as possible helps—you want good financial projections and to be able to justify your projections by including your market research (reports, interviews, and comparables). You are selling yourself as much as your project, especially if the success of the projects depends solely on your ability to execute on the business plan. The credit committee will issue an approval with some "conditions." Unlike a term sheet, this is an actual commitment to lend.

Sample Bank Term Sheet

Thank you for choosing _____ for your financing needs. This proposal does not represent a commitment to lend, is not all-inclusive, and merely reflects the parties' discussions to date. I am pleased to present the following proposal:

Borrower:	Commercial Investors Group, LLC
Loan Amount:	Lesser of 75% of appraised value or 80% of cost, approx. $6,552,000
Type:	Commercial Real Estate Term Loan
Term:	10-year term, 25-year amortization
Interest Rate:	Option A) Rate fixed for the full 10 years at 3.91% Option B) Rate fixed for the first 7 years at 3.61%, resetting to the 3-year US Treasury + 2.00%
Repayment:	Payments of monthly principal and interest (option to escrow for real-estate taxes available)
Prepayment	There will be no prepayment penalty
Fees:	0.25% plus all out-of-pocket expenses including items such as appraisal, environmental and title
Collateral:	First real-estate mortgage and assignment of rents on property located at _____
Guarantees:	Mike Sowers (and any other owners of entity >20%)
Additional Requirements:	• Borrower to maintain a minimum Debt Service Coverage Ratio of 1.20 to 1.00 pre-distribution and 1.00 to 1.00 post distribution • Sufficient and acceptable appraisal, environmental and title per Bank standards • Borrower agrees to execute all documents as the Bank or Bank's legal counsel may reasonably require. • Annual business tax return and rent roll required. • Annual PFS and tax returns required on all guarantors. • All other items deemed necessary by _____ in order to close the loan.

We truly appreciate the opportunity to work with you on this project. Please feel free to contact me directly if you have questions or need additional clarification. If you find this acceptable, please sign the letter below and provide a check in the amount of $7,000 to get the process started. Should the loan request not fund, all proceeds net of expenses incurred will be refunded back to you. I look forward to working with you.

Signature _____

FUND

CLEAR TO CLOSE

You must clear all the conditions that came with your approval in order to actually close. In the next chapter, we cover how to do that.

Key Reader Takeaways

☐ Work with community banks and credit unions for upfront loans and refinance with larger lenders once you have stabilized the property.

☐ Lenders care about income, credit, and equity (ICE).

☐ Don't ever agree to a yield maintenance prepayment clause.

☐ Select which folders within your deal folder hierarchy you want to share with your lender.

☐ Make it easy for your loan officer to present a compelling story to the credit committee.

☐ Back up your projections with third-party data.

Action Items

☐ Figure out what information you want to share with your lenders and send out at least three loan requests.

☐ Follow up and get three term sheets to compare.

☐ Move forward with one lender for your project, but don't close the door on others until your deal comes back approved with conditions.

Chapter 18

Close the Deal

Objective: Fund and Close the Deal

My stomach sank to the floor, and I literally almost cried. I had already cashed the check mentally, so losing the deal was like writing a check back for the amount I stood to make—which was a six-digit number.

I had been working on this deal with one of my team members for a couple months, and we were literally about to sign the paperwork when the buyer we were whole-saling the deal to cancelled at the last minute. I don't want you to experience what I felt that day, but human nature says that you will make the same mistake of mentally cashing your check before you actually close. At least you can be aware of it. Then when it happens, you'll be able to say, "Dammit Mike. You told me not to do that."

This is the hardest part of all of the parts and probably the most important. You need to get a bunch done in this part to make it all come together. Here's your checklist:

- Tenant Estoppel Certificates
- Final Sworn Construction Statement
- Final Sources and Uses
- Form Your Entity
- Signed Operating Agreement or Subscriptions
- Collect Equity Funds
- Clear Lender Conditions
- Legal Review
- Closing Statement Review

Tenant Estoppel Certificates

An estoppel is a form that the tenants sign that certifies their understanding of the terms of the lease. It also serves to subordinate the tenants' rights in title to the new loan you are recording against the property. Most lenders require them.

Have the lender draft them if possible, then have your attorney review it and redline it. Redlining is a term used for tracking the changes in Microsoft Word, which makes the changes show up in red. This is your protection so the tenant doesn't come back and say they had a different agreement with the prior owner after you close.

Make sure you cover these key lease items in the estoppel:

- Lease end date.
- Renewal or cancellation options.
- Rent rate and calculations.
- Cam/Tax estimates and payments if net, triple net, or modified gross leases.
- Status and value of any work the landlord or tenant is required to complete.
- Certification that there are no open work orders or issues.
- Security deposit and unused tenant improvement allowances.
- Subordination to lender.
- Description of the condition they need to leave the space in when they vacate the space.

Final Sworn Construction Statement

We call this a "sworn." You may have submitted a sworn to the lender and title company, but if you get further information prior to closing that changes anything, this is the chance to change your numbers.

Be sure to include your contingency for construction in this number. (We'll cover all of this in the Fix step that's coming up).

Final Sources and Uses

This is the *final* sources and uses of capital that they will base the loan amount on. Some lenders will allow for some or all of the closing costs, leasing fees, and holding cost reserves in the loan-to-cost calculation, and some will not. Be sure to check with your lender early on for what "costs" they allow when calculating their loan amount.

Make sure your total uses of capital matches up with the amounts you are sourcing for equity and debt to be sure you don't raise too much or not enough equity capital.

Form Your Entity

You will file articles of organization with your Secretary of State to make your LLC official. Then you will go to the IRS website and file for your Employer Identification Number (EIN). Your state may also require you to create a Taxpayer ID. In Minnesota, we do that right on the Department of Revenue website.

You'll need your articles of organization from the Secretary of State and the Federal Employer Identification Number to open a bank account. We open an operating checking account and a trust account for security deposits (unless our leases allow us to comingle security deposit funds with our general operating funds). Make sure your general partners come with you to open this. If you don't know who they are yet, you can always add them later. Also, make sure the bank you select has good online access and remote deposit for rent checks. You don't want to have to drive to the bank every time you get a check.

Most times, the lender who does the main loan will want you to put all your rental income into a checking account that you open at their bank. I push back on this condition, and you should too because you want all your accounts at one lender. You can agree to open a bank account there, but try not to agree to run all your income and expenses through that account for the property, or you will regret it. Trust me. If you own multiple properties and have loans from different lenders that you have committed to running operating accounts through, you'll have to log into ten different online accounts, drive to ten banks to make deposits, or have ten deposit machines sitting on your desk. That gets old—fast!

Signed Operating Agreement or Subscriptions

The partnership operating agreement is your prenuptial agreement for your marriage to your partners. You will have one whether you do a fund or a JV.

In a JV, all the partners sign the operating agreement. In the fund, the general partners sign the operating agreement but the LPs sign subscription agreements that subscribe them to the investment.

These are critical items! Of course, you are going to choose your partners wisely, but since I've made mistakes in the past, here's what you need to know:

- Don't make written promises to investors that deviate from the private placement memorandum, operating agreement, or subscription agreement.
- Make sure you have an attorney who specializes in securities draft this. Do NOT use your general counsel.
- Have a strategy call with your full team of advisors when structuring this. If you only talk with one advisor at a time, your overall structure could have holes in it.

You will want to have a call with your advisory team. Here is who I usually have on the call:

- Qualified CPA with experience in funds and JVs for commercial real estate
- Attorney who specializes in securities
- Your general partner(s), if any

Do not invite your potential limited partners to be on this call. The purpose of the call is to determine the final structure of your deal. Hot talking points are as follows:

- Fund or joint venture structure?
- Who are the general partners? Who are the limited partners? Are they all in one state or multiple states? Are they all accredited investors or are some of them non-accredited?
- What is the business plan with the property? Fix and sell to owner-user, fix, fill, and sell to financial buyer, or fix, fill, refinance and hold long term?
- Are you raising money as preferred equity or mezzanine debt, or a combination?
- What are the sources and uses of capital?
- How much of the sources of capital are coming from the limited partners and how much is coming from the general partners?
- What is the price per membership unit? (We usually do $1 per unit to make it simple.)
- What is the lot size? These are the chunks they can buy. We usually set this at $10K or ten thousand membership units, so they could do $100K, $110K, $120K, etc.)
- What is the minimum you can raise and still do the project, and what is the cap or maximum you will want to raise?
- What is the minimum investment for one limited partner? (We usually set this at $100K depending on how much we want to raise. I like to have fewer than ten investors if possible.)
- If you don't hit the minimum, what happens? Does everyone just get their money back, or does the deal sponsor have to put in the rest? If the deal cancels, does everyone share in the loss for money spent in due diligence, or does the GP eat the whole thing?
- What is the preferred return (hurdle rate)? How does the profit get split after that (waterfall structure)?
- What are the buyout provisions for the active partners in case of a dispute?

I know it's boring stuff, but it's a critical part. Spend time here and ensure this document accurately reflects your intentions with regard to how you will actually operate the property. An ounce of effort here saves many pounds of pain later. This is your prenuptial agreement, and I recommend you don't take it lightly—you don't want to end up in a nasty divorce later.

FUND

Collect Equity Funds

Get your investors to actually send their funds into your operating account. You can use an attorney to have a funding closing prior to your actual closing so everyone funds on the same date. I like to write up the agreement so the preferred return timeclock doesn't start until the funds go into use when you actually close on the property.

Clear Lender Conditions

This is where you methodically clear any remaining conditions that the lender has to close. Most commonly, these are: appraisal review, environmental report review, lender's title policy review, and final review of sworn construction statement and sources and uses. If they have any additional conditions, make sure you work to clear them quickly. Things get stressful if you wait until the last minute.

Legal Review

At this point, you will be tired. You just want this thing to close. But beware: some lenders are sneaky and slip in legal terms you never agreed to. You should have your attorney review the final note and mortgage before you sign it at closing to make sure there aren't any prepayment or other acceleration clauses they slipped in there that you might need to be aware of.

Trust but verify! Don't be cheap and skip this part, or it might be very expensive in the long run.

Closing Statement Review

The closing statement shows all the debits and credits for your closing. Is your acquisition fee on there? Broker taken care of? Did the lender throw in some "junk fees" like doc prep fees in addition to their origination fee? What about the prorations on rent, security deposits, and other items that should transfer from the seller—are those accurate?

In my experience, 95 percent of the time, the document is *not* accurate when I first review it. Buyer beware!

Once you have successfully cleared all the conditions to close, you should be able to attend your first closing and sign the deal.

Congratulations! You have completed the marketing, sales, and finance pieces of your business plan. You just bought your first commercial property and should be excited that you saw it through to this point.

The next three steps are operational and are all about creating value in the property. For now, take a deep breath and enjoy the moment. This is a big victory for you!

Key Reader Takeaways

- ☐ Pay attention to the details to make sure nothing slips through the cracks.
- ☐ Get legal help.
- ☐ Review the closing statement thoroughly.

Action Items

- ☐ Select a securities attorney, CPA, and general partners.
- ☐ Hold a conference call to finalize your deal structure.
- ☐ Clear your lender's conditions.
- ☐ Collect signatures on the operating agreement and subscriptions.
- ☐ Get your equity partners' money into your operating account.
- ☐ Close your deal.

FUND

Step 4
Fix

This step is all about construction. As you do the improvements that create value in the building, it allows you to charge a higher rent, fill vacancies faster, and reduce operating expenses that kill your NOI. The key to success is having a super tight final budget. We call this final budget the "sworn construction statement."

Cost estimating is an iterative process, and each iteration gets more detailed. Your first cost estimate is actually done at the end of your property tour. You use those numbers in your original MACO worksheet to determine your offer price. It is just an educated guess you make using the renovation cost worksheet.

After you get the property under contract, you will write a detailed scope of work and get some concept drawings done. Then you'll send these packages out for bids before your contingency expires. You will start getting more granular with your estimates, including materials and actual pricing from vendors and suppliers. You will lock in final numbers and use them when you revise your MACO worksheet to decide if you should walk, renegotiate, or move forward with your deal.

After that, you usually finalize selections, have construction drawings done, and sign construction contracts. Once you get to this point, you will have your final construction contracts and budget—the sworn construction statement. You will submit these to your lender prior to closing, to determine your final loan amount and set the schedule for the draw requests.

After you close on the property, it's go time!

Here are the parts to the Fix step:

- Estimate Repair Costs
- Gather Bids
- Sign Construction Contracts
- Complete Construction Draws

The Fix step is a critical one, and it's where many newbies go over on timeline or budget. Keeping a process early on, maintaining proactive communication with all parties, and making frequent site visits is what makes this step a success.

Let's dive into each part further.

FIX

Chapter 19

Estimate Repair Costs

Objective: Estimate Your Costs to Fix the Building Up

We are taking a leap back in time here. This part is actually done at the end of the tour step, and it's where you take the first step to locking in your construction budget.

The idea behind renovating to create value is that everything you do has a purpose. If it doesn't create more value than it costs, you don't do it. There are a few different ways something can create value. That is, they either increase the NOI or the Market Multiple:

- Increase rent tenants are willing to pay.
- Reduce or eliminate certain expenses.
- Speed up leasing efforts.
- Make tenants want to renew.
- Reduce the perceived risk a buyer might have when you sell.

By now, you should understand the concept behind creating value, but how do you quickly analyze if a particular repair will create more value than it costs? Remember calculating our Magic Multiple when we were figuring out our MACO in the Figure step? Ours was 9.0 for Center Drive.

That meant we could invest up to nine times the NOI into the property in order to achieve our desired profit margin. Now we are using it in a different way—to evaluate if a renovation item makes sense or not. The total investment in this case is your investment into the particular renovation item you are evaluating. If you can figure out the incremental increase in NOI that will result from your renovation, then you can apply a Magic Multiple to figure out the most you could afford to pay for that renovation.

I've rehabbed over a thousand properties, so I know how important this step is in figuring out what renovation items to do and which ones not to do. I have also found that this is the hardest part for most of my students. If you worry that you won't be able to accurately estimate repairs, then I have good news for you. I am going to give you a shortcut!

I call it the renovation cost worksheet, and like the others, you can also download a spreadsheet version on our website. If you want to get even more detailed, you can use an estimating software. RS Means is the one I recommend.

At this stage in the game, you are just estimating the renovation costs (with a reasonable level of accuracy) in order to make an offer for the Figure step. If you are getting bids during the Figure step, you are probably spending more time than you should on it. Use the spreadsheet to get a quick idea.

I lump the improvements into categories:

- Big-Ticket Items
- Energy Upgrades
- Cosmetic Upgrades
- Tenant Improvements
- Contractor Costs

If your offer gets accepted, you will have a contingency period where you can write a formal scope of work, get concept drawings made, and solicit bids from contractors. If your numbers are way off, you can always back out of the deal, so you really have no risk here. With that being said, getting good at estimating renovation costs quickly will increase your long-term chances of success and reduce the likelihood that you will be way off on your fix-up costs in your preliminary MACO worksheet.

Download the template from my website or duplicate the worksheets and fill them out with pricing for your area. Feel free to add more line items to your template as they come up in your deals. This should be a working template that gets better each time you use it.

In the examples I'm going to show you, I used the real numbers for Center Drive that I estimated up front when doing my MACO analysis.

Big Ticket Items

Big-Ticket Items

Division	Item	Unit	Rate	Qty	Total
Roof	Flat Roof – Overlay	SF	$5.25		
	Flat Roof – Complete Tear-Off	SF	$9.50		
	Roof – Redo Perimeter	LF	$30.00		
	Skylight Replacement	EA	$5,000.00		
	Perimeter Flashings	LF	$6.50		
Parking Lot	Asphalt Repair	SF	$10.00		
	Asphalt Overlay	SF	$3.00		
	Asphalt Replacement	SF	$5.00		
	Sweep, Sealcoat and Restripe	SF	$1.00		
	Concrete	SF	$7.00		
HVAC/ Mechanicals	Indoor 100K BTU Furnace and A/C	EA	$8,500.00		
	Unit Heater	EA	$2,000.00		
	Rooftop Unit	EA	$8,500.00		
	Smart Thermostats	EA	$450.00		

These are the items that blow your budget completely if you miss them, so focus on them first:

- Roof
- Parking Lot
- Mechanicals

If you factor replacements in on the front end, the seller will feel the pain, not you. Some will argue they don't add "value," but if a tenant doesn't renew their lease because their roof is leaking, you'll have costly turnover. Lost rent, costs to renovate, leasing commissions, and tenant improvement dollars that you have to allocate to the tenant are all real costs associated with turnover. Don't downplay how important it is to keep your tenants happy! This is a business, and your tenant is your customer.

Even if you don't plan to renovate the building, check the age and remaining useful life of these three critical items. If the remaining useful life is less than ten years, I usually prorate the cost with the seller. At five years left, I deduct half the cost; at two years left, I deduct 80 percent of the cost. I have a column on the spreadsheet version of my renovation cost worksheet for a depletion percent that adjusts the cost based on the remaining useful life you plug in.

There are three ways you can handle each repair item:

- **Deduct and Finance:** You deduct the cost from the MACO, and you add it to your sworn statement so the bank will finance it. You do this for items you plan to do within the first six months. This would include everything you know for sure you will renovate on the property right away.
- **Deduct and Reserve:** You deduct the cost from the MACO and raise the funds as a reserve up front. Do this for big-ticket items you plan to do in six to twenty-four months. Add it to the sources and uses, but don't put it on your sworn statement. If you know your item will need to be done in the near future, but not immediately after closing, you should raise the money up front, so you don't have to do a capital call in a year. It's best to raise capital for items that may need to be replaced in a year or so, but that you're not 100 percent

certain you will. An example would be some old HVAC equipment or a parking lot. Maybe it's the middle of winter and you want to wait until next summer to see how things go. You can always distribute funds back to investors to pay their capital accounts down if you decide not to do the repairs. This is a better option than doing a capital call within the first year, which looks bad.

- **Deduct Only:** You deduct the cost from the MACO, but don't raise the funds for the repair at all. Do this for big-ticket items that may be two years out or more. You don't want to raise money for something you won't do for several years or you'll be paying a preferred return on that cash for a long time, which will water down the returns to investors. An example would be to adjust the MACO to account for 50 percent of the cost of a roof with five years life left on it.

Pro Tip

Learn how to get really good at estimating the remaining useful life for these items. The best way to do this is to meet contractors at the property who specialize in roofing, asphalt, and mechanicals, and ask them to do a condition report. Ask them a ton of questions about what they look for to estimate remaining useful life, so you know **how** they arrived at their conclusion. Then on the next property, you can estimate it yourself with reasonable accuracy, put your assumption on your offer sheet, and account for the partial cost to replace in your renovation cost worksheet.

ROOF

Most flat roofs last twenty years. Some last as long as thirty but will start having ongoing maintenance issues toward the end. Issues here cost you time, money, and pissed-off tenants, so get educated on how to estimate the remaining useful life.

There are two ways to replace a flat roof system: overlay and replacement. Ask your roofing contractor for options. If they don't "do" overlays, ask them why, or find someone who will. There are some great options that come with a fifteen-to-twenty-year, non-prorated warranty on labor and materials for overlay roofs at a fraction of the cost. Options here are PVC, rubber, or TPO. I prefer PVC for value, even though it's not the best of the three options. How long you plan to hold the property should impact your decision on what roofing system to do.

I measure them using Google Earth.

PARKING LOT

Parking lots can be as expensive as a roof. Don't miss them! I measure this using Google Earth too. Just like the roof, you can do a tear-out or an overlay, though you might not need to. You might just need a sweep, seal coat, and stripe. The condition of the parking lot and the timeline you plan to hold the property will drive your decision on which route to go. Get smart on this. During due diligence, bring a few subcontractors by to have them educate you on the matter.

MECHANICAL SYSTEMS

Picture of a Rooftop Unit (RTU)

FIX

Commercial rooftop units, often called RTUs, are like the furnace and air conditioner you have in your house. They pump air through ductwork like any other forced-air system. The only difference is these combos sit on the roof.

You can figure out the year it was built, usually by looking at the model number. The third and fourth digits are often the year it was manufactured. Another trick I learned is to pull up the property in Google Earth satellite view in my iPad and take a screenshot. Then I number the rooftop units in sequential order using my stylus and take pictures of these labels in exactly the same order as I numbered them on the screenshot. The result is a full inventory of all of my units in less than ten minutes that I can reference later to determine how much money I'm taking off the price, how much cash I need to set aside for starting reserves, and how much annual maintenance I should plan on.

Unit heaters are the garage heater style that hang from the ceiling of a warehouse. These usually last ten to fifteen years and vent up and out.

Office buildings and apartments usually have interior furnaces with an A/C condenser on the outside and refrigerant lines running back and forth. If the building has boilers, you may want to consider deducting the cost of a new forced-air system since boilers are usually very costly to operate.

Picture of a Unit Heater

Energy Upgrades

Energy Upgrades

Division	Item	Unit	Rate	Qty	Total
Electrical	LED Lighting and Motion Sensor Upgrades	SF	$1.00		
	Automated Door Locks	Door	$1,250.00		
	New Service Panel	EA	$4,500.00		
	Additional Metering	Meter	$2,500.00		
Insulation	Spray Foam Insulation	SF	$3.00		
	Fiberglass Batt Insulation	SF	$2.50		
Plumbing	Remodel Bathroom – Full Gut	EA	$15,000.00		
	Remodel Bathroom – Cosmetic	EA	$6,500.00		
	LED Lighting and Motion Sensor Upgrades	SF	$1.00		

Now that you've taken care of the big-ticket items, the remaining decisions revolve around what upgrades create more value than they cost to do. This is important.

Energy upgrades almost always pay for themselves.

How do you know if they pay for themselves?

Remember the Magic Multiple? Your Magic Multiple is the multiple of NOI that you can be all-in at in order to hit your desired profit margin. I gave you five scenarios that all increase NOI. Simply figure out how much NOI they would create, multiply it by your Magic Multiple, and that's your break-even cost for that item. If the cost is below that number, do it.

For example, let's say I can separate the utility meters and have the tenants pay those directly. If it saves $15,000 in annual utility costs, then my NOI goes up by

$15,000. If my Magic Multiple is 9.0, I can spend up to $135,000 to separate those meters and have it make sense. If it costs me less than $135,000 to separate them, then I do it. If it costs more than that, then I don't, unless it creates some other benefit that is non-financial.

$$\textbf{Top Limit for Cost of Improvement} \ = \ \frac{\textbf{Increase}}{\textbf{in NOI}} \ \times \ \frac{\textbf{Magic}}{\textbf{Multiple}}$$

If you decided to separate the meters, in this example, you would factor the actual cost into your Fix costs and reduce your utility expenses by $15,000.

You can run different scenarios to see what scope of work gives you the best numbers. Let's focus on some items that almost always pay for themselves. That is, the value increase is usually much higher than the cost of the improvement.

LED LIGHTING

There may be a tax credit available for upgrading your building to LED lighting, but even if there is not, it still makes sense to do this upgrade. I usually re-device the existing fixtures as opposed to getting all new fixtures. As a general rule of thumb, I have been spending around $1 per square foot to upgrade my buildings to LED lights, but it cuts the electric bill in half.

At one of our projects, I spent $12,500 to upgrade a fifteen thousand-square-foot office building to LED inside and out, and it reduced my electric bill $6,000 per year. The market cap rates for that building are 8%, so that $6,000 per year equates to $75,000 in value. Would you spend $12,500 to increase the value of your building by $75,000?

MOTION SENSORS

Another big electrical upgrade is motion sensors. All bathrooms and closets should have motion switches installed. Make sure you get a motion switch above the stalls in the bathroom too. I learned this the hard way!

We now use motion sensors combined with timers in the hallways. During normal business hours, the lights are always on at a regular brightness. After hours, they drop down in brightness with a motion sensor triggering them back to normal brightness. Overnight, they are off, but motion still works.

AUTOMATED DOOR LOCKS

Automating your security system will save a lot of time and money. If you have to hire someone to show up every day and lock and unlock the building, you're out of your mind. Install an automated door locking system that is programmable so you can set the lock and unlock times and people can use keycards outside of those hours.

SMART THERMOSTATS

Having programmable smart thermostats that you can operate remotely is a game changer. When a tenant complains to your property manager about temperature, you can have your property manager adjust the temperature without sending someone out to the property. This quickly shaves maintenance dollars.

INSULATION

The goal is to reduce energy costs. Often, insulation below the new roof membrane or in the exterior walls makes a huge difference. Blow fiberglass in attics in wood-framed construction, and seal air gaps around penetrations.

PLUMBING FIXTURES

Being cheap is expensive. Cheap fixtures have plastic valves and nice ones use ceramic. To get the right ones, buy your fixtures from a specialty plumbing store, not from the big box stores. An hour of plumbing labor is as much as the entire cost of the fixture, and if the fixture you select lasts two years until it craps out, you will end up spending much more in the long run than getting the nice one that lasts eight years.

Cosmetic Upgrades

Cosmetic Upgrades

Division	Item	Unit	Rate	Qty	Total
Siding & Trim	Vinyl Siding	SF	$5.00		
	Cement Siding	SF	$7.00		
	Custom Fascia	LF	$22.00		
	Tuckpointing Existing Brick	SF	$45.00		
	New Stone/Brick	SF	$30.00		
Exteriors Doors & Windows	Exterior Doors Single	EA	$2,500.00		
	Overhead Garage Door	EA	$4,200.00		
	Window – Glass Only	SF	$50.00		
	Window – Glass and Frame	EA	$1,000.00		
	Cut In New Drive In/Dock Door	EA	$20,000.00		
Drywall & Painting	Hang, Tape, and Mud	SF	$4.25		
	Interior Painting	SF	$2.00		
	Exterior Painting	SF	$1.50		
	Acoustic Ceiling Tiles and Grid	SF	$6.50		
Flooring	Carpet Squares	SF	$2.50		
	Carpet Base	LF	$2.50		
	Carpet Stairs	EA	$150.00		
	Tile	SF	$15.00		
	Vinyl Plank	SF	$7.00		
Cleaning	Deep Cleaning	SF	$0.25		

We do these items to make spaces more desirable so they rent at higher rates, which dramatically increases our NOI. Plus, any new buyer will be impressed with the condition of the property, which reduces perceived risk and increases the multiple they are willing to pay for your NOI.

SIDING, TRIM AND TUCKPOINTING

The exterior wall surface is the biggest thing people see when they arrive at the property. The average exterior paint job lasts three to five years. Wrapping all exterior wood in aluminum is a great way to improve the curb appeal of the building but also saves ongoing maintenance dollars. Changing large wall surfaces makes a huge impact on the curb appeal of the property.

WINDOWS

Light equals money—rent rates for offices increase dramatically when people have natural light. Where can you add natural light with windows or skylights to drive rent rates up?

Be careful about how you install skylights, as they can be a big maintenance cost that actually increases expenses. When you cut in a window or door, you have to add support across the top, so make sure you get a structural engineer's opinion during due diligence before you lock in your final sworn construction statement for the bank.

PAINT

Large surface area cosmetic upgrades like paint and carpet make the largest impact per dollar. We use the same color scheme for all of our buildings to keep things consistent and to simplify the maintenance process going forward (Sherwin Williams SW7029 Agreeable Gray on the walls and SW7009 Pearly White on trim and doors). Our railings and partitions in bathrooms are usually gloss black. You may choose a different color scheme, and you may elect to do pops of bright colors, but I would caution against anything that may go out of style in five years. You want your color scheme to be evergreen (always relevant).

Call your local paint store to see if they do color consultations or know someone who does. If you have ever selected a color using one of those little 2" × 2" squares, painted a whole room, and decided you hated it, you'll know how much a consultant can save you. Imagine doing a $20,000 paint job and realizing it doesn't look good. Spend the $300 on the color consultant!

FIX

FLOORING

Here, I tend to like multi-color products because they don't show wear and tear as much. We use carpet squares instead of rolled carpet. That way, when someone spills or one gets ruined, we can pop it out and replace just that one square. We get the matching color in a roll for stairs, and we have it bound into a carpet base that matches.

For entryways and bathrooms, we use luxury heavy-duty plank flooring and go right over the tile if the city allows it. Mud-set tile is very expensive to remove. If you prepare the floor properly with a floated embossing leveler and glue the material down properly, it will last for a really long time even with high wear and tear. Make sure you get a waterproof product and something meant for commercial use. Do not use laminate or hardwood-type products for commercial use.

Pro Tip

I was touring a property with an owner, and one unit looked atrocious. It needed carpet and paint and smelled horrible, like mold had been growing in there for years. It had been vacant for *two years*. When I asked him why he had not investigated the smell and had the unit remodeled, he said, "That would be stupid. The tenant will want to pick out their carpet and select their paint colors. If I do it now, I may end up having to redo it again in the future."

I don't think he realized how stupid he really was!

With the exception of a few rare individuals who watch HGTV 24/7, most people want move-in ready, turnkey spaces. And after designing and remodeling thousands of properties, I can tell you with 100 percent certainty, people are horrible at visualizing. People have trouble seeing things as they would be with new carpet and paint, or a wall moved here or there. For this reason, you will have trouble getting top dollar in rent and filling your spaces if you don't clean them up. This seller could have redone his carpet and paint five times with the rent he would have received if he had filled the space two years prior.

> Don't ever let the tenant pick the carpet and paint for office and multifamily buildings. Always remodel the unit—just be sure to use a neutral color scheme that appeals to the largest amount of people.

CLEANING

Budget for a deep clean once your remodel is complete. Contractors will only clean to a broom-swept condition. Having a super clean property that smells good is not only a good way to win new tenants but also to keep existing tenants. Whoever you hire to do the regular janitorial work will usually do this cheapest up front because it will make their job easier long term.

Tenant Improvements

The final category includes the things tenants want to help grow their business or enjoy the space more. There are two ways to give tenants money:

- Tenant Improvement Allowance
- Building Improvements

TENANT IMPROVEMENT ALLOWANCE

A tenant may need to build out their space to fit their needs. Sometimes they will ask you to reimburse them for some or all of these costs by giving them what's called a Tenant Improvement Allowance or TI.

Tenant Improvements

Division	Item	Unit	Rate	Qty	Total
Tenant	Tenant Improvement Allowance	SF	$5.00		
Demolition	Dumpsters	EA	$700.00		
	Demolition	HR	$75.00		
Carpentry	New Partition Wall (Up to 10')	LF	$50.00		
	New Partition Wall (10' to 20')	LF	$120.00		
	Interior Doors	EA	$900.00		
	Cabinets	LF	$150.00		
	Countertops	SF	$60.00		
Furniture	Mailbox Bank	EA	$1,250.00		
	Furniture/Art	Bldg	$1,500.00		
Signage	Outdoor Sign Bank	EA	$10,000.00		
	Directory in Lobby	EA	$1,500.00		
	Tenant Suite Signs	Unit	$100.00		
ADA Upgrades	Passenger Elevator (Existing Shaft)	EA	$200,000.00		
	Passenger Elevator (New Shaft)	EA	$325,000.00		
	ADA Bathroom	EA	$12,500.00		
	Signage	EA	$10,000.00		

In a tight market where lots of space is available, landlords need to spice up the deal by pitching in for tenant improvements. Check with brokers in your area on what is typical. In our area, it's $3–$7 per square foot per year for office space. On industrial leases, there is usually an allowance of $1–$2 per square foot total for warehouse square footage. Retail is all over the board depending on the space and the needs.

I try to specify in the lease how the TI dollars can be spent. You want the money to go for upgrades that will increase the rent if this tenant defaults or doesn't renew at the end of the lease term—basically any of the items we have discussed in this chapter that add value. Try to limit them from being spent on furniture, fixtures, and equipment or other upgrades that do not add any value to your building.

It's common for the landlord to amortize some or all of the tenant improvement allowance into the lease. Basically, you are financing their improvements by adding the monthly payments that a bank would charge to their monthly rent. It's all part of the negotiation.

For example, let's say I want to budget $5 per square foot per year allowance for a five-year office lease. So if I have ten thousand RSF of office vacant, I need a line item for tenant improvement allowance for $250,000. The actual may end up being a different number altogether once I actually negotiate a deal with a tenant, but at least I'm budgeting something.

BUILDING IMPROVEMENTS

Sometimes it's better to control the remodel for certain items the tenant wants to have done since it may impact other tenants. If you hire the contractor and oversee the work prior to turning the space over to the tenant, we call these building improvements or BIs. Building improvements can consist of many areas. Let's cover some of the big ones.

DRIVE-IN AND DOCK DOORS

Industrial tenants want access. Can you add more drive-in doors, entry, or dock doors to give tenants better access to their space? Drive-in doors are at ground level, and dock doors are a few feet off the ground. Sometimes you can convert a drive-in door to a dock door by digging down or vice versa by ramping up. Small tenants usually want drive-in doors, whereas larger tenants usually want both.

DEMOLITION

If you have warehouse or retail spaces that are really chopped up, you will probably want to remove interior walls that aren't load-bearing prior to taking photos. I also recommend "whiteshelling" warehouse and retail spaces. This is where you basically take it back to a shell and paint everything white. Use shellac paint to take any smells away. I like gray paint for concrete floors and white on the walls and ceiling.

CARPENTRY

Tenants sometimes want walls built. This would include rough and finish carpentry, like dividing spaces, trim, doors, cabinets, and countertops.

FURNITURE AND AMENITIES

Don't skip out on the amenities, but make sure they will actually be something the tenants will use. I interview all of the current tenants during due diligence and ask them what amenities they wish the building had. Some won't care; some will want certain things. Don't assume.

In office buildings, I have found that things like shared conference rooms with digital whiteboards and nice chairs add a lot of value, especially if you are going to have small office units. Electric chargers for vehicles can be a perk in some areas as well.

ADA UPGRADES

In the state of Minnesota, you have to put 20 percent of your remodeling budget into ADA upgrades. This was a big oopsy for me when I started estimating project costs. So if you have a $100,000 remodel and none of the items are for ADA upgrades, you need to spend an additional $25,000 on ADA upgrades (25K ÷ 125K = 20%). You are required to do this!

Check with your municipality on what they require, or you're going to get caught off guard. If that budget is big enough for any of these, you have to do them in this order:

- Elevator
- Access to Building
- ADA Bathrooms
- ADA Signage

If 20 percent of your remodeling cost isn't enough to buy an elevator and you have wheelchair access to the building, then you would need to add an ADA bathroom or signage.

Check with the local building official when you visit the city during the due diligence part of the Fund step to get the exact details for your area. An architect can help you with this piece, but they cost money too. If you don't check on this, you may be missing a huge part of the budget.

SIGNAGE

Signage for retail tenants is critical. For office and warehouse tenants, it's a very nice luxury. For apartments, it's not as critical. On strip-mall buildings, adding pylon and rooftop signage is a very nice way to increase your ability to win new tenants and increase the value for existing tenants, especially if the signs can be viewed from a highway or freeway.

Contractor and Soft Costs

Contractor Soft Costs

Division	Item	Unit	Rate	Qty	Total
General Conditions	Permit	EA	$2,000.00		
	Project Manager Hourly	HR	$90.00		
	Builder's Risk Insurance	EA	$500.00		
	Temporary Bathrooms	WK	$200.00		
Contractor's Fee	Contractor Overhead and Profit	Fee	5%		
Drawings	Space Measurement Studies	SF	$0.05		
	Media Package for Listings	SF	$0.08		
	Architectural and Engineering	Bid			
Contingency	Contingency		10%		

GENERAL CONDITIONS

These are all of the things the contractor incurs for overhead and other items they pay directly that they bill back to you. This is where most contractors pad their profits. I'm going to show you how to evaluate whether the general conditions are fair or not later in the book.

CONTRACTOR'S FEE

Most contractors charge a fee between 3–40 percent of the total costs of the project. It varies dramatically across the size, scope, and contractor type. Make sure you factor one in. In the following chapters, we go into great detail on how to work with contractors and understand their fees.

DRAWINGS

These include your initial concept drawings, construction drawings, and your space measurement study.

CONTINGENCY

Build in a contingency for unforeseen circumstances. Even the best estimators miss stuff. If you feel confident in your numbers, use 10 percent. If you have a complicated project and are new to the game, use 15 percent or even 20 percent to cover your ass...ets.

Remember that a dollar of additional NOI creates ten to twenty dollars in value for the property. Be thinking about renovations that either increase rent or reduce expenses, and don't forget the big-ticket items and building in money to do the things that will drive revenue and reduce or eliminate expenses.

Key Takeaways

☐ Big ticket items are roof, asphalt, and HVAC.

☐ Energy upgrades return the most.

☐ Use your Magic Multiple to calculate your break-even cost for a given repair.

☐ Cosmetic and tenant upgrades are worth it.

☐ Don't forget a TI and contingency budget.

☐ Do your best to estimate accurately and then move on.

Action Items

☐ Estimate the NOI savings for a particular item and figure out if it makes sense or not using your Magic Multiple.

☐ Figure out the scope of work and quantity of each line item for your renovation cost worksheet.

☐ Plug it into your calculator to spit out a prelim budget for your initial MACO worksheet on the "costs to fix" line item.

Chapter 20

Gather Firm Bids

Objective: Finalize Your Sworn Construction Statement

You used the renovation cost worksheet to estimate your renovation costs in order to make an offer. However, once you have an offer accepted, you need to lock in some exact numbers. That means it's time to get bids.

You need these numbers to make a final decision on whether you move forward or not because the renovation cost drastically affects the price you can pay. Plus, if you blow this part, you could ask for the wrong amount of capital from your lender or equity partners and have to come back later and raise more money.

Here is the high-level process you'll follow:

- Drawings and Specifications
- Bidder List
- Request for Pricing
- Site Review
- Gather Bids
- Sworn Construction Statement vs. Reserves

Drawings and Specifications

Here, you'll make a set of drawings accompanied by a written scope of work that you'll break down by trade.

DRAWINGS

There are two types of drawings: concept drawings and construction drawings. At this point, you want to hire an architect or designer to prepare "concept" drawings. These will detail any changes you plan to make so the subcontractors can have a solid idea of what you plan to do. What walls are coming down? What walls are being added? You can communicate a huge portion of the scope through drawings in order to ensure your subcontractors are bidding the right stuff. You'll begin working on these drawings right after you get the property under contract and use them to gather bids before your contingency ends.

After you remove your contingency or successfully re-trade the deal, you will then ask that same architect to convert the concept drawings to construction drawings, which entails adding code sheets, cross-sections, callouts, and other details that the city will require in order to issue a permit. You will use this final set for your construction contracts and to pull permits.

SPECIFICATIONS

Attach a specification sheet along with your drawings that includes a narrative for things that can't be communicated through a drawing, like the make and model of plumbing and lighting fixtures you want to use and the scope of work to be done. Specifications include things like scope, size, color, SKU number, and model number. It's also a good idea to detail what the contractor should include in their bid and what they should not include. The more detailed the scope of work is on your specifications, the better off you will be, and the less change orders you will have down the road.

Make sure they don't have to guess. If they think working with you will be a pain in the butt, you will get what I call the "I don't want the job" price.

Pro Tip

Ask them to include "potential change orders" for items that might come up that they would foresee. For example, a plumber might include potential change order pricing for "insulating the pipes if the inspector requires it," or a roofer might include pricing to "replace rotted decking if they encounter that during demolition." Concealed conditions usually equate to change orders. Get pricing for how you both agree to handle the stuff buried underneath if you encounter a problem. Get this pricing up front because your negotiating power decreases dramatically once you sign a contract.

Bidder List

Where do you find good contractors? The answer depends on whether you will hire a GC and have them bring in the subs, or whether you will GC the project yourself and bring in the subs on your own. There are pros and cons to each method. I've done both and I still do both.

You find good general contractors from referrals from other investors and brokers. That's it. If you plan to GC yourself, you have to assemble a lot of subcontractors, and that is a little more difficult.

First, you *don't* find them online. You find them by getting referrals from specialty suppliers, and other subcontractors and investors. Good subcontractors don't advertise. What you'll find on Angie's List, HomeAdvisor, Thumbtack, and pretty much any other online site is the retail-polished contractors. Good subcontractors usually don't even have online profiles, and many still use a flip phone. Do you really think they have their Google Places profile all set up and operating properly? No. They probably don't even have a business card.

Figure out where they buy materials from. I'm not talking about the big box stores like Home Depot—it's the specialty suppliers like your roofing supplier, plumbing supplier, electrical supplier, HVAC supplier, drywall supplier, or lumber yard. Go into those stores and network with the front desk folks. They see these people every day. Ask them who the best subs are that are buying the most materials and have a good reputation. If they don't have anyone for you, show up at 7:00 a.m. on Monday, sit in the parking lot with a box of donuts and coffee, and collect names and numbers. If you see a sub working at another property, stop and get their information. You have to get grimy to get the good subs!

When you call a potential subcontractor to interview them, ask questions like:

- What percent of your work is for investors or other general contractors?
- What trades do you specialize in?
- Do you have standard piece rate type pricing (per square foot, per linear foot, per unit)?
- How far out are you booked right now?
- What do you need in order to bid the job?
- Are you union?

Get a feel for whether they primarily work for investors and other contractors, or a high percentage of their work comes from working with homeowners. If they are doing work directly with homeowners or building owners, they may be too expensive. Understand how they price jobs and what they need from you to give you a detailed estimate.

Request for Pricing

Now that you have a list of subs or contractors to bid the job, simply send them a request-for-pricing package that includes:

- Drawings
- Specifications
- Bid Sheet
- Deadline

I send out a bcc to them all at once to save me time—just *make sure* it's bcc.

A bid sheet is nothing more than a blank version of the renovation cost worksheet, filtered to only show the line items you want bid, and with the prices redacted. I accompany that with a Word document that spells out the full scope of work and specifications along with my concept drawings and a deadline for the bid to come back.

I'm controlling how I want them to present the numbers to me: I want them to simply fill in their numbers on my form so I can update my renovation cost worksheet. If you don't do this, you will get apples and oranges and have a tough time comparing bids.

Set a deadline for a week or two out and be firm and clear on it. Get verbal acceptance that they can meet the deadline. Require them to submit their pricing on your forms by then or they will be eliminated from consideration.

Site Review

We do a virtual tour using a 3D camera called a Matterport camera. It allows us to share our 3D model with the subcontractors and embed virtual tags that include notes on various items in the 3D model. With this virtual model, contractors can walk through the project anytime they want, in full-color 3D. This is a massive benefit for anyone bidding the job, and for you. If you are going to walk contractors through the actual property, remember a few things.

- Schedule tours with enough time in between, so you don't have more than one trade or general contractor there at the same time. It's tacky, and their interest in bidding the job will dwindle.
- Schedule a full day and do rounds of tours, usually two hours apart. Leave enough downtime in between in case people linger after.

- Have detailed drawing sets emailed in advance, but also a hard copy on the day of the site visit in case they forget to bring a set.

Gather Bids

Check in with your bidders regularly, and make sure they are on track to submit their written bid on time. Answer any questions. Make sure they understand the deadline, and let them know you are excited to develop a relationship with them. You can't afford to get to the end only to find out everyone decided not to bid on your job.

When you get the bids back, organize them in your online folders and extract the numbers. Put the numbers into your renovation cost worksheet that you will use to update your final MACO. Compare their numbers to your original estimates. How far off are you? You can also use this as an opportunity to update the pricing on your template for your next deal.

Read their submittals and make sure they bid your entire scope of work. Make sure you read the "Work Not Included" or "Exclusions" section to see what they are *not* bidding on. See what potential change orders they put on there; maybe you need another line item. Make sure the subcontractor's bids don't have gaps between them or overlaps. For example, who is providing the bath fans—the HVAC company or the electrician? Who is puttying the nail holes and caulking the new trim—the carpenter or the painter? Who is doing the reglet flashing at the perimeter of the building—the siding crew or the roofing crew?

Dot your i's and cross your t's by reviewing the inclusions and exclusions that have been submitted, and be prepared to have to go back and ask them to make revisions. The best subs are not great office people. Oftentimes they don't follow your instructions well because you are asking them to deviate from their normal process. If it's your first time working with them, have patience. You are laying the groundwork for an ongoing relationship, and eventually they will get your process down.

CONSTRUCTION CONTINGENCY

Now that you've collected all your bids on your forms and transferred the pricing back into your renovation cost worksheet, add 10–20 percent to that as a contingency for things that are bound to come up in order to achieve a final construction budget. That final budget number flows into your final MACO worksheet as the cost to fix, then gets split up into two categories on your sources and uses worksheet: the items that will be financed through your lender (sworn construction statement) and the items that will not (beginning reserves).

Sworn Construction Statement vs. Reserves

You should include the items the lender will finance on a sworn construction statement to the lender and include the items you will not finance as starting reserves on your sources and uses, to ensure you raise enough capital to fund them down the road, since the bank isn't funding them. The sworn construction statement should include your final construction numbers, summarized by trade (i.e., roofing, siding, carpentry, windows, etc.). Remember that your lender will include the items on the sworn in your loan calculation, so it's usually best to finance as much as possible, as long as you plan to for sure do the renovation in your initial remodel. If you are not sure, you should still raise enough capital up front if you plan to do them in a year or two. If you don't think they will be done in the next two years, you can raise the capital later on or siphon cash from the holding years to build a reserve to do them further out.

Your title company may have a specific version of the sworn construction statement they want you to use, but in general, a signed statement like this will suffice. I use a pivot table in Excel from my renovation cost worksheet to summarize my line items. Then I filter out the zeros or just have my contractor submit one if I hire a general contractor. On the next page is an example of what one looks like.

Now that you have a process for converting your rough estimate numbers to a solid sworn construction statement, we can cover how to structure your construction contracts.

Sworn Construction Statement

Row Labels	Sum of Sworn
Asphalt and Concrete	$8,500
Drywall and Painting	$12,000
Exteriors Doors and Windows	$2,000
General Conditions	$4,531
HVAC	$8,500
Other Soft Costs	$900
Roofing	$12,945
Grand Total	**$49,376**

The undersigned contractor and owner of the Property state that the attached list contains the names of all subcontractors and suppliers for specific portions of the work on this Property. All material costs shown are correct. The items mentioned include all labor and material required to complete the building according to plans and specifications and there are no other contracts outstanding. There is nothing due or to become due for materials, labor or other work other than as above stated. To increase the cost of construction, owner or contractor must furnish to the Lender and the Title Company with additional owner deposits (if requested) to cover the increase. In the event of an increase, no orders or claims will be made until the information and additional deposits shall have been made. The purpose of this Statement is to induce the Title Company to pay out of the proceeds of a loan of $_____, secured by a mortgage on the Property; and that upon payment of the specific unpaid items listed herein, the undersigned contractor hereby agrees to waive all claims of priority to said mortgage. The undersigned hereby authorizes Lender and Title Company to disburse the proceeds of the above real estate mortgage, together with such additional funds as undersigned furnishes and makes available, to the Contractor and/or subcontractors from time to time as work progresses, on the basis of the Construction Statement and lien waivers presented. The undersigned specifically agrees to pay any unpaid bills for construction or site improvements, to remove mechanic's liens should any be filed against said Property, and to pay all bills, costs, expenses and legal fees; and indemnify said company against any loss should it become necessary for the company to bring action to remove the lien or to pay the bills. The parties agree to appoint the Title Company as Escrow Agent; and the Lender is authorized to advance to the Escrow Agent from time to time during the progress of construction adequate funds to pay for costs of construction as warranted by lender's periodic inspection of progress of construction. A facsimile signature on this Statement is valid as an original.

Subscribed and sworn to before this _____ day of _____

Notary Public _____

Contractor _____ (Date) _____

Signature _____ Contractor (Title) _____

Owner _____ (Date) _____

Key Takeaways

☐ Prepare organized big-request packages and send them to the GCs you are considering or to subcontractors you find at specialty suppliers if you plan to GC yourself.

☐ Review the submittals that come back for inclusions and exclusions, and ask for revisions if necessary.

☐ Have the subs submit their bid on a blank version of your renovation cost worksheet.

☐ Break your construction costs into "reserves" and "sworn construction statement" items.

☐ Lenders will only include the sworn items as costs when calculating the loan size.

Action Items

☐ Decide if you will GC the project yourself or hire a GC.

☐ Get a few referrals from local investors for good general contractors and subcontractors, or visit specialty suppliers to start assembling good subcontractors.

☐ Create an online folder that contains drawings, specifications, and a blank spreadsheet for subcontractors to enter their pricing on.

☐ Share that folder link with some contractors.

☐ Give them a deadline to submit their bids.

☐ Collect the bids and revise your renovation cost and MACO worksheets.

FIX

Chapter 21

Sign Construction Contracts

Objective: Sign Construction Contracts

To hire or not to hire a general contractor—that is the question.

If you don't have construction experience and a Rolodex of subcontractors, then trying to manage your own projects is probably a bad idea. If you have a project manager working for you, or you have acted as the general contractor on projects before and you are good at it, you may consider doing the project management for your first commercial deal.

I have done it both ways, and there are pros and cons to each.

Self-managing can save quite a bit of money but should really only be done if you already have experience and a list of good subcontractors. Hiring a general contractor can save you time and get access to subcontractors you might not otherwise have access to, but you'll lose some control over your budget, and your fees will be higher.

Pros and Cons of Hiring a General Contractor

Contract Type	Pros	Cons
Hire a General Contractor	Professional Advice. Have More Time to Find and Fund Deals. Leverage Existing Relationships.	Exposure to Potential Change Orders and Cost Overruns that You Can't Control.
Be Your Own General Contractor	Increased Control over Costs. Save on Fees.	Get Stuck in Day-to-Day Management. Subcontractor Cost May Increase or Decrease Depending on How Good Your Network Is.

We're going to focus on hiring a general contractor—either way, you should always maintain the right to choose the subcontractors.

Ways to Hire a General Contractor

In commercial construction, you usually contract in one of two ways:

- Design/Build (Construction Manager)
- Lowest Qualified Bidder (General Contractor)

DESIGN/BUILD

This is where you hire a construction manager to design the project and then oversee the build. They will hire an architect and assemble a team of subcontractors early in the process to give input on the design. This may cost a little more on the front end, but because the design is so much better, it will almost always reduce the number of change orders and decrease the construction timeline.

This can also be referred to as "cost-plus." It's an open book type arrangement where they are just passing through their "costs" plus a fee. That means your budget will fluctuate throughout the project as your costs change. The construction manager is likely to use reliable subcontractors that are easy to work with and on the more expensive end. After all, that will mean less headache for them plus a bigger fee. This contract is basically outsourcing the project management for your project.

The major drawback to this arrangement is that the only way the construction manager makes more money is by costing you more money! That's why I usually ask them to put a GMP on the project—a guaranteed max price.

For example, let's say they estimate the total project costs plus their fee to be $500,000. They may put a guaranteed maximum price of $550,000 for the project so there is a $50,000 contingency fund baked in. If something comes up that changes the scope of work—like you deciding to add an elevator—of course, they are going to charge you a change order fee where you'll cover the additional costs beyond the GMP. The GMP will put some risk on them to make sure the numbers are tight and the project doesn't go over budget.

LOWEST QUALIFIED BIDDER

Here, you are working directly with an architect to make a set of drawings and then sending them out to one or more general contractors who bid the work and put a firm number on it.

This only works if you have a tight scope, specifications, and drawings—otherwise, you are going to get change ordered to death! The risk is on the contractor for any cost fluctuations, so they will generally bid a risk factor into their project. For example, the same project that they might have estimated at $500K with a GMP of $550K, they might bid at $550K. If their costs are $600K, they'll lose money on the project. If they come in at $400K on cost, they make out like a bandit. Because of this, the general contractor will generally hire the cheapest qualified labor—the lowest qualified bidder.

Here's how the selection process for the subcontractors usually works:

They remove anyone they think can't perform because they aren't large enough, aren't professional enough, or can't meet the deadline. Then they take the lowest bidder of the remaining candidates. Usually, this is the middle-priced bidder, but not always. Often the lowest bidders are not qualified for one reason or another.

Contract Details

The general contractor fee is not where the money is made in contracting. The margin is in the general conditions, self-performed work, and change orders. Let's dive into each of them.

GENERAL CONDITIONS

General conditions include overhead and general project items. Regardless of the way you contract, a contractor will have costs of operating their business that are not direct costs to your project—monthly payroll charges, hiring expenses, office personnel, general liability insurance, licensing costs, etc. They will bill some of these costs to each of their projects.

A lot of hidden margins can be captured in the general conditions category. A contractor may have an annual liability insurance cost of $10,000, but bills $8,500 of that to five different projects over the course of a year. The general contractor usually hires a project manager to manage your project, and they'll bill time and materials for that project manager to your project at rates approaching or even exceeding $90–$100 per hour. So you're paying the project manager as part of general conditions costs and then a construction management fee on top of that.

How much they bill to you is usually a "pluck from air" type calculation, and that is why you have to be very careful when reviewing the general conditions.

SELF-PERFORMED WORK

The project manager may only cost them $45 per hour, but they are billing it for $90 per hour. They may get three bids for concrete at $10,000, $12,000, and $15,000, and if your contract stipulates that they select the lowest qualified bidder, they may say that the $10,000 bidder isn't qualified because they aren't large enough to meet the timeline. That may be valid. Or they may select to match the $12,000 bid and then self-perform the work for $6,000, thereby making $6,000 in profit.

It is not necessarily a bad thing for them to make money on both the line item and the fee because they are managing the crew, ordering the materials, and doing all of the work the subcontractor would have also done. Just be careful to audit these things to make sure they aren't only collecting bids that are high to maximize their margin on self-performed work.

INFLATED BIDS

Remember that a construction manager gets paid a higher fee when they drive the costs up. If you don't know what things should cost, ask them to get multiple bids. I've had the best cost savings from subcontractors that may require a little more hand-holding but that saved big dollars.

I have had projects where the roofing bids presented by the general contractor were $200,000–$250,000, and I got the work done for $100,000. I'm not kidding! I have had projects where the drywall bids have ranged from $125,000 to $450,000 for the same exact scope of work.

This is why I taught you how to start building your own list of subcontractors, to double-check your GCs when they are putting together the budgets for your projects if their numbers seem off. Always maintain the right to request they get pricing from one of your vendors.

CHANGE ORDERS

I got a project done on my own for almost a full million dollars cheaper than the identical project around the corner that the other developer had a large GC in town do. Controlling the project doubled my profit on that building—I made a million on the development and a million as the general contractor.

FIX

If something pops up unexpectedly, you will likely be forced into signing an urgent change order instead of having the luxury of having your own crew on-site already to do the work at relatively inexpensive rates.

If you are going to write a change order, use the AIA standard G701—Change Order Form to change the scope, price, and timeline for the project with your general contractor (or with your subcontractors if you are acting as a general contractor).

NOT INCLUDED IN CONTRACT (NIC)

Buyer beware! Read the fine print. You want consistency in how you contract with everyone.

Look for things like "by owner," "not included," and "by others." Make sure the gaps in their bids are accounted for by someone else's scope and that two people aren't including the same thing. We already talked about this in the last chapter when reviewing bids, so make sure your audit from before makes its way to the actual contract. Transfer the scope from the proposal they give you and clean it up. Make sure you clearly spell out what's included and what's not included in the contract itself.

This is why I recommend you have your attorney draft the construction contracts rather than signing the contracts of your vendors, so you have one template for all of your contracts that you are familiar with.

Making the Choice

I've hired a GC and been my own GC on projects, so I'm not partial to either method. For really large projects, I hire my own project manager in-house. If I have too many deals going on, I may hire a general contractor so I can continue finding and funding deals. If it's just a couple of trades, I might manage it myself.

Figure out what you are capable of and contract the rest out. If you only need to do carpet and paint, maybe you can find a carpet guy and a painter. If you are doing an extensive remodel with ten to fifteen different trades, it probably makes sense to hire it out unless you're in the business already. Be careful not to buy yourself a project just to make money as a general contractor.

No matter what the case is, never be the person actually swinging the hammer!

You may think you are saving money on the investment, but you are really just paying yourself a carpenter's wage. Your time should be spent finding and funding deals. And your deal had better be profitable when hiring a GC to do all of the work, or else you're in a mess. In select cases, you might want to do some of the management yourself to maintain control, eliminate risk, and reduce fees. Just be careful not to think you are saving money managing your own project when it may take longer and reduce the number of other deals you can do.

Now that you know how to contract with people and where to find good subcontractors, let's sign contracts and get your project started! In the next chapter, we cover how to manage the schedule and submit draw requests to the bank as the work is completed.

Key Reader Takeaways

☐ Double-check subcontractor bids.
☐ Write the contracts on your own forms that your attorney put together.
☐ Have a contingency budget.

Action Items

☐ Weigh the pros and cons of managing your own project.
☐ Decide if you will do the design/build or use the lowest qualified bidder approach.
☐ Award the bids.
☐ Have your attorney draft the construction agreements.
☐ Sign the construction agreements.

FIX

Chapter 22

Complete Construction Draws

Objective: Manage a Schedule and Get People Paid

On one of my projects, I hired a sub that was quite a bit cheaper. I thought I was saving money, but in the end, it cost me more. It took him an extra two months to complete the drywall portion of the project while my project manager spent hundreds of added hours micromanaging him to get his guys working in the right areas and on the right stuff.

That property brings in $50,000 in rent per month, so being delayed by two months equated to $100,000 in lost rent. I guess that $20,000 I saved by going with his bid didn't help me much! For this reason, it's absolutely critical that your general contractor and subcontractor agreements have a firm start and end date and a strict per diem charge—a daily deduction from the contract price for every day they go late, equal to what you will lose in rent. In the prior example, it would be $1,667 per day for every day they are late.

A per diem is just one of several ways to keep a schedule on track and money in everyone's pockets. Let's also look at:

- Gantt Charts
- Weekly Construction Meetings
- Draw Requests
- Receipt Tracking
- Lien Waivers

Gantt Charts

Request that your contractor sets up and uses a Gantt chart for your project. Google "Gantt chart Excel free" to find a template, or you can find software to do it for you.

The main benefit of a Gantt chart is being able to create dependencies. If you can't start the drywall until the insulation inspection happens, then the drywall is dependent on the insulation inspection. If you can't insulate until the framing inspection is done, then there's a dependency there too. The idea is to create all the work items and then create the dependencies until all of the necessary pieces are accounted for.

Here is an example of a real project I just finished:

Once you have the dependencies created, you can track what's called the "critical path." The items in black are critical path items. If there is a delay on a critical item, it delays the overall completion of the project. Some items will have some flexibility; some won't.

Gantt Chart

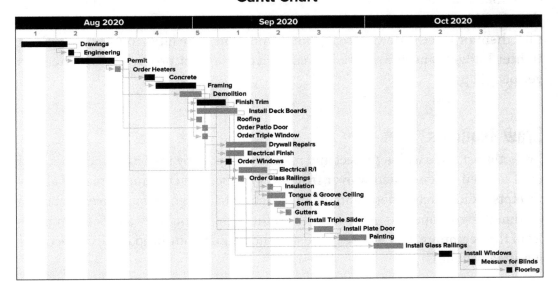

Even if you hire an outside contractor, you should look for one who is going to use scheduling software and allow you to see the ever-changing schedule. Your role as asset manager and deal sponsor is to ensure the business plan is executed properly; that is, on time and on budget. While you may hire out the construction and property management, you will never hire out asset management.

Start thinking of your property management, leasing, and construction management partners as actual partners that you should be collaborating with and holding accountable to your goals as asset manager. You need tools like this in place to do that. Another thing that helps keep you on track is having a weekly meeting with the construction team.

Weekly Construction Meetings

I recommend a weekly meeting with the subs who are actively working on the project and the project manager or site superintendent. Set this expectation early on and require it in the contract itself. By having a set day and time each week to hold this meeting, everyone can be prepared and ready. This is a great time for problem-solving, scheduling updates, change order discussions, or questions that can wait. Of course, there will be questions that can't wait, and those will be answered on a daily basis by your site supervisor, whether you hire them or the GC does. Great communication translates to a faster build, a tighter budget, and fewer headaches. As your project progresses you need to get people paid.

Draw Requests

I was almost done with a project and ready to get paid by the bank when they told me I needed a signed lien waiver from every subcontractor and copies of all my receipts. I didn't have them, and the nightmare I had to go through to collect them is something I hope you never have to go through. If you have a process in place from the beginning, you will keep most of the hair on your head (unless, of course, it's already gone).

A draw request is something you submit when you want to get paid—remember, the lender based their loan on your total costs, some of which included your "costs to fix" that you chose to finance. The renovation cost portion of the loan gets distributed through a title company as you *request draws* on those funds.

Ask your title company what they need early on in the process before you ever even close on the property. Most title companies and lenders have their own forms but will also accept the AIA Standard G702—Application and Certificate for Payment.

When you use a draw request form to submit your draw requests to the lender and title company for approval, you will generally state which line items on your sworn construction statement have work completed, how much is complete, and the subcontractor invoices showing those costs, as well as your materials receipts showing paid in full.

Here is an example:

Draw Request Form

Item	Division	Original	% Complete	Amount Due	Payable To
1	General Conditions	$4,531	45%	$2,039	CCG
2	Asphalt and Concrete	$8,500	15%	$1,275	Mitch's Asphalt
3	Cabinets and Countertops				
4	Carpentry				
5	Demolition				
6	Drywall and Painting	$12,000	0	$0	Mitch's Drywall
7	Electrical				
8	Equipment				
9	Ext. Doors and Windows	$2,000	20%	$400	Metro Construction
10	Flooring				
11	Furnishings				
12	HVAC	$8,500	22%	$1,870	Joe's HVAC
13	Insulation				
14	Int. Doors and Trim				
15	Masonry				
16	Other Soft Costs	$900	0	$0	CCG
17	Plumbing				
18	Roofing	$12,945	100%	$12,945	Rigos Roofing
19	Siding and Trim				
20	Signage				
21	Specialties				
22	TI Allowance				
	Grand Total	**$49,376**	**37.53%**	**$18,529**	

Contractor _____   Owner _____

The title company's form will have some additional information like the loan number and job address, but this is the basic meat of the draw request form. You, as the manager of the LLC, and your general contractor will sign each draw request, and the lender will also hire someone to verify that the value of work stated on the request matches what was actually completed up to that point.

To complete this form, pull the line items from your sworn statement and tell them how much of it is complete, what amount is owed, and who it's owed to.

Receipt Tracking

You'll need to submit receipts for paid materials. Don't forget this item! Small expenses will usually come out of pocket and then the title company will reimburse you. For large materials like ordering cabinets or lumber for the whole project, you will usually get an invoice from the vendor; submit it as part of your draw request, and have the title company pay them directly.

We use a shared online folder in Google Drive to track our receipts, but any service would suffice. The team members take a picture of the receipt at the checkout counter and then upload the receipts directly into the online folder from their phone. Then my bookkeeper attaches them in our accounting system to the credit card charges as they hit our account. The title company and lender get the link to the folder at each draw.

I've always been a fan of doing your work as you go. It reduces stress and streamlines the process. Teach your team early on not to wait until the end of the week to scan in their receipts. If they wait until the end of the week, guess what! They'll lose the receipt and you'll have to track it down. And without receipts, your draw is going to get messy.

Lien Waivers

A lien waiver is a form people sign that waives their right to place a mechanics lien on your property. In most states, when someone provides labor or materials, they automatically have a right to place a lien on your building if they aren't paid. It is usually a standardized form that your title company should be able to provide you with. Since they are the ones insuring the title of the property, they want you to collect these when you pay people.

You can get conditional and unconditional lien waivers and indicate whether the payment is a partial payment or final payment. A **conditional** lien waiver is something they sign stating they waive the lien rights, on the condition of getting paid the amount you owe them. You can use this to get a signature *before* you pay someone. An **unconditional** lien waiver is something you get *at the time* you pay someone, so it does not contain the condition that they get paid.

When you pay the vendors or suppliers, get lien waivers signed as a condition of payment. Don't pay the vendor and rely on them sending the lien waivers back, or you will have to hunt them down when you go to submit your next draw. Give to get: they need to give a lien waiver to get paid. Plain and simple. I like to have the title company require the subs to come into their office to sign and pick up the check, so I don't have to deal with it. Set that expectation early on when interviewing subcontractors or your general contractor.

Continue managing the schedule using your Gantt chart, submitting effective draw requests, tracking receipts, and filing lien waivers until your project is closed out. At that point, the lender will order the original appraiser to come back out and certify the project is complete. They do this to ensure you have met their criteria for the as-stabilized value they projected, and then you will get your final term loan. The loan payments will then convert from interest only to principal and interest.

With a nice, pretty building ready for tenants, you can list the vacancies for lease for top dollar. In the next step, we cover how to list your property, generate leads, and sign leases!

FIX

Key Reader Takeaways

☐ Require your site supervisor to use a Gantt chart to track scheduling and hold weekly construction meetings.

☐ Use the title company or AIA draw form to get people paid.

☐ Have a system to organize materials receipts as you go.

☐ Collect lien waivers every time you pay someone.

Action Items

☐ Find a software to create a Gantt chart for your project schedule.

☐ Create an online folder system for receipt and lien waiver tracking.

☐ Fill out a draw request form for your first draw.

FIX

Step 5
Fill

The Fill step is all about filling vacancies and raising rents to market rate on existing leases as they renew. Here are the parts we'll cover:

- List the Property
- Generate Leads
- Conduct Showings
- Screen the Tenants
- Negotiate and Sign Leases

By the end, you'll be able to list your property like a pro with a world-class media package and have a strategy to drive traffic to your listings and generate leads. We'll cover marketing strategy, showings, screenings, and clauses you should consider having in your contracts.

Vacancies are very costly, so it's wise to spend money to fill them quickly. A dollar of lost rent is the same as a dollar of expense on your P&L. By the time you are done reading this step, you are going to know exactly how to fill your spaces at lightning speed and how to weed out the good tenants from the bad ones. You will also know how to structure your leases in a way that protects you and your bottom line.

Chapter 23

List the Property

Objective: Hire a Broker to List Your Property

Early on, I was talking to a developer friend of mine and he was flabbergasted that I was trying to do my own leasing for one of my retail projects. I said, "But Brian, the leasing commissions are ridiculous in this business; I can't afford to pay them!"

He sternly replied, "You're wrong, Mike. You can't afford *not* to pay them. Don't cost yourself $2M in value by trying to save $50K in leasing commissions."

He was right. The building I was leasing had been sitting vacant for almost a year. I had already lost $180K in potential rent, which would have translated to over $2M in value at an 8% cap rate. The commission to fill the entire space would have been under $50K. I put my tail between my legs and admitted I was wrong.

Filling your vacancies is the most important aspect of your business plan. As you learn how leasing commissions work in the coming chapters, you're going to be tempted to do your own leasing to save on fees as well.

FILL

> **Don't be an idiot. Being cheap is expensive.**

Don't lease your own spaces unless you are a licensed broker and do leasing full time for a living. Separate your role as asset manager from your temptation to also be the leasing agent for the project. Your duty is to deliver the highest returns to your investors. You should only do the leasing if you are the best-qualified candidate in town to do it.

Leasing commissions, lease concessions, and advertising dollars are investments that you will get a return on—just like the money you invested into fixing the building up.

Do whatever it takes to get the building full—even if you have to sign leases at rates below market. It's much easier to maintain high occupancy and increase rents once your building is full than it is to wait it out and fill it up slowly at ideal rents.

I'm not saying that you should hire out the leasing 100 percent of the time. Sometimes the spaces are small enough that no one wants to take on the project. In those cases, sure—do your own leasing. For the rest of the time, learn how to source, select, and secure the best leasing agent for your project to deliver the best ROI to your investors.

In this chapter, I'm going to teach you what a good leasing agent should do so that you can either do it yourself when necessary or know how to hire the right person for the job.

Here is the listing process:

- Consultations
- Proposals
- Listing Agreement
- Listing Documents
- Capture
- Create
- List

Consultations

You already had some of these when you were doing your market research. Look up stats on who has done the most leasing transactions in your area. Look at active listings and see who has the most. Ask around to see who is doing a lot of landlord rep assignments for the type of tenants you want to target for your building. Once you have some agents and brokers identified, it's time to do some interviews.

I recommend hiring agents with a CCIM designation. Ask them these questions:

- What asset types do you specialize in?
- What kind of results have you gotten?
- What do you think this would rent for?
- How long would it take to fill?
- What is your marketing strategy?
- How are your fees structured?

If you're interested in more, you can also request that they submit a proposal.

Proposals

You've interviewed the agents and requested a proposal. Now you need to go through them and learn what the agents will do to get your spaces filled. Dial in specifically on their marketing plan and who they think is the best fit for the property. Don't hire the cheapest broker—hire the one who has the best marketing strategy. Even if you decide not to hire this out and do it yourself, collect proposals anyway. You will learn a lot of useful information along the way.

Listing Agreement

There are two types of agents: the "landlord rep" represents the landlord, and the "tenant rep" represents the tenant. Find a good landlord rep and sign a listing agreement with them.

The agreement can be exclusive or non-exclusive, though I recommend exclusive. Lots of people recommend a non-exclusive arrangement where the agent only gets paid if they bring the tenants, but if the landlord brings the tenants, they don't get paid. If you were an agent and had some exclusive listings and some non-exclusive listings, which ones would you spend more time working on? The one where you know you'll *for sure* get paid, or the one where you only *might* get paid?

We already made the point that being cheap was expensive. Don't half-ass trying to hire someone cheaply, only to have the agent give you a half effort. In fact, I would argue that you should structure your deal to give them a bonus if they can fill the space faster. Remember my retail spaces? Rent was $15K a month. I could bonus them $15K to fill the spaces one month sooner and come out the same financially.

No one says you can't structure a graduated compensation structure or pay them more if they bring you a higher net rent rate. Get creative with how you contract with people.

Listing Documents

Here are some things you should have ready for your agent after you sign the listing agreement.

- Marketing Description
- Floor Plans
- Property Highlights
- Tenant Profiles

The more information you have, the better your media package will turn out and the faster they can get the property listed. I like to organize all of this in the same online folder I'm using for all of the property information.

Capture

The next step is to capture the best media package available for the property. Most people do their shopping online, so your media is what will get them excited to request a showing. Don't take shortcuts here either.

I usually order two rounds of media: one right after I remove my contingency or successfully renegotiate the deal, and another once I finish the remodel. I use the first one to start marketing the spaces right away before I've even closed on the property. Then I update all of the marketing once the property is fixed up and send everything out again.

Here is the raw media we capture for our listings.

- Wide-Angle Photos
- 3D Virtual Tour
- Drone Video
- Agent Video

Create

Once you have captured the media, pay someone to create all of the finished products. Here are the deliverables we usually get:

- Offering Memorandum
- Property Video
- Web Landing Page

OFFERING MEMORANDUM

This is a fancy name for a long-form brochure. Your listing agent will do all of this for you, but if you list it yourself, you should know what makes a good offering memorandum.

Include highlights about the opportunity and lease comps to justify your asking rates. Show the site plan and where the property is located on a map. Include copies of your floor plans that show rentable square footage by suite, and highlight the suites that are available. Show what other tenants are in the building on the floor plan. The graphic designer will use the photos your photographer took and all of the property data you gathered to make the brochure.

PROPERTY VIDEO

The property video can be whatever you want. Get creative and spend money on it to make it amazing. I like to have a mixture that includes drone footage, a 3D walkthrough, floor plans, pictures, and clips of me talking about the property, all edited together with nice transitions and music.

Look for agents who have really good videos for the properties they have listed, or if you hire someone with proven performance who is older and doesn't have the knack for technology, tell them you will provide them with a video for them to market your space.

WEB LANDING PAGE

You need a top-notch landing page that is designed to wow the visitors and call them to action. Your desired action could be requesting a showing by filling out a form, or it could be scheduling a showing directly from that page. We usually embed the 3D tours on these. Include a gallery of the photos, property details, and showcase the property video.

List

Now that you have captured some awesome footage and weaved it into a killer media creation, you are ready to list your property.

Very few deals are done on the MLS for leasing, so you want to get your ad out there on every platform available. We use MLS, Catylist, Craigslist, CoStar, LoopNet, 42Floors, Apartments.com, and any other website we can get our hands on.

Go to Google and type in whatever search terms you think a tenant would type in if they were looking for space. For example, you could type in "Office for lease Minneapolis." See what comes up. Click through to the websites, and see which ones are your competition and which ones are third-party vendors that you can get your listings on.

We also post the listings on Facebook, Instagram, and LinkedIn, and we try to use geofenced Facebook, Google, and LinkedIn ads to target specific people in specific buildings. If you do ads, set a pretty healthy budget for these ads, and you may want to consider upgrading your LoopNet ads to get more exposure too.

Summary

As the asset manager, your job is to drive the NOI and NOI multiple. Part of that role is hiring the best leasing agent possible. If you are the best fit for the job, then do these tasks yourself. Otherwise, you now know how to interview brokers, review their proposals, sign a listing agreement, give them the key data they need, and ensure they capture and create a world-class media package to post your listing on all the major platforms.

These are fishing tactics. In the next chapter, we cover how to hunt for tenants with direct marketing and how to farm your network to drive additional traffic to your listings.

Key Reader Takeaways

☐ Being cheap is expensive.
☐ You will learn a lot from soliciting leasing proposals from top brokers in town.
☐ Always sign an exclusive listing.
☐ Have your property information well-organized for the agent you hire.
☐ Don't rely on your agent to make your media package.
☐ Spend the extra money to do a better media package than the competitors.

Action Items

☐ Collect the key data for your property.
☐ Interview a few leasing agents/brokers and hire one.
☐ Interview a few media vendors and select one.
☐ Interview a few graphic design vendors and select one.
☐ Create your media package, and list your property on all major websites.

Chapter 24

Generate Leads

Objective: Schedule a Showing with a Qualified Potential Tenant

Don't do what the largest brokerages in town do to lease their space: list it online, put a sign in the yard, send it out to their network, and wait for the phone to ring. I call this the "post and pray" method. That's what we covered in the last chapter and it works sometimes, but it's lazy. Your investors deserve better than that.

You can't afford to wait for the phone to ring. You need to *make* it ring by designing and executing a direct marketing strategy like you did for property owners. You will literally use the same contact methods—phone, email, ringless voicemail, direct mail, LinkedIn InMail, and text messages. It's all the same tactics you know, just a different audience.

Make sure the person responsible for filling the space commits to a certain number of outbound contacts every week. In this chapter, I'm going to show you how to follow this proven process to proactively drive traffic to your listings:

- Design a Marketing Strategy
- Brainstorm Whom to Target
- Create a Tenant Prospecting List
- Execute Contact Campaigns
- Schedule Showings
- Trial Close

Design a Marketing Strategy

Forget clicking around and trying to call people one at a time. It's better than nothing, but it's not the most efficient method available. Design your campaign so you can take massive action with little effort.

Use the same exact strategy you used to contact property owners in the Find step, leveraging technology to get you bigger results, faster. You can literally do the same exact gather, fish, hunt, and farm sequence or mix it up a little bit. Get creative!

Let's recap each of the four sustenance strategies you learned in the Contact part of the Find step, and show how they can be used to secure tenants for your building.

GATHERING FOR TENANTS

Gathering is finding tenants by luring brokers that already have a tenant rep contract signed with them. In the Find step, we looked at properties listed by brokers. Now the objective is to have brokers bring you tenants in exchange for you paying them a commission.

Simply reach out to tenant rep brokers directly and ask if they already have any clients under contract that meet your criteria. Let them know you have a bonus for them if you can get a deal done by the end of the month. You already created the broker list back in the Find step, so just do a blast email, ringless voicemail, or text campaign to them.

FISHING FOR TENANTS

You've already started fishing by listing your properties online. This doesn't take much time, and once it's done, it's easy to update and maintain the listings. Remember to refresh your listings every week on the websites you are using.

You should also put a very large sign out front. Make it easily visible with a unique, eye-catching color. You can use social media too—just put the link to your new landing page into a post and share it with friends. You can also do social media ads to get your post in front of people who aren't friends with you on Facebook.

If you created a tenant prospecting list that includes emails, you can upload that list to Facebook to create an audience for targeted ads. You can also target ads to people who have key "interests" on their Facebook profile, like "insurance agents" or whatever you think your target audience would have typed into that part of their profile.

HUNTING FOR TENANTS

Hunt for tenants by building the tenant prospecting list and sending out direct mail, emails, texts, and ringless voicemails.

You can hit up hundreds if not thousands of people using a ringless voicemail saying something like, "Hey, it's Mike from Commercial Investors Group, and we just had a really nice unit become available at 2738 Winnetka in New Hope, and I was wondering if you guys were looking for office space in the next six months or so. If you are, give me a ring at 612-xxx-xxx. Chat soon." Then wait for the phone to ring, or as you scale up your operation to automate the process, set up a separate leasing number to go to a 24/7 call center with a script.

FARMING FOR TENANTS

Farm for tenants by pushing your listings out to people in your network who may do business with your ideal tenants. Do not format your email to be nice and pretty. Use plain text, make it one or two sentences, and include the link to your property listing landing page. This at least puts it on their radar. The key to all of this is using a consistent touchpoint strategy that keeps you top of mind without feeling pushy or contacting them too frequently.

Brainstorm Whom to Target

Here's how you build a list so you can prospect tenants effectively. Visit the city and get a zoning packet. This will tell you what the permitted and conditional uses of the property are. Compare this list against the current tenants in the building. Would any of these types of tenants share a customer base with your existing tenants? For example, if it's an office building that has an insurance agent, a realtor, and a title company, then maybe targeting a mortgage company as a potential tenant would make sense. If it's a light industrial flex building that has various car services, maybe another car service type business makes sense. Brainstorm the types of businesses you think would do well in that building. Literally pull out a sheet of paper, and write down every type of tenant you think would be a good fit for your building. Then rank them from best to worst fit. You can expand your list even further by finding the NAICS code for one of those tenants. Google "NAICS" codes to go to the website, and you can explore different types of tenants and figure out which kinds are closely related.

Create a Tenant Prospecting List

Let's say you decide that you want to target mortgage companies to come into your building. Go to Google and type "mortgage companies, Austin, TX" or whatever city your building is in, then copy and paste the business names and phone numbers of the results into a blank spreadsheet.

You could also click into each listing and scroll to the bottom of their website to see if you can find an email address. The objective is to create an Excel spreadsheet with business names, contacts, phones, and emails that give you the power to do direct marketing.

Execute Contact Campaigns

You will need to spend money here. Lots of it. This is where the rubber meets the road. Set action-based goals, not results-based. A good goal looks like "send out two thousand pieces of mail" or "hit 500 potential tenants this week with a ringless voicemail." You control your activities—you don't control your results. If you are doing consistent activity over a long period of time, the results will come.

Pay attention to your raw activity levels and your conversion ratios to see where you are having success and where your pipeline needs help. If you aren't getting the results you want, you may not be doing enough activity, or you may have bad timing, messaging, or delivery. One side of the equation is a commitment issue and the other is a skill issue. By tracking your numbers, you can figure out which one it is and enlist someone to help you in that specific area.

Remember, the goal of your campaign is to generate leads of people who are interested in seeing the space. Track them in your database so you can follow up effectively and not let any slip through the cracks. If you follow up well, your leases-to-leads ratio will increase dramatically.

Schedule Showings

Leads go cold about as fast as a bucket of hot water if you throw it out in the middle of winter (you southerners won't get this joke). So be sure to call them immediately when they come in, and keep calling them until you get ahold of them. Don't waste time showing units to people who aren't qualified. Here are the things you should ask a tenant before you schedule the showing:

- How did you hear about us?
- What building and unit are you interested in?
- Space Info:
  - When does your current lease end?
  - What is your desired move-in date?
  - How much space do you need?
  - What are you going to use the space for?
  - What is your monthly all-in budget?
- Verify Contact Information
  - Full name
  - Phone
  - Email
  - Business name
  - Business type

If you have a space that you think will meet their needs, schedule the showing.

Trial Close

After I set the appointment, I do a trial close before I hang up. "Mr. Tenant, if we meet out there and the space meets all your needs, are you going to want to submit an application right then?"

See what they say and listen for objections. Are there other decision makers who should be there? Sometimes they will say they would need to show it to their partner or someone else at the company. Tell them this space has had lots of activity, and ask if it would make sense to get everyone there on the first visit so they can actually make a decision. You will save yourself a second trip across town. If they push back, schedule it anyway. Don't offend them; just offer it as a suggestion. I usually say something like, "I've found when I show everyone who would weigh in on the decision, it's easier for people to come to a consensus quickly."

Pro Tip

We send the tenants our listing package including the 3D virtual tour before the showing. I encourage them to walk through the space virtually and let me know right away if they don't think it will be a good fit. I have saved a lot of time with people who did the virtual tour and knew for sure it wasn't a good fit. Follow up with them by phone and cross-sell them to another location. Even if it's not in a building of yours, give them tips on where to look and how to search. You will bless their lives, and that's what living is all about.

Now that you've scheduled a showing, we are going to cover what to do before, during, and after a showing to maximize your effectiveness. It's time to secure the good tenants and let the bad ones go.

FILL

Key Reader Takeaways

- ☐ Gather, hunt, fish, and farm for prospective tenants.
- ☐ Use the city zoning packet and NAICS codes to spur ideas for who to target.
- ☐ Create a list with contact information to unlock your ability to mass market.
- ☐ Set activity-based goals.
- ☐ Track your numbers.
- ☐ Filter leads so you aren't wasting time.
- ☐ Track leads and follow up until you mark it dead or schedule a showing.
- ☐ Do a trial close.

Action Items

- ☐ Use the zoning packet and the NAICS codes to brainstorm the types of tenants you want to target.
- ☐ Record yourself making a prospecting list by scraping Google Places, then send the video to potential VAs and select one to create a prospecting list for you.
- ☐ Design and install a sign at your property.
- ☐ Send out a direct marketing campaign to brokers and prospective tenants with your brochure and links to your listing page.
- ☐ Follow up on leads and schedule some showings.

Chapter 25

Conduct Showings

Objective: Get a Rental Application

Leasing is sales, and sales requires negotiations. The key is to make them feel like they got a smoking deal, while you still get exactly what you need to make your proforma come to life.

Qualify them early, then ask temperature-taking questions throughout the process. These are questions like, "Would that work for you?" "Can you see your business operating from this space?" and "What would you want to change in order for this to work for you?"

In this chapter, we are going to cover what to do before, during, and after the showing to get the right tenants to submit a rental application. But before we cover the showing process, I want to help you understand that the size of the tenant dictates the process in many ways.

FILL

Small vs. Large Tenants

You can categorize tenants as large or small based on the size of the space they need or the size of the company they have. Smaller tenants operate very much like residential apartment renters.

For space, I consider tenants under three thousand square feet small, from three thousand to ten thousand square feet medium-sized, and over ten thousand square feet, large tenants. For company size, I consider national or regional companies large and local companies small.

You could have a large company in a small space or a small company in a large space, but for the most part, small companies take small spaces, and large companies take large spaces.

Small companies are usually quick to make a decision, want to move quickly, want shorter-term leases, and usually don't hire an attorney to review the lease. Strike while they are hot! Don't wait a couple days to write up the lease. As mentioned in the last chapter, I have my leasing agents prequalify them on the phone with this trial close: "So if I come out there and show the space, and it meets all of your needs, are you going to be ready to place the deposit down to tie up the space and sign a lease?"

If they say no, figure out what their objection is. Is it someone else who has to sign off or approve the space? Then respectfully request that person to attend the showing, or suggest you reschedule for a time when everyone can attend to keep everybody on the same page.

If they say yes, or "Yes, if I like it," then say, "Okay great. We have had a lot of interest in the space. Do you want to maybe bring your checkbook in case you like the space, so we can take care of the paperwork right away?"

Since these are smaller spaces, you need to show them quickly, sign them quickly, and make sure you go through the entire lease clause by clause so they fully understand what they are signing.

A legal document is not just for a court case. If you end up in court because they didn't read their lease, you may win the battle, but you still lost the war. Make sure they understand details like your expense stop or expense pass-through procedures (we cover these in the next chapter). They need to internalize how things work, so they don't think you slipped in some clauses to screw them later. That is not good for referrals and renewals.

I usually qualify tenants based on other sources of income. I look to see that they have been making at least three times the annual rent payments on their tax returns for the last two years, from a reliable source of income. If they are a new business owner with a dream but no verifiable income, it's up to you on how you want to handle it. If you are reliant on that income to make your deal work, you may need to take a pass. If this is the last little vacancy and you've had trouble filling it, read their business plan and consider giving them a shot. You can be a blessing for these people, and they will stay loyal to you as a result.

Larger tenants don't work as fast. They will usually have an agent, but not always. If they don't have an agent, you can explain that you may be able to offer better terms if you aren't required to pay a commission so that an agent doesn't convince the tenant they are better off having representation and that their services are free "because the landlord usually pays their fees" halfway into your negotiations. While it's true the landlord usually pays their fees, the landlord will also be able to give better terms when they don't have to pay leasing fees to the tenant rep broker.

Larger tenants will visit the space and then submit a request for proposal. They are essentially asking you to put forth a term sheet that spells out the basic terms with which you are willing to lease the space.

Be willing to spend more time with larger tenants. Have patience. Work proactively to get feedback from the agent on what's happening behind the scenes and see how you can make your proposal more attractive. The agent wants to get paid and will help you get to where you need to be in order to win their client.

While the sense of urgency is different for large tenants, overall, you still do the same things before, during, and after the showing.

FILL

Before the Showing

Set expectations and confirm the meeting by phone, email, or text prior to the showing. I usually send a templated email that includes the process, the property brochure, and a link to the property listing page on our website with a virtual tour. Remind them to have all decision makers there. Give existing tenants notice if they occupy the space you are going to show. In most states, you don't need to give notice if you are visiting the property but not entering their space.

During the Showing

Arrive on time and dress professionally. It's amazing how much more respect people give you when you dress to impress. Try it. Do a showing in sneakers and a ball cap and then do one suited and booted. See how they respond differently. Here is the process we use for our showings:

- Build Rapport
- Set Expectations
- Tour
- Needs Analysis
- Presentation
- Close

BUILD RAPPORT

Find common ground quickly. Set them at ease. I do this with a smile, a handshake, and a compliment of some sort. Make sure you are well kept and professional-looking. Mirror their mannerisms. If they cross their arms, cross yours. Ask them what part of town they live in and how long they have been in business. Their business is their baby. People love talking about their babies. Don't spend too long here—make sure you are the one to transition quickly to the expectations.

SET EXPECTATIONS

I say, "Well, let's get down to business. I propose we tour the building, and you can ask your questions along the way. At the end, you can decide if you want to apply for the space, or tell me if it's not a good fit. How does that sound?" Let them know you'll be taking notes throughout the tour, then hand them a floor plan and a brochure, and any pertinent information on the space.

TOUR

Next, I start physically moving through the property. Do the tour methodically. Be friendly with existing tenants, and call them by name if possible. This shows you are a good landlord who cares enough about their tenants to remember their names.

NEEDS ANALYSIS

This is where your discovery questions come in. Ask any question beginning with who, what, where, why, when, and how, then follow up with "tell me more." Dive deeper into each response.

Who would actually be signing the lease? What is your timeline for making a decision? Where else are you looking? When do you want to move in? How long of a lease do you desire? You get the idea. Ask these questions as you are touring the property, and it will feel natural. Write their responses down.

PRESENTATION

I transition to the presentation when the tour is done by asking, "What questions do you have for me that I can answer to help you decide if this space is right for you?" They will start asking questions, and you can use this opportunity to present information on the property or your company. Now you are giving them the information they actually want, and when they run out of questions, it's time to move to the close.

CLOSE

Repeat back all of their needs (which you wrote down), and ask them to confirm if you're understanding them correctly. Then simply ask, "Do you think this space will work for you?" If they say yes, and they are a small tenant, email them the application right then and there from your phone, and confirm they received it on their phone. If they say yes, and they are a large tenant, write down the specific needs they have, so you can send them a term sheet.

If they say no, get specific feedback on why, to see if you can tweak your space to meet their needs. You may also want to cross-sell them to another property you have. Always end the discussion on a good note, keep the door open, and follow up with an email thanking them for their time. You may get another property under contract tomorrow or come across a friend of yours who has a property that you can fill for them and create value. Who knows? Maybe they'll even cut you in on the GP Units as a partner if you have enough tenants in your pocket to fill the whole building.

After the Showing

Follow up. Follow up. Follow up until you get a yes or a no. The goal of the showing is to get an application, and the next chapter covers how to screen those candidates effectively to make sure you are only signing leases with winners.

FILL

Key Reader Takeaways

☐ Ask open-ended questions and probe.

☐ Listen and take notes.

☐ Ask for the application or send a term sheet promptly.

☐ Follow up until you get an application or a no.

Action Items

☐ Write down ten questions you will ask each potential tenant during your tour so you will know what you're asking when you arrive.

☐ Jot down five features of the property you want to highlight and three features of your company that make it easy to work with you.

☐ Conduct a showing and get a rental application.

FILL

Chapter 26

Screen the Tenants

Objective: Issue an Approval or Denial on the Tenant's Application

Trust but verify.

Don't take anything on the rental application as gospel. You should have a written matrix for your decision criteria, especially if you are doing apartments.

A decision matrix is a written list of the bare minimum and preferred criteria for a tenant that you have for every candidate, so you can defend your decisions if you ever get sued. Issue a denial letter if you turn down any tenants, stating specifically what on the matrix made them not qualify.

Income Verification

Require them to submit proof of income. Tax returns, pay stubs, bank statements. I require one of these documents to prove to me that they make at least three times the total rent in gross income. If the rent is $2,500 per month, I want to see $7,500 per month in gross income. This is how I gauge their ability to repay.

Credit Verification

Our system allows an online application where they can put in their credit card for the application fee. Then I get notified once they fill it out, and I simply hit a "screen now" button, and it comes back with the credit decision. There are screening services out there you can use to do this.

We look for unlawful detainers and major delinquencies on the credit report, especially in the last two years. If they got evicted somewhere, it is a big red flag for us. It's not always a deal killer, but you can request a letter of explanation and then speak to the company that evicted them to see if the issue was indeed resolved. Sometimes they paid up and the issue was closed out. If their credit issues are really old, I don't put much weight on that. I tend to focus on the most recent two to three years.

Criminal History

We don't allow felonies for any fraud, violent crimes, or misrepresentation. If the felony is ten-plus years old and was for something I don't think would affect their tenancy, like drug use, then we will consider it if they can demonstrate how their life has changed. We are Christian at our core and believe it was finished on the cross, so we treat our tenants that same way. You have an obligation to protect your other tenants and your investors, so the nature and recency of the crimes matter.

References

Call the references, knowing that bad tenants will list their friends as references. My friend Lenny Frolov taught me a trick on how to get to the bottom of this. Most properties are owned in an LLC. Every property owner knows the name of the LLC that owns the property. He checks how the title is held on the property before he calls the references. In the middle of the reference call, he slips in, "What's the name of the entity that owns this property?" If they can't answer the question immediately, he knows it's a bogus reference.

I would get at least two solid references for leases over one thousand square feet. Don't skip this part. Turnover is ridiculously expensive in time, energy, eviction fees, legal fees, lost rent, renovations, leasing commissions, and tenant improvement concessions.

A good tenant is worth their weight in gold. A bad tenant will make you think twice about doing real estate ever again. I once had the worst tenants in the world in one of my buildings. They drove me so crazy, we ended up canceling their lease and selling the building. (Yes, I was one of the motivated sellers you are looking for, and the buyer got a smoking deal!) Make sure you sell good tenants on coming to your building. If you have to give them concessions like free rent, tenant improvement allowance budgets, or reduced rates, do it. They will pay dividends in the long run.

I know you're excited and possibly desperate to get your spaces filled, but take the time to do it right. Have urgency, but do your homework. Implement a solid marketing plan so you have more options to choose from. Don't marry the wrong person, or you will end up going through a nasty divorce.

If your tenant passes your screening process and is approved, you can now write the lease. The next chapter covers the different types of leases and what kinds of clauses you should have in them.

FILL

Key Takeaways

- ☐ Having a written decision matrix saves you from a lawsuit.
- ☐ Verify rental history and income.
- ☐ Ask the reference how the property is titled to weed out bogus references.

Action Items

- ☐ Work with your property management company to set up your screening criteria on paper.
- ☐ Secure a credit and criminal screening vendor.
- ☐ Get a paper application from that vendor for your tenants to fill out or get set up for online applications.

Chapter 27

Negotiate and Sign Leases

Objective: Sign Long-Term Leases with Good Credit Tenants

Leases have lots of naming conventions, but none of them really matter. What matters is who is paying what, when, and how because you need to estimate your NOI. Part of that is figuring out how much income you will have coming in and what expenses you will have going out. This information is usually detailed in a series of contract clauses that spells out who pays what, when, and how.

All leases fall on a spectrum, and only the extremes of the spectrum can really have a name that is meaningful; everything else is just a hybrid. The extremes are full-service gross and absolute net lease, but in the real world, almost all leases are hybrid leases, where the tenant and the landlord are each responsible for at least some expenses.

> **All that matters is who pays what, when, and how.**

Here is the spectrum. Don't overcomplicate this.

Spectrum of Lease Types

Full Service Gross	Gross + Utilities	Modified Gross Lease	Triple Net Lease	Absolute Net Lease

←——→

Expense Fluctuation
Risk Falls on Landlord

Expense Fluctuation
Risk Falls on Tenant

Landlord Pays All Expenses

Tenant Pays All Expenses

Lease Names You Will Hear

People love attaching naming conventions to stuff. You may hear these commonly used naming conventions for types of leases, but I bet if you asked ten highly qualified, competent brokers what a triple net lease is, you would get a wide variety of answers.

Lumping leases into broad categories is about as useful as lumping humans into races. Sure, they help you determine the overall color of their skin, but every single person is completely different and unique.

The type of lease will be useful to give you a broad idea of who pays what, but you have to read the lease to really figure out the specifics, just like you have to meet a person to really learn who they are.

Here are different lease types you might hear used:

- Absolute Gross Lease (Gross)
- Gross Plus Utilities
- Modified Gross

- Triple Net Lease (NNN)
- Absolute Net Lease (Net)

If you are confused beyond measure because this all seems to be over your head, you are the norm, not the exception! Let's cover each.

ABSOLUTE GROSS LEASE

This can also be called a full-service lease. In an absolute gross lease, the landlord is responsible for 100 percent of the expenses, and the tenant pays a fixed gross rent. If the expenses go up, the landlord takes the hit. If they go down, the landlord wins. Expense fluctuation risk is on the landlord.

These are common in apartments and office buildings where the landlord pays 100 percent of the utilities and operating expenses for that space. If the tenant pays a single item, then it's a hybrid lease and not a true full-service lease.

GROSS PLUS UTILITIES LEASE

This is like a full-service lease, but the tenants pay some or all of their own utilities. These are common in cases where the meters are separate, such as multi-tenant apartments, and really small retail or warehouse properties where each unit has its own meter for gas, electric, or water.

Remember, it's wise to always have the tenants pay utilities directly if they have their own meter, to remove the utilities expense from your NOI equation. If the landlord pays all of the expenses but bills the utilities back by submetering or a ratio utility billing system, then it still qualifies as a Gross + Utilities lease type. We cover what a ratio utility billing system is in the next step.

MODIFIED GROSS LEASE

A modified gross lease is a gross lease, but the landlord puts a "cap" on the expenses they will pay. It basically reads that the landlord will cover the operating expenses up to a certain dollar amount, then the landlord stops paying the expenses—an expense stop.

A gross lease with an expense stop functions like a net lease with a few key differences. The reason it's called an expense stop is because it's the amount of expenses the landlord agrees to pay before they "stop" being responsible for the expenses and then the tenant is responsible.

Please note that *being responsible* and *paying for* are not the same things. The landlord still pays the overage, and then they collect back from the tenant at the end of the year because the tenant is responsible. If a tenant moves in or out during the calendar year, the numbers are prorated. The reconciliation process for an expense stop is almost identical to reconciling a net lease—it is a way to keep your upside while protecting your downside on a gross lease. We cover how to do this shortly.

TRIPLE NET (NNN) LEASE

This is the most commonly misused term in real estate. NNN lease and triple net lease have been used in this book interchangeably. The reality is that many leases could qualify as triple net leases, but all have very different terms.

A triple net lease is a lease where the tenant pays a net rent to the landlord net of taxes, insurance, and common area maintenance, or CAM for short. Those are the three Ns that give it its name.

As you know, there are seven categories of operating expenses. Remember the acronym TUMMIRA (Taxes, Utilities, Maintenance, Management, Insurance, Repairs, and Administrative).

Taxes and Insurance are two of the three Ns, with the third N being CAM. CAM stands for common area maintenance and is usually where it gets hairy because it varies so widely across leases and can include expenses across the remaining five expense categories. If you read a triple net lease, oftentimes they allow the landlord to bill back utilities, management fees, repairs, and certain admin costs.

The real question is this: what specific expenses within these categories can the landlord bill back for? You have to read the leases to see. Are repairs within a vacant unit billable or only in common areas? If the landlord restripes the parking lot, is that billable back to the tenants, or is that considered a capital improvement? Can they bill back capital improvements, and if so, how do they do it? Do they bill the actual cost in one year, the depreciated value each year, or do they bill the reserve that they are setting aside before they do the improvement altogether? Is there a cap on the management fees a landlord can charge back to the tenant?

You have to get into the weeds in the lease to figure all of this out. Each lease will include a clause that discusses what expenses can be "passed through" to the tenants and which can't.

I despise the term "triple net," because the reality is that no two leases are alike because the definition of CAM is never the same. The idea of a triple net lease is that the landlord pays some expenses and then bills them back to the tenants as "additional rent." You will generally see a base rent plus the expense pass-throughs. Remember when we analyzed a deal we did a gross rent approach and a net rent approach? This is the type of lease you would use for a net rent approach.

The landlord will absorb some of the expenses in a triple net lease. Typically, we see the landlord being responsible for capital improvements, legal fees, leasing, advertising fees, and costs associated with vacant units, such as utilities and repairs, to get them rented again. Since most leases leave some of the responsibility on the landlord, it's your job to read the lease itself and figure out what expenses the landlord (you) would absorb, and factor that into your analysis. People often make the mistake of looking at the base rent on a triple net lease and using that as their NOI and not accounting for the expenses the landlord will not be able to pass through to the tenant. If the landlord is not responsible for any expenses at all and passed 100 percent through to the tenant, then you actually have an absolute net lease.

ABSOLUTE NET LEASE

In an absolute net lease, the tenant pays the landlord a fixed net rent. These are most common in single-tenant buildings. It's called a net rent because the tenant is locking in a net operating income for the landlord, and the tenant is responsible for 100 percent of the expenses.

The key difference between this and a triple net lease is that the tenant is also usually responsible for leasing fees, capital improvements, and all associated costs. Oftentimes they pay these expenses directly as opposed to the landlord paying them and then passing them through as additional rent.

An absolute net lease guarantees a specific NOI to the landlord. Large corporations sign these to have other investors buy the real estate and essentially finance the building for them. This makes their balance sheets look better because they don't have to capitalize the leases, but the accounting laws have changed, so you will probably see less of these as we move forward in time. The tenant operates the building as if they own it. Net rent and NOI are different. Net rent is the income. Net rent equals NOI only if there are zero expenses, which there are only zero expenses in a true absolute net lease.

Most standalone, single-tenant retail buildings are absolute net leases. Think McDonalds. No matter what happens on the property, the tenant is responsible. Roof caves in, tenant's problem. Taxes go up—sorry, tenant. City assesses the property, tenant is S.O.L.

The lease guarantees the landlord will "net" a certain amount each month and locks in that amount. Because they are basically renting the land, sometimes people call them land leases.

Term Sheet

The clauses in the actual lease agreement dictate who pays what, when, and how, but 90 percent of the lease document is legal jargon that doesn't really mean anything. If you are doing small leases—three thousand square feet or less—I recommend you have your attorney put together a template for the building. Then you can fill it in as you get tenants ready to sign a lease. If you have a larger lease, you may consider doing a term sheet first to make sure you are on the same page before you start spending money on an attorney.

This is an LOI for the lease. When larger tenants represented by an agent make a request for a proposal (RFP), this is what they are asking for.

Your lease template or term sheet will lay out the general terms of the lease that you are willing to accept. Expect that they will counter your offer with more aggressive terms, so you may not want to put out your bottom line first, or you won't have any room to negotiate. Don't let their attorney draft the lease either; that will be a one-sided lease.

If you can agree to terms on the term sheet, then you can get signatures and let the attorneys draft up a formal lease. I usually ask larger tenants to put forth a non-refundable legal drafting fee. Usually, it's $1,000 to $2,500, depending on what I anticipate my costs to be at the time the term sheet is signed and agreed to, in order to cover my costs on drafting the lease. If they decide not to move forward, this fee ensures you are not out the money. For smaller tenants, just draft the lease using the template you already paid for. Then you're only out your time if they flake.

Another option would be to agree to "split" the cost of having a neutral third party draft the lease. I've been burned too many times on tenants changing their minds and me being out the money. Here are some of the terms I cover in my term sheet.

Expense Pass-Throughs

You can decide what expenses you want to pass through to the tenants. An expense pass-through can either be paid directly by the tenants, or it can be paid by the landlord and then "recovered" from the tenants as additional rent. In multi-tenant buildings, it would be extremely difficult to bill all of the tenants their proportionate share of every expense on a monthly basis.

Instead, your property manager will prepare a budget for the property for an entire calendar year, showing the projected totals for each category of expenses. This is typically done around November or December for the next year. Then the tenants pay one-twelfth of their proportionate share of the expected expenses each month. Their proportionate share is determined as follows:

$$\text{Tenant's Proportionate Share} = \frac{\text{Tenant's Rentable Square Footage}}{\text{Total Building Rentable Square Footage}}$$

At the end of the year, your property manager will reconcile the budget.

Expense Reconciliation

Modified gross leases with an expense stop, triple net, and net leases all require a process called "reconciling." This process is typically done in January or February for the prior year to ensure you haven't included any expenses that aren't allowed to be passed through based on each tenant's lease language. Hopefully, all of the leases are written similarly, or you're going to have a lot of fun doing this.

Your property manager will do this for you, but you should understand how it works so you can double-check their work. I find errors all the time even with the best property managers out there. Here is what an annual budget and tenant's proportionate share might have looked like at the Center Drive property if I had chosen to do net leases instead of gross leases.

Calculating Tenant's Proportionate Share

Annual Budget

Expense Category	Budget
Taxes	$10,000
Utilities	$500
Maintenance	$7,000
Management	$7,000
Insurance	$3,000
Repairs	$9,800
Admin	$2,700
Total	$40,000

Tenant's Proportionate Share

Tenant	RSF	Share	Exp/Yr	Exp/Mo
Tenant A	2,400	12.0%	$4,800	$400
Tenant B	1,220	6.1%	$2,440	$203
Tenant C	3,300	16.5%	$6,600	$550
Tenant D	2,610	13.1%	$5,220	$435
Tenant E	3,050	15.3%	$6,100	$508
Tenant F	3,420	17.1%	$6,840	$570
Tenant G	1,740	8.7%	$3,480	$290
Vacant	2,260	11.3%	$4,520	$377
Total	20,000			

The expenses are projected to be $2 per square foot per year. This is the amount you would include as an expense stop in the case of a gross lease with expense stop, or what you would charge each month on top of the net rent for the escrow for the pass-through expenses on a net lease.

Then you reconcile at the end of the year.

If the actual expenses were over budget and ended up being $50,000, each tenant would owe their share of the actual expenses but get a credit for what they had paid in. For example, Tenant A would owe 12% of $50,000 or $6,000, but since they already paid $4,800, they would write a check to the landlord for $1,200.

Let's see what happens if the actual expenses were under budget at $30,000: Tenant A would owe 12% of $30,000 or $3,600, and since they paid in $4,800, the landlord would write them a check for $1,200 *only* if it were a net lease type of lease. If it were a gross lease with the expense stop at $2, the landlord would keep the upside and not owe a refund.

Modified Gross versus Net Lease Comparison

Type	Example	Actual Expenses Are $50,000	Actual Expenses Are $30,000
If You Do Gross Leases with Expense Stops	Tenant A pays $1,600 a month in rent of which $400 is included for expenses.	Landlord bills tenant $1,200 for the year.	Nothing happens.
If You Do Net Leases	Tenant A Pays $1,200 a month in base rent plus $400 a month for their share of CAM/TAX as their estimated share of the expense pass-throughs for the building.	Tenant pays landlord $1,200.	Landlord pays tenant $1,200.

A gross lease with an expense stop is actually better for the landlord than a net lease because they get the same benefits of locking in their net income from that lease, but they keep the upside if they manage the expenses better than projected instead of refunding it to the tenant. This incentivizes lower costs, like updating the LED lights and doing other things that would save the tenant money as well.

FILL

Gross-Up Clause

You lose a lot of money on net leases if they don't have gross-up clauses. If the building is only 75% occupied, then you are only recovering 75% of your expenses. This means you are not only losing the rental income on the 25% vacancy, but you are absorbing the expenses on the 25% vacancy. That will kill your NOI.

Certain expenses such as taxes and admin costs are fixed and do not change based on occupancy. We don't gross these types of expenses up because I personally don't believe it's fair. Other expenses such as utilities, management, maintenance, and repairs *will* change with occupancy and we *do* gross those expenses up.

A gross-up clause lets you recalculate the tenant's proportionate share by adjusting the denominator in the proportionate share calculation to only be the square footage of occupied units instead of the total building square footage. Basically, you only pass the expenses on to the people who are occupying the building.

You use the adjusted proportionate share percentage to bill the expenses for things that would change based on the occupancy of the building. For instance, in our example, we had one vacancy. In this case, we would recalculate the percentage share using the 17,740 square feet as the denominator to recalculate the percentage each tenant who actually occupied the building was responsible for. That way you always recover 100 percent of the expenses you are allowed to pass through.

At the end of the day, it's all about what's fair. If the expense would legitimately be lower because you have a vacancy—which is the case with utilities, management fees, and repairs—then the expense should be shared among the tenants that just occupy the building. Whereas, if the expense were the same either way—like property taxes or insurance—then the tenant shouldn't bear the burden of your vacancy issue.

If you don't believe what you are doing is fair in your heart, your tenants will sense that when you explain it and they may not agree to it. Don't try to structure your deals to just benefit you. Structure them so it's fair. If you do that, you will have no problem selling the terms and why they are fair.

FILL

Step-Ups

These are scheduled systematic increases in the rent. Typically, step-ups are done every twelve months of the lease term. They are typically either a fixed percent of the prior year rent, or a fixed incremental increase in the dollar amount each year. For example, you could have a 3% per year or a $100 per year bump. They are meant to keep the rent in line with inflation. You can see what the actual inflation rates have been over the past ten years by checking the CPI on Google.

Technically, while these are called step-up leases, a true step-up lease steps up much faster than inflation. It is a great way to get somebody in the space now and have your lease grow with them as they grow. If you start under market rate and end over market rate, the average is at market rate.

This works great for smaller, startup-type businesses or if you want to get a tenant in at a price point they need to be at.

Free Rent

I love using free rent to get tenants into a space. It is going to sit vacant anyway. I prefer free rent over a rent reduction. When the lease is up and it comes time to renew, it's easier to renew at the higher rent rate because it's not as big of a jump as it would be if you give them a price reduction for every month of the original lease term.

Percent of Sales

These are not commonly used anymore. Typically, they were used for retail leases. I don't use them because of how easy it is for the tenant to cheat. However, in certain circumstances, you might want to use them if the tenant is a larger tenant with audited financials.

Personal Guarantee

I highly recommend getting a personal guarantee from all owners owning over 20 percent of the LLC or corporation leasing your spaces, for small and medium-sized leases. Look for personal guarantees on leases you are assuming when you buy a property. They are weak if they don't have one—anyone can walk without recourse.

The only problem with a personal guarantee is that when you have issues, the owners are smart enough to siphon off all their liquid assets so you have nothing left to collect. That's why I started doing letters of credit instead for larger tenants.

Letters of Credit

A letter of credit is a surety bond that their lender issues that guarantees your rent. They will have a line of credit at the bank open that must maintain an available balance of the amount on the letter of credit they have with you—let's say it's $50,000. If the tenant defaults, the lender draws on the line of credit to pay you, and then the tenant owes the bank just like with any other secured line of credit.

These tend to be more reliable than personal guarantees but should not be used for smaller tenants under ten thousand square feet, because they don't usually qualify for them.

Options

Options of any sort have value. Options you give away are value you are giving away. If you include an option to renew, an option to purchase, or a first right of refusal to lease the space next to them if it becomes available, then you have given away something of value. If you give a tenant an option to renew their lease, that is a unilateral arrangement that benefits them. If they exercise it, you have to comply—but they don't have to exercise it.

If market rates at the time of renewal are higher than you have pre-agreed to renew for, they may exercise their option, saving them money. If market rates at the time of the renewal are lower than the rate on their option, they simply don't exercise their option, and they enter into a negotiation with you to lease the space under new terms, or they look elsewhere.

When I issue a term sheet, I don't ever give options. I make the tenant, or their agent/ broker, come back and ask for them as a concession. When I give that concession (which is giving something of value), I usually get a concession on something else. Although a five-year lease with a five-year renewal seems like it's as good as a ten-year lease, I can assure you that your lender and appraiser will not give as much value to the five-year deal with a five-year renewal because the income stream is not as predictable. For that reason, neither will your financial buyer when you go to sell this thing. Try to get ten-year terms with no renewal options, and work from there.

Leasing Commissions

Speaking of agents. My head spun 360 degrees and I almost fell out of my chair when I figured out how much commercial real estate agents wanted me to pay them to bring me a tenant for my first retail location. The commission was $50K, and that was the market rate. I had not accounted for that in my proforma! Holy buckets!

Because these vary widely by market, you will want to check with a few commercial real estate agents to see what the leasing commissions are in your area. Here is how they work in my market, and yours might be similar:

Common Leasing Commissions by Asset Class

Asset Class	1 Agent Involved	2 Agents involved
Office	$1.00 per SF per year for first 5 years, then $0.50 per year after that.	$1.50 per SF per year for first 5 years, then $0.75 per year after that.
Warehouse	7% of first year net rent, 6% of second year net rent, 5% of third year net rent, 4% of fourth year net rent, 3% of fifth year and any year after that net rent.	150% of that schedule, split 50/50 between the two agents.
Retail	3% of total net cumulative rent or same as office commission.	150% of that schedule.
Apartments	One month's rent.	N/A

FILL

As you can see, the commission goes up when there are two agents involved—one agent representing the landlord and one representing the tenant. Sometimes it goes up 50 percent and sometimes it goes up 75 percent. It is not typical to see a renter for an apartment be represented, so I didn't put a commission in for that category for two agents.

Cumulative gross rent is the total rent obligation the tenant will have over the entire course of the lease, including base rent and additional rent for expense pass-throughs. This is the total amount the tenant is obligated to pay under the lease. Think of it as the sales price for the lease.

Oftentimes you will pay commission based on this number. It's rare I see commissions based on the net (base) rent, though sometimes it does happen for triple net properties. Cumulative net rent works the same way, but you only add up the base rent and leave the expense pass-throughs out of the equation.

I found a little mathematical workaround to calculate a cumulative rent obligation:

$$\text{Cumulative Rent Obligation} = (1 + \text{Annual Increase \%})^{\text{Lease Years}} \times \frac{\text{Gross Rent in Month One}}{} \times \frac{\text{Number of Months of the Lease}}{}$$

For example, your agent signs a lease for a one thousand-square-foot office that starts at a gross rate of $1,000 per month and increases every year by 3% for a total of sixty months.

$$\text{Cumulative Rent Obligation} = (1.03)^5 \times \$1,000 \times 60 = \$69,556.44$$

You can double-check your math by multiplying the months of the lease by the starting rent. If your answer is just slightly higher, then you are probably correct. For example, if we didn't have an annual increase, the cumulative rent obligation would simply be sixty months at $1,000 per month for $60,000. The extra $9,556.44 is the additional rent from the annual rent increases.

FILL

If you paid $1.00 per square foot per year, you would have paid a commission of $5,000. If you agreed to do it at say 5% of cumulative gross rent, you would have paid 5% × $69,556.44 = $3,477.82.

Amortizing Tenant Improvements

Tenant improvement allowances are a great way to incentivize tenants to move into your space. You budgeted for them on your renovation cost worksheet, which flowed to your costs to fix on the MACO worksheet. The tenant pays for their remodel and then you reimburse them or pay the contractor directly.

You can "amortize" some or all of this TI allowance into the lease—it's completely up to you. Amortizing is a fancy way of saying you are going to finance their improvements and add the payments to the lease.

Let's do this for the Center Drive deal. The final actual WACCC was 7.054%, as calculated on the sources and uses worksheet, and let's say your tenant wants you to give them $2.00 per square foot per year of tenant improvement allowances on a three thousand-square-foot space for a five-year lease. They are basically asking you to finance $30,000 of their build-out for them (3,000 × $2.00 × 5).

Now let's say you are willing to just charge them your cost of 7.054% on this money. Simply run these numbers through a time value of money or loan calculator to determine that their payments to you are $594.80 per month for sixty months.

I know I told you that you were done with finance class, but you're not. Go download a financial calculator app on your phone that does time value of money. I recommend the HP 10bii app.

Here is what it looks like if you plug it into a time value of money calculator:

Time Value of Money Calculator

594.80_				≡
P/YR:12				End Mode
60.000	7.054%	−30,000.000	594.801	0.000
N	**I/YR**	**PV**	**PMT**	**FV**
INPUT	MU	CST	PRC	MAR
K	%	CF$_j$	Σ+	←
+/−	RCL	→M	RM	M+
	7	8	9	÷
	4	5	6	×
C	1	2	3	−
HELP	0	•	=	+

Make sure your N=12 in your calculator meaning twelve payments per year. To use this calculator, you can enter any four of the five variables and then solve for the fifth.

N—Number of periods is sixty for the five years you want to finance the TIs for.

I/YR—Interest per year is 7.054% for the rate you are charging them, which is the same as your final, actual WACCC from the sources and uses worksheet.

PV—Present value is negative $30,000 because you are shelling out $30K to them in TIs. Negative values are money going away from you, and positive values are money coming toward you.

PMT—Leave blank for now because this is what we want to solve for.

FV—Future value is the payment they will make to you at the end of the five years, which would be zero.

Once you have those four items plugged in, you can hit the PMT button and solve for the payment. The payment would be $594.80 which is a positive number indicating the money would be coming *to* you.

Therefore, if you wanted to finance the TIs, you would add $594.80 to the monthly rent you were going to charge them if you wanted to pass through 100 percent of the TI allowance. You could also choose to charge them half, like $300, and absorb the other half of the TIs as part of your concessions to get them into the space. See what you already budgeted for in the renovation cost worksheet. Remember, as long as the money is spent on improvements that would increase rent for any other tenants, it's money well spent.

End of Finance 201 class.

Turnover Is Costly

There are four main costs to turnover:

- Lost rental income
- Expense absorption
- Leasing fees to re-lease the space
- Repair costs to make the space lease ready again

This is why it makes sense to think of your tenants as your customers. Their success is your success. You are their partner, not their adversary. How can you help their business succeed so they see you as a strategic partner, not just a landlord? People don't stay at their job just because of money, and tenants don't stay at their building just because of rent rates.

Can you drive business to your tenants by referring them? Can you give them your business? Can you give them little random gifts here and there to show them you appreciate them? Can you handle maintenance requests very quickly to show you care about their needs, even if you have to pay a little more to get it done quick or after hours? The extra effort you take to make them a happy customer will make a dramatic impact on your NOI in the long run.

Just like structuring a purchase or a partnership, by using creativity, you can achieve the same result in different ways and make the deal work for your tenants. For example, if I know I need to make $69,556.44 over five years from my space, I could give some free rent on the front end of the lease but increase my annual rent bump to 5% per year.

Get creative with the terms of the lease, and don't get too stuck on the base rent if you can achieve a similar cumulative rent over the period of the lease. As a general rule of thumb, if I can get to within 90 percent of my proforma rents, I will do the deal to get the tenant in the building.

Summary

Small tenants just want to know how much they are paying each month. In fact, they are willing to pay a little more per square foot in exchange for certainty. They generally don't understand net leases and hate the idea of not knowing how much they are going to be paying.

I rent spaces under five thousand square feet using a gross lease with an expense stop. With larger tenants, if they are going to take the risk on the downside protection for the landlord, they will also generally want to keep the upside benefit, so spaces over five thousand square feet usually go to NNN leases. These tenants are usually represented by an agent who explains net leases and convinces them that this is a better option.

I hope you can see that the net and gross parts of the names of the lease simply refer to the part of the P&L that the lease locks in for the landlord. What I mean is that a gross lease only locks in the gross income number for the landlord, and an absolute net lease locks in the net operating income for the landlord.

However, most leases are hybrid leases, where the landlord and tenant are each responsible for some expenses. You have to read the entire lease to figure out exactly what expenses are paid by the tenant and what expenses are paid by the landlord and if there are any limits to those payments for either party.

FILL

Don't forget to have an attorney review your leases to create a template you can use over and over for smaller spaces or on a case-by-case basis for larger leases. The goal is to get your building 100 percent occupied. Now that your building is filled, the final step is to drive the financial performance of the building in order to force appreciation.

Key Reader Takeaways

- ☐ Read the lease to see who pays what, when, and how.
- ☐ Don't get too caught up in lease naming conventions.
- ☐ Understand how to reconcile expense pass-throughs or expense stops.
- ☐ A tenant's proportionate share is simply the percentage of rentable square footage that their suite is as a percentage of the overall building rentable square feet.
- ☐ Use gross-up clauses to insulate against expense absorption from vacancy.
- ☐ Use gross leases with an expense stop for spaces under five thousand square feet and NNN leases for spaces over 5,000 square feet.
- ☐ Lease negotiations should include creativity and persistence to find win-win situations and lock people in.

Action Items

- ☐ Review the existing leases in place on a new target property with this new information, and see who pays what, when, and how.
- ☐ Have an attorney draft your form lease you will use for your building.
- ☐ Decide if you will include a gross-up clause or not in your leases.
- ☐ Calculate a sample payment for financing a tenant improvement allowance using your WACCC as the interest rate you are going to charge them.

FILL

Step 6
Financials

This step is all about freeing up your time by putting a property management company in place to help you achieve the higher NOI. There are three parts to driving the financials to realize the higher NOI and achieve the appreciation you have been working toward:

- Select Management Company
- Onboard the Property
- Stabilize the Financials

This is where you will interview and hire a property manager, though once again the seven steps are not necessarily linear. You should start interviewing property management firms early in the process and be ready to sign a contract with them right after you get through the due diligence part of the Fund step. If you wait until closing to hire them, you're going to end up doing most of the onboarding work yourself.

I'll also teach you how to actually take over the property the week after closing and stabilize the financials so that you have a history of improved NOI on paper for your refinance or sale of the property. Finally, you will learn different ways to realize the added value and drive the multiple up.

This is where the rubber meets the road. Let's go through each part in more detail so you can finish the race strong.

Chapter 28

Select Management Company

Objective: Find the Right Firm to Manage Your Property

In the beginning, I tried multiple management companies and wasn't happy with any of them. They did not put in the effort that I wanted them to, so I decided to have my brokerage company manage it. I brought on a full-time property manager in-house to ensure that our properties were getting the attention they deserved.

It was going pretty well until my business coach screwed it up for me.

One day, he asked me why I was doing my property management in-house. I gave him a perfectly crafted speech about how we controlled our assets better, maintained our tenant relationships better, and saved tons of money on maintenance costs.

Then he dropped a bomb on my logic. "Mike, what is your competitive advantage in property management? I mean, what are you doing better than the best firms in town that make your management division unique?"

"I care more," I responded. Other than that, I couldn't answer him.

He said, "Shut it down. Remove the overhead of your salaried employees, convert the expense to a variable cost, and focus on your core business where you do have a competitive advantage: finding and funding deals. Just find a company that cares about *their* core business as much as you do about yours."

He was right. I had made the mistake of convincing myself that managing our own properties was benefitting me when the reality was that I just needed to spend more time finding the right property manager and structuring a compensation package that aligned our interests.

That's exactly what I did, and it was one of the best decisions I've ever made. I had found myself spending a tremendous amount of time and energy putting out fires, selecting vendors, handling maintenance calls, and doing budgets. These are not where you make the money in this business—and you can't try to grow two companies at the same time.

Grow your investment business and outsource your management. Maybe when you grow it to the size where you want to (and are able to) start a property management business, you can do it, but don't start off that way. To find anyone decent to work directly for you as an employee, you will have to buy more capacity than you need, thus paying a salary that far exceeds the variable cost of outsourcing it.

The good news is I learned a lot while doing it myself, and I'm going to share all the secrets I learned so that you can start where I left off after three years of doing it myself. Then you can select a management company like a pro.

Here are the key lessons:

- Get Referrals
- Ask the *Right* Questions
- Align Motivations with Creative Compensation
- Work *with* Them, Don't Delegate *to* Them

Get Referrals

The reality is that good property management companies are not always easy to find. You don't want a massive company that's all over the country, like a CBRE. Nothing against these companies, but they are so big your property is just another number to them. They make their money on volume. You need someone who will get into the trenches and be your biggest ally. You'll have to pay them above market to get there, but you need someone who is local and willing to go the extra mile.

The best companies I have found came through referrals from other investors who have used them successfully. Get into whatever commercial real estate investing networks are available in your area and start asking around. When you interview brokers in the research step or as you are soliciting leasing proposals in the Fill step, ask them for the top three management companies they would recommend with contact info. If they don't have a specific person's name and number, it's probably not the best referral.

Ask the Right Questions

Here are the questions I ask the property management company to determine if they are a good fit or not:

- Can you describe the portfolio you are managing, including size, asset class, and locations?
- How much of that do you own?
- Do you work on Value-Add properties?
- What is your approach to creating value?
- What software(s) do you use?

- Do you do your maintenance in-house?
- How are your fees structured?
- Are you open to a structure that incentivizes you to drive the NOI?
- Who is the actual manager and how many properties are they responsible for?

You are looking for a company that has at least a million square feet of property under management, primarily in your local market. Interview the actual person who would manage the property, not just the owner or sales rep. Ask them how many assets they are currently responsible for to see how spread thin they are.

Look for someone who uses a real property management software with a tenant portal, autopay for tenants, and maintenance tracking capabilities. If they use QuickBooks to run their operation, just hang up the phone. They are not your company.

Most mid-sized companies like this will do maintenance in-house and have a guy or two. See what they charge. Rates should be around $50 an hour. If it's $100 or more, they are robbing you. I cover my ideal fee structure in the next section.

Align Motivations with Creative Compensation

Finding a good property management company is like finding a life partner: you might have a lot of first dates, but don't propose unless you're sure they are the one!

I hired all the wrong management companies early on. It was painful. That's why I came to the conclusion that "getting married" was a bad idea. The reality is that the right partner can be the biggest blessing ever!

In this case, the right partner must be experienced with Value-Add property management. Value-Add real estate is extremely labor-intensive. They have to work three to five times as hard as they would on a stabilized property, for half the income. Under that type of arrangement, who wouldn't be frustrated!?

For this reason, I recommend you pay above-market management fees. That probably seems counterintuitive, since you are so focused on your bottom line, but let me defend my statement here for a second.

If you set it up so all the horses pull the cart in the same direction—in other words, if they get a portion of the incremental profit they help secure for you—then it's not really a cost to you. It's a benefit.

Remember when I told my mentor that my only competitive advantage was that I cared more? No one gives a rip about your $500 commission for that last five hundred-square-foot office space in the dark corner of the building except you, unless you make them care by incentivizing them. Find a way to compensate them for helping fill these spaces:

- Pay a percent of revenue, or a fixed monthly fee, whichever is greater.
- Offer them a higher percent of revenue for each month if the building is 100 percent occupied and they collect 100 percent of the rent that month.
- Pay them an NOI bonus at the end of the year.

Here is what it looks like graphically:

Property Management Fee Chart

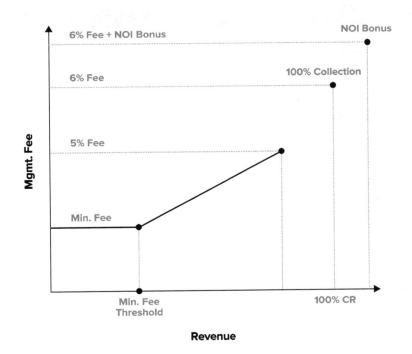

This way, you protect their downside risk but give them the upside potential. This directly aligns their interests with yours, which is getting the building 100 percent occupied, collecting 100 percent of that rent, and keeping operating expenses as modest as possible while still keeping tenants happy and the building in good condition.

Here's how we could do it for Center Drive.

The going-in revenue was $110K per year, and the stabilized revenue was $141K. What if we offered 5% of revenue with a $500 per month minimum, but if the building was full and they collected in full, they got 6%? I usually set the minimum at a little over what the starting rent is so that the starting percent is higher than the normal fee.

Here's how that would play out:

Management Fee Scenarios

Scenario	Fee	Notes
Rent Is under $10K for the Month	$500	Minimum Fee
Rent Is over $10K per Month	5% of Revenue	Normal Fee
100% Occupancy and Collection for the Month	6% of Revenue	Bonus Fee

Essentially, you are paying them a higher percent up front as a bare minimum fee because you know your rent amount is artificially low. You could also choose to throw in an NOI bonus at the end of the year. Here is a sliding scale you could use:

NOI Bonus to Property Manager

NOI Goal	$90,000	$95,000	$100,000	$105,000	$110,000
% Goal	90%	95%	100%	105%	110%
Bonus	$500	$1,000	$2,500	$5,000	$7,500
Net to You	$89,500	$94,000	$97,500	$100,000	$102,500

Most management companies will have never done an arrangement like this. You have to sell them on the idea.

Find ways to make the property manager think like the owner. What does the owner want? The owner wants 100 percent occupancy, 100 percent collection, and a high NOI. Most management companies prefer to manage stabilized assets because they have the highest revenue and least amount of headaches, but by using a creative approach to structuring compensation for your property manager, you can both drive toward the same goal.

My business coach helped me realize I had come to the wrong conclusion about property managers. Outsourcing the management wasn't the wrong idea. Outsourcing the management *to the wrong company* with the wrong comp plan was the wrong idea.

Keep searching until you find the right management company. Structure your compensation so they get paid more when you achieve a higher NOI, and they will be your best ally in driving the value of your property.

Don't Delegate to Them

Just remember, you are still the asset manager. You still have a very large role in executing the business plan. Don't ever hand off management completely. The mindset that you can sit back and do nothing is the wrong one to have. The only passive investors in your deal are the limited partners you raised your capital from. They are relying on you to be Johnny-on-the-spot with your team.

FINANCIALS

Set NOI and occupancy goals with that team, and have them check in with you regularly on their progress toward achieving those goals. Remember that the incremental wins impact your sponsor fees dramatically because you really don't start earning big dollars until you get into the uppermost tiers.

A property at 90% occupancy might have an NOI that is only 70% of an NOI for a property that is fully occupied—that last 10% in occupancy makes a tremendous impact on NOI. That's why it's critical to proactively manage your management company and work alongside them to stabilize the property.

Once you find, interview, and secure a property management company that is naturally incentivized to think like an owner, it's time to learn how to onboard your property at closing to start implementing your business plan.

Key Takeaways

- ☐ Look for a company that has a good management software.
- ☐ Pay a higher fee when they achieve 100 percent occupancy and collection for the month.
- ☐ Pay an NOI bonus on a sliding scale.
- ☐ Be willing to pay a minimum management fee.

Action Items

- ☐ Get referrals and interview thoroughly to find a local firm that has at least 1M square feet under management.
- ☐ Interview the actual manager who would manage your property, and ask them about capacity and their approach to adding value.
- ☐ Select a firm to use for your property management, and sign a contract with them.

Chapter 29

Onboard the Property

Objective: Execute a Smooth Takeover of the Property at Closing

The first question that comes to a tenant's mind when they hear their property has been sold is "Dude, what's going to happen to my rent?" Most of them experience anxiety about the unknown just like the rest of us. Address that anxiety quickly and professionally. This is their first impression of you and your management company. First impressions matter and will set the foundation for the future.

That's why the first week after closing can be the hardest week of the whole seven-step process if you don't do it right. The key is to put everything in place early while balancing the other things you're doing to wrap up the Fund step and start the Fix step.

There is a right way to onboard your property, and there is a wrong way. I did it the wrong way with Center Drive. Here's what I learned:

- Your job is to create value *for* your tenants, not to extract value *from* them.
- The amount of rent they will pay you is in direct proportion to the success of their business within your space.
- **It's not about you and your agenda; it's about them and their business.**

That's where I blew it on Center Drive. If you recall, the guy who sold me the property was not billing back the utilities like he should have been, and the rent was way under market.

I went around to each tenant right after closing and explained they were not paying market rent and that they were not paying everything they were supposed to pay on the lease. I pissed a lot of people off, and it only increased their anxiety and made my job harder as the property manager.

This is not what you want; trust me!

Instead, meet each tenant individually and make the focus of the conversation about learning their business, their needs, and their wants. They will not care how much you know until they know how much you care.

Try not to rock the cradle too much. Reassure them their current lease terms will be honored. Figure out how you can help drive business to them, and ask them what changes they would like to see made on the building. Do they need more or less space? Are they happy where they are at? Would they renew if their lease were up right now?

If you approach the tenants in a service-oriented manner, they will begin to trust you, and you may uncover opportunities to rewrite the lease based on what they need, not based on what you want.

Reduce their anxiety by reassuring them that you are their friend and not their enemy. If your heart is to help them and their business grow, you will find they respond much more warmly to the needs of your business plan over time.

Zig Ziglar said it best: "You can have everything in life you want, if you will just help enough other people get what *they* want."

Let's go through each of the steps you need to complete in order to successfully onboard a property with your management company:

- Sign Vendor Contracts
- Tenant Welcome Letter
- Rekey Building
- Amenity Scheduling System
- Change Utilities to Your Name
- Management Software
- Annual Budget

Sign Vendor Contracts

If you haven't already done so, select your leasing vendor, contractors, and property management company, and sign contracts with them so they can start working on the project as soon as possible. Also do a 3D tour, space measurement study, and media package if you haven't yet.

Tenant Welcome Letter

Have your property manager mail out a welcome letter prior to closing if possible. Here is what the letter usually covers:

- Which day management will (or already has) transferred
- Let them know you will rekey the building
- Let them know their lease terms will remain in effect
- Let them know how to pay rent
- Let them know how to submit maintenance requests
- Let them know how to contact management

The sooner they get the letter, the better, to help alleviate anxiety.

Rekey Building

For security reasons, you should rekey the entire building as soon as possible. Account for this in your renovation costs. Get a master key for the whole building, and then get a maintenance key that only does your common area rooms.

One client I represented purchased a twenty-unit office building with over 120 keys! It was a nightmare trying to figure out what key operated what door. It required one of our staff members to go to the property multiple times a day to meet contractors, tenants, vendors, and so forth.

Any money you spend rekeying will pay dividends in the long run. We recommend also installing a digital lockbox with a code that can be updated remotely and expires after twenty-four hours. That way you can give vendors temporary codes for access to the building. Depending on your lock types, you can build this functionality right into your door locks themselves.

Game changer.

Amenity Scheduling System

Figure out a way to automate the scheduling for common area conference rooms and amenities. We created a Google calendar for each amenity and allowed people to schedule on that calendar using Calendly. There are other options, and any kind of scheduling software works.

Change Utilities to Your Name

Have your management company call all of the utility companies and change the utilities into your new LLC's name. Ask for a budget plan quote if you haven't already done so and get one. Remember, consistency in financials matters. Ask them how you can save money while you're at it.

Management Software

Would you build a house without power tools? I hope not. Property management software is your power tool. Hopefully, you hired a management company that uses an actual property management software. Software should help with leasing, maintenance, lease administration, and accounting.

We tried to use QuickBooks to manage our properties. QuickBooks is a great accounting software, but it's not a great management software. Any money you spend on a good property management software will increase your rent collection, reduce your expenses, and save you time.

I made a complex spreadsheet to weigh the pros and cons of every software out there. You might just rely on whatever software your management company uses, but insist that they set you up as a user in their system, so you at a minimum have viewing access to your property.

To get the best of both worlds, let your property management company use the software they are already using, but require them to summarize the data into a weekly and monthly tracker that you create that is consistent for all of your properties and management companies. This normalizes the output of the data from their software programs, so you have consistency in reviewing the performance of your portfolio. Making quarterly reports for your investors is easier too.

Any good property management solution will work, but some are a better value than others. Here are some things to look for:

1. Mobile friendly
2. Online portal for tenants
3. Ability for tenants to set up autopay
4. Ability to create recurring charges to the tenants, including coding rent increases in the future
5. Have late charges automatically hit tenant ledgers
6. Track maintenance tickets

7. Bill pay and direct deposit for vendors
8. Owner reporting function

Since being cheap is expensive, look for a management company with one of the top softwares out there. The software the management company uses is their toolkit. How good their tools are should weigh in your decision of who you hire.

Software changes all the time, so do your research. A great property management software will allow tenants to set up auto ACH for rent and automatically record those receipts for you. It will auto charge late fees and remind tenants who haven't paid automatically and will automate the maintenance tracking process. These are the types of features that drive that incremental revenue.

Annual Budget

The last but probably the most important piece of taking over a property after closing is having your management company create the proforma budget for the remainder of the year. I share my MACO worksheet with them and then let them use their own experience to form the budget for the year. This budget forms the basis for your NOI goal for the year and is how you will rate their performance overall. Once you have it, be sure to read it (especially the CAM budget for the expense pass-throughs) and approve of it yourself before sending it out to your investors.

If you have done the onboarding well, you have signed contracts with your property management company, your contractor, your leasing agent, and your maintenance vendors, and you have set the building up for success. You have rekeyed the building, set up all the tenant ledgers with auto charges, and added the online portal to your website. You have a budget for the year, and your management company communicated to your tenants how to pay rent and submit maintenance requests.

Your property is up and running, and it's time to maximize the NOI and stabilize the property.

Key Reader Takeaways

- ☐ Your first interaction with your tenant is critical.
- ☐ Overcommunicate to reduce anxiety.
- ☐ Have a heart for delivering value to the tenants.

Action Items

- ☐ Have your management company deliver welcome letters to each tenant.
- ☐ Have a conversation with each tenant that is all about them and nothing about you.
- ☐ Create your annual budget for the property.
- ☐ Set goals with your management company, and communicate these goals to your investors.

FINANCIALS

Chapter 30

Stabilize the Financials

Objective: Generate a Stable History of NOI

This journey you've been on to fix and fill your building is like getting a diploma—it doesn't mean anything unless you use it to increase your income. Whenever you want to sell or refinance, they will ask for your financials. Those financials should show a history of a consistent, high NOI in order to get the best appraisal or sale price.

> **Remember that value comes from NOI and the NOI multiple, which is higher when your NOI is more sustainable, predictable, and transferable.**

Be deliberate in operating your business so that the NOI is maximized and consistent over a period of time so you can cash out as effectively as possible.

In this chapter, we are going to cover the six things you need to do in order to maximize the value of your property. These are things that drive the NOI and increase the NOI multiple, and you can literally follow them down the MACO worksheet as they impact each line item. They are:

1. Increase the Rent Rate
2. Bill the Correct Square Footages
3. Increase the Occupancy (decrease the vacancy rate)
4. Increase the Collection Rate (decrease credit loss)
5. Decrease Operating Expenses
6. Increase the Market Multiple (decrease the cap rate)

You'll work with your property manager to implement all of these over the course of a year or two, and then you will reach the final step: *Freedom.*

Increase the Rent Rate

The Fix step impacts this rate the most. Renovating the building, adding value, and doing better marketing all equate to higher rent rates. Curb appeal matters, just like it does for single-family homes, perhaps more. People want to have pride in customers visiting their business.

In the Center Drive case study, we spent $35,000 remodeling the building. We seal coated the parking lot, replaced some bad heaters, updated some tenant bathrooms, separated some utility meters, and fixed the roof leaks.

Remodel the building, and have the spaces well lit, move-in ready, and smelling good when you tour people through. Update the bathrooms and hallways, and make sure you hire good vendors who'll keep them pristine. Amenities drive value.

If you have a good marketing plan, you can get multiple people to apply and use that to your advantage to negotiate higher rents.

Bill the Correct Square Footages

Often, the square footages being billed to the tenants are wrong. Calculate the correct rentable square footages, and bill this amount back to the tenants. This is all done through the space measurement study and is a critical step to have in place before you finalize your marketing for the vacancies and sign leases.

Increase the Occupancy

You do this in the Fill step. Vacant spaces should be as clean-looking as possible, and online listings should have immaculate-looking photos and video tours. Hire superstar listing agents.

For warehouse and retail spaces that require build-outs, demo unnecessary walls and take them back to a white shell. Don't build out the spaces prematurely. Paint walls and ceiling white and the floors grey. Make it bright and clean looking.

For apartments and office space, make them move-in ready. Install fresh flooring, paint, and update bathrooms and common areas. Spend a ton of money on media packages, listing platforms, online lead tools, and whatever you need to do in order to cast the net as wide as possible to get top-quality candidates. When we raised rents to market on Center Drive, several tenants moved out. But we cleaned the spaces up, did 3D tours, and rolled out an aggressive marketing strategy to get them leased up with better tenants at higher rates per square foot.

Increase the Collection Ratio

Manage the property effectively over time by using great systems. Automate the collection of rent by adopting software that allows autopay and ACH payments. Use a management company that auto charges late fees and evicts tenants in default in a timely manner. Do more thorough screening to get more reliable tenants.

At Center Drive, we had to pay to get a couple tenants out that were deadbeats. It's always better to negotiate an informal surrender than to have to do a formal eviction.

FINANCIALS

Decrease Operating Expenses

Focus on cutting utility costs with smart building upgrades like LED lighting, motion sensors, new heating systems and controls, and new plumbing fixtures. Challenge your property taxes every single year like clockwork. Shop your insurance carriers, but don't ever get actual cash value policies—always get replacement cost value policies. If the existing leases don't allow you to implement these strategies, then insert them when you sign new leases. Put an expense stop clause or gross-up clause in your leases going forward to protect NOI.

The key is shifting responsibility and reducing the absorption of expenses that can be passed through. In most of our deals, the biggest decrease in operating costs is from finding a way to get the tenants to pay for the utilities.

There are four main things you can do to reduce or eliminate utility costs:

- Separate the Meters
- Install Submeters
- RUBS
- CAM

SEPARATE THE METERS

You'll rarely be held accountable for utility bills that are in the tenant's name, except for water. You'll have to get quotes for separating the gas, electric, and water meters and run a cost/benefit analysis using your Magic Multiple. If you have to rewire the entire building to separate the meters, it is usually cost prohibitive and you'll have to look at other options.

INSTALL SUBMETERS

If it's really expensive to separate the meters, sometimes you can just install sub-meters on the utility lines as they enter each space to track who is using what. You'll pay the utility bills, but you bill them back to the tenants based on their *actual* use. This is a low-cost way to get tenants paying directly, but you will still absorb some costs if they don't reimburse you and it adds administrative work.

RUBS

RUBS stands for Ratio Utility Billing System. It's like submetering, but you bill back the utilities to the tenants based on their proportionate share of the square footage as opposed to actual use. Here's how you calculate it:

$$\text{Meter Pro-Rata Share} = \frac{\text{Tenant's Rentable Square Footage}}{\text{Total Rentable Square Footage on that Meter}}$$

Let's say we have three tenants on one gas meter:

Example R.U.B.S. Billing

Tenant	RSF	% of Bill	Amount
Tenant A	5,000	50%	$50
Tenant B	3,000	30%	$30
Tenant C	2,000	20%	$20
Total	10,000		$100

In my example, if a bill comes in for $100, you would pay the bill but then charge each tenant their share of the bill—$50, $30, and $20 respectively. Most old-school property owners don't do this because of the accounting work that it requires, or they didn't write their lease to allow for it. But any decent property management software lets you set this up and does the calculations automatically for you.

Sometimes walls have been moved around and things weren't rewired, so it becomes very difficult to try to figure out which meters run which spaces. Billing back utilities using this method is a good option if locating where utilities enter the space is difficult so you can't effectively submeter.

The main drawback to this approach is creating disputes among tenants. If one tenant is using far more than another who has the same square footage, they will likely complain.

COMMON AREA MAINTENANCE (CAM)

If none of those options work, you can always include it in the CAM budget if you have expense pass-throughs or expense stops in your lease, and the leases are written to allow you to pass through the utilities to the tenants. We covered reconciling these expenses in the "Negotiate and Sign Leases" chapter. Be careful, though. Most leases don't allow you to bill back utilities for vacant spaces in the building, so make sure you either have a gross-up clause, or only bill back the percentage of the utility bills for what the occupancy in the building is. This isn't as good as the other three methods because the tenant doesn't feel the direct pain of leaving their lights on all night, but it's still better than nothing.

In the Center Drive case study, I rewired a couple units to get all the meters separated and had the tenants pay them directly. This was a major factor in improving the NOI.

Decrease Market Cap Rate (Increase the Multiple)

The NOI multiple is determined by how predictable, sustainable, and transferable the NOI is. We increase the multiple or decrease the cap rate by decreasing the perceived risk of property. We call this de-risking. Here are practical ways you can de-risk your property, so it's worth more for the same NOI.

PREDICTABLE

- Get better credit tenants and include a clause for financial reporting from them.
- Lease the building to multiple tenants—more tenants decreases the risk if any one single tenant defaults.
- Contract with lawn/snow/cleaning vendors on fixed monthly rates, not pay per visit type contracts.
- Tackle all of the big-ticket items up front, so you can better ascertain the annual repairs budget.
- Get on the budget system offered by the utility companies, so your utilities are the same every month.

SUSTAINABLE

- Sign longer-term leases.
- Show consistent financials over time on paper.
- Include lease clauses that protect the upside for the landlord, like expense stops, expense pass-throughs, and gross-up clauses.

TRANSFERABLE

- Put third-party management systems in place.
- Put leasing systems in place.
- Have a superstar due diligence package when preparing to sell, so you are perceived as having run the property very professionally—organized knowledge reduces perceived risk.

At the end of the day, the financial history that you can document will determine the value of your property. Be sure to execute your Fix, Fill, and Financial steps in tandem, keeping your eye on the prize: it's all about driving the NOI and the multiple of the NOI. The key is increasing the value more than it costs to increase that value.

That is exactly what we did at Center Drive. We increased the NOI from $40K to $100K and almost doubled the value of the building.

FINANCIALS

This doesn't happen overnight. You will likely want at least one full calendar year and corresponding tax return to justify your new value to a lender or buyer. In the next step, we discuss how to refinance or sell your property, and how to analyze when it's the right time to do it.

Key Reader Takeaways

☐ Increase the rent, occupancy, and collection rates.
☐ Decrease expenses by passing on utilities, writing smart leases, challenging taxes, and negotiating better vendor contracts.
☐ Sign fixed-rate recurring service contracts, not pay as you go.
☐ Spend more time and money securing more reliable tenants on longer-term leases.

Action Items

☐ Work with your management company to create a written plan to improve the financials over time.
☐ Figure out how you are going to bill back utilities before you sign new leases.
☐ Set NOI goals with the property management and leasing companies.

Step 7
Freedom

How do you know when to sell or refinance your property?

This step answers that question.

The "Refinance" chapter shows you how to replace expensive equity with low-cost debt. This increases your risk of default because debt *must* be paid, but it does improve your overall cash flow position as the deal sponsor. Find the right balance between cash flow and risk that comes from over-leveraging your property.

The "Sell" chapter teaches you how to calculate your return on equity and know when moving that equity to another property would yield a higher risk-adjusted return. If you decide to sell, you'll need to think of how to structure the deal to maximize cash out while minimizing taxes. You could also get creative and do seller financing of various sorts to keep a residual income stream coming in while getting a higher price.

This is the final step of the seven. It's where you'll free up your capital, pay off your partners, hold for long-term cash flow, and eventually sell to begin your next adventure.

Chapter 31

Refinance the Property

Objective: Pay Down the Capital Accounts to Zero

Are you going to slaughter the cow or keep milking it?

If you slaughter the cow, you will have a delicious steak dinner—but then what? Is there a way to keep enjoying the milk for years to come?

Selling is not the only way to maximize your commercial investment. Keeping the property but refinancing can help you cash out tax-free without losing your cash cow. The decision is ultimately up to you and how you pitched the investment to your partners on the front end.

Now that you fixed the building, filled it, and stabilized the financials, you should have increased the value at least 30–40 percent and doubled your equity. When you refinance, you'll get a new loan based on a new appraisal, and the new appraiser will review your financials from the time you bought it to now.

If you did the Financials step well, you'll be able to demonstrate a history of improved NOI and make a case for the higher value. I can't emphasize how important it is that you sell the story to the appraiser! Appraisals are an opinion of value, and that opinion can be heavily influenced by property data, repair receipts, and an organized set of financials.

In this chapter, we cover the benefits of refinancing and how to do it like a pro.

Choosing a Lender

Sometimes I value the relationship with my local lender over the interest rate savings a larger bank can offer. After all, you want to do more Value-Add deals with this same lender, right? With that being said, you should shop around.

The most important terms to evaluate are:

- Loan-to-Value (LTV)
- Interest Rate
- Closing Costs
- Amortization Period
- Term
- Prepayment Penalty

LOAN-TO-VALUE (LTV)

Be cautious about doing more than 75% loan-to-value. You don't want to take out too much money and have the property go south on you—leverage equates to risk.

Get the new loan at no more than your initial costs. Try to keep the debt service coverage ratio above 1.25 (the NOI is at least 1.25 times the annual debt service). I have found that to be the sweet spot between not overleveraging the property and not extracting enough cheap capital.

INTEREST RATE

Your community bank or credit union may or may not have the best rates. Shop around. Be willing to give up a little bit on interest rate to get a better term, longer amortization period, and higher loan-to-value.

CLOSING COSTS

Here, you are looking for minimal refinance fees and points. I usually pay a 0.5–1% origination fee plus appraisal and all hard costs.

AMORTIZATION PERIOD

Your lender will generally want a twenty-year amortization. Try to hold firm for a twenty-five or thirty-year amortization. The longer the amortization, the smaller the payment, and since your goal is cash flow, paying less principal each month is better for you.

TERM

The term is how long the loan goes before you have to pay it off. This payoff is called a balloon. Most commercial loans are on a five-year term. Sometimes you can get one that automatically renews for another five years at a pre-agreed-upon rate based on an index plus a margin. If you go with institutional money or large lenders, you can sometimes get a seven or ten-year term, but be careful—there are sometimes prepayment clauses on these loans.

PREPAYMENT PENALTY

You don't want any prepay penalty, but if you have to agree to one, make sure it only applies if you refinance and doesn't apply if you sell. I usually agree to 2% in the first year and 1% in the second year, only if I refinance with another lender. This is always negotiable.

Earlier, you learned that yield is measured by the internal rate of return (IRR). If the lender tells you they do yield maintenance to determine the prepayment penalty, run as fast as you can. It means that your payoff amount is determined by discounting back all of the future payments due under the loan at the lender's cost of funds at the time of the prepayment to determine the payoff amount.

On most loans, the payoff amount is simply the principal balance. On a yield maintenance loan, the payoff amount is the present value of the future payments, discounted at the lender's new cost of funds, which is controlled by them. This is the kiss of death!

Remember the story I told you earlier about the property I just bought, where the guy couldn't sell because he originated the loan at 4.9%, the current rates were 4%, and his prepayment penalty if he sold the building was over half a million dollars? Don't pigeonhole yourself by agreeing to a yield maintenance clause.

Cash-Out Refinance

If you get an appraisal value that is favorable—140 percent of the total costs or more—then you can pull out your initial capital tax-free and earn a nice residual income on the equity you leave in the deal. You'll distribute the cash in accordance with the operating agreement. You set this waterfall in the operating agreement during the Fund step, so go back to review what your operating agreement says.

REFINANCE FEE

It's customary for the sponsor to receive a "guaranty fee" of 0.5%–2% at the time of the refinance for guaranteeing a larger loan amount and for your time spent reviewing and securing the new financing. This can generate the active income you need to hang onto the property and keep going.

PAY DOWN CAPITAL ACCOUNTS

I often get asked what happens to the partners when you give them their money back. We discussed this in the Fund step, but the answer is that it's completely up to you. You will dictate this up front in your operating agreement and in the PPM if you do a fund structure.

If you don't get a high enough value on the appraisal to pay everyone back in full, that's okay. It may still make sense to refinance and pay down the capital accounts as much as you can or choose to pay off certain investors and leave other ones in. Remember, the main benefit of paying down capital accounts is reducing or eliminating the high preferred return payments that are based on the capital account balances.

BUY BACK UNITS

Earlier in the book, you learned that paying capital accounts down and buying back membership units are two different things. You should include a buyback clause in your operating agreement. The cleanest way to do it is to calculate a payoff based on an agreed-upon IRR, such as 20 percent. Basically, the LLC has the option to buy back membership units as long as you provide a 20 percent IRR.

What investor out there wouldn't be excited to make 20 percent annually on their money? Here is an example if you bought the membership units back halfway through the fourth year:

Limited Partner Buyout Calculation

Year	CF Operation	Return of Capital		Upside		Total CF
0	−$100,000				=	−$100,000
1	$8,933					$8,933
2	$15,033				=	$15,033
3	$15,134				=	$15,134
4	$6,000	+	$100,000	+	$46,120	=	$152,120
			IRR			20.00%

You can solve for a payoff amount using the "Goal Seek" Function in Microsoft Excel. This forces the IRR cell to equal the agreed-upon percent, in this case, 20 percent, by

FREEDOM

having Excel change the payoff cell, in this case, $46,120. The payoff here is $146,120, and they have earned $6,000 for the year in quarterly payments prior to that.

CHANGE IN OWNERSHIP PERCENTAGE

The initial upside split between GP and LP was based on risk. The LPs had their capital at risk, and you personally guaranteed the loans, took the risk of default, and did all of the work.

If you pay them back with the proceeds from the refinance but don't give them the upside to buy them out, one of two things should happen: they should either sign on the new debt with you to stay in the deal with the split at the highest tier of the waterfall, or their split should be reduced to like 5–10 percent of the upside because they no longer have any risk in the deal.

For example, if they sign on the new debt with you, in our example, the pref would be eliminated and we would split each dollar 70 percent to the GPs and 30 percent to the LPs. If they don't sign on debt with you, you might give them 10 percent of the cash flow until you sell, at which point you give them the 70/30 split you agreed to originally up to a 20 percent IRR.

However you structure it, make sure you pay off your partners in a way that makes them want to keep doing deals with you. Get as creative as you would like. You can make these as complicated or as simple as you want. Just remember you have to explain all of this to someone and get them to sign off on it and give you their money. Don't make it so complicated no one understands it.

Your Job Is to Make Your Partners Money

Try not to think of your partners as an expense on your analysis, where the less you can make them, the more you make. This is the pie theory. If you cut them more of the pie, that means you have less. Instead, use your creativity to figure out how to make the pie bigger, so you both get more and can be excited to make your partners a ton of money.

Greed is the surest path to not having people reinvest with you. I am only happy with a deal when I can deliver ridiculous returns to my partners—we're talking 12–20 percent—and I wake up every morning and work hard to achieve that.

There have been times where I'm structuring a deal and a general partner will ask, "Why are we giving away so much equity to the LPs? I think we can raise all of the money without offering that additional upside." I tell them that it's our job to make as much money as possible for our partners.

Just like with your tenants, your investors are your customers, and you want to create raving fans, so they'll tell all of their high-net-worth friends about your little investing program, and you'll never, ever have to worry about raising money again.

On Center Drive, we achieved an NOI of $100,000 and got a valuation of well over a million dollars. I had just over $750,000 in actual costs into the building. I bought my partner out early on in the process for an agreed-upon fee of $20,000. I took out a new loan about two years later and got 100 percent of my money back out. Now I make around $50,000 a year in cash flow from that one property, with zero dollars into the deal. I kept repeating this process and building my portfolio, selling some assets along the way, and mixing in some wholesaling too.

After you refinance, you can hold the property indefinitely until it makes sense to sell. The next chapter covers how to figure out if, and when, that time has come.

FREEDOM

Key Reader Takeaways

☐ Shop the terms for your refinance.

☐ Make sure the terms sheets clearly spell out the closing costs and fees on the front end and the prepayment penalties on the back end.

☐ Take a refinance fee of 0.5%–1% for yourself.

☐ Don't ever agree to a yield maintenance prepayment clause.

☐ Be sure to leave a DSCR of at least 1.25 (NOI ÷ ADS).

☐ Pay back all the equity capital to eliminate preferred payments.

☐ Buy back membership units if you have excess cash after you return capital.

☐ Agree on an IRR with the limited partners that you can buy them out at any time. This is the cleanest way to calculate a buyout price for their membership units.

Action Items

☐ Try using the Goal Seek Function in Microsoft Excel to calculate a payoff.

☐ Create a banker list and make note of who is good for "going-in" money and who is good for "coming-out" money.

☐ Get three terms sheets for your refinance and compare them.

☐ Calculate *your* split of the cash flow before and after your refinance (partnership cash flow should go down, but GP cash flow should go up).

☐ Refinance your property.

Chapter 32

Sell the Property

Objective: Get a Higher Return on Equity in a Different Project

Some properties cash flow really well, and some don't. Sometimes it makes sense to cash in your chips and move the equity you created to another property.

If you bought using my strategy, you used the MACO worksheet and bought for Value-Add. You used equity partners on the front end, created value, refinanced, and paid those equity partners off to hold long term for cash flow. If you were able to get a creative deal done (i.e., contract for deed, master lease, or seller carryback), then you likely paid a premium but didn't need to raise much, if any, equity. Perhaps you could fast-track to the cash flow stage from the start and wouldn't need to refinance.

> The goal is to create value and eliminate expensive equity, so you can hold long term for cash flow. This is how you build a true legacy of wealth for generations to come.

However, everything is for sale at the right price, isn't it? How do you know when it's the right time to sell?

Keep in mind that if you sell before you have owned the property for one year, you will likely pay ordinary income taxes on the profit. Whereas if you hold for at least one year, you will probably pay taxes at the long-term capital gains rate.

It's all about return. When you can move the SPBT (Sales Proceeds Before Tax) to another project and get a better risk-adjusted return, it's time.

You may have heard the terms "cash-on-cash return" or "cash-on-equity return." Here are the formulas for them:

$$\text{Cash-on-Cash Return} = \frac{\text{Stabilized Cash Flow}}{\text{Total Capital Invested}}$$

$$\text{Cash-on-Equity Return} = \frac{\text{Stabilized Cash Flow}}{\text{SPBT}}$$

The first formula is used to calculate the cash-on-cash return for the project—that is, how much cash you have coming in from your rental operation as compared to how much cash the partnership has put *into* the investment.

The second one is used to determine the rate of return you are getting on the equity you have sitting in the property—that is, how much cash you have coming in as compared to how much cash you can *pull out* of the investment.

The numerator is the same for both formulas. The denominator in the first one is the total capital invested, whereas the denominator in the second is the total capital you could pull out of the property if you sold. You can run either formula at the project level, LP level, or GP level.

I usually run it at the project level, since I'm a steward over the GP and LP funds and have to make good decisions for both positions at the project level. Most people don't calculate either one of these formulas, or if they do, they only calculate the cash-on-cash return.

Net Proceeds from Sale

Review the sales proceeds calculator in the "Sales Proceeds Worksheet" section of Chapter 15 again or pull it up in your deal analyzer spreadsheet. Remember that we capitalized the Year 5 NOI of $112,411 at a cap rate of 8.34% to project the sales price of $1,348,355. Then we deducted the closing costs of $79,316 to solve for net proceeds from sale of $1,269,039. This is the amount we would net at the sale before paying off any debt or returning any capital to the partners.

Bank Debt Balance

The next item on the SPBT worksheet is the payoff for the loan. In our case, we financed our deal with bank debt, so we had the mortgage balance to pay off. You can look at the amortization schedule or run a future value calculation in a time value of money calculator to predict this.

On the next page I show you how to calculate a bank payoff using a financial calculator.

Using TVM Calculator to Calculate Future Value

-484,318.474				
P/YR:12				End Mode
60.000	4.500	551,250.000	-3,064.000	-484,318.474
N	**I/YR**	**PV**	**PMT**	**FV**
INPUT	MU	CST	PRC	MAR
K	%	CFj	Σ+	←
+/−	RCL	→M	RM	M+
	7	8	9	÷
	4	5	6	×
C	1	2	3	—
HELP	0	•	=	+

Put the interest rate, original loan amount, and monthly payment for the loan in the I/YR, PV, and PMT fields. Put the number of periods from the loan start date you want to calculate the payoff for (in this case, sixty months). Then solve for FV, which is future value.

The payoff in this case is $484,318.47. The number in the calculator is negative because we are paying the money out (money is going away from us). Please note that in the calculator above we used "end mode" which charges interest at the end of the month. In the Sales Proceeds Before Tax Calculator we calculated the payoff using "beginning mode" so the payoff was slightly different ($484,316). Ignore this difference.

Always check to see if your result is reasonable. Make sure you do a negative number of the payment since it's money going out. Remember positive numbers are money coming in, and negative numbers are money going out.

You would walk out of the closing at this sale with a check for $784,723. This is the Sales Proceeds Before Tax (SPBT). This would be distributed to the members based on the waterfall structure you agreed to, and everyone would pay taxes based on their unique situation.

If you only have a few partners and they are all willing to 1031 exchange into another property, then you don't need to calculate your taxes because you won't pay them. However, if you raised money from lots of people and any one of them wants out, you may not be able to do a 1031 exchange to defer your capital gains taxes.

Therefore, you should calculate what the tax impact would be on most people to calculate your sales proceeds after tax (SPAT). Let's look at how the taxes at sale work.

Gain on Sale Components

If you do decide to sell and pay taxes, hopefully, you have a gain on sale. That gain will be taxed in three different ways:

- Capital gains tax on appreciation
- Recapture tax on the depreciation
- Ordinary income tax on the personal property

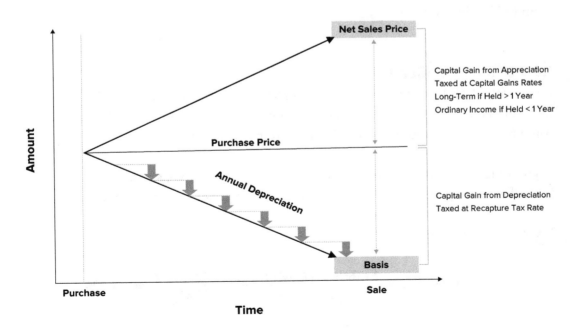

Capital Gains Breakdown

CAPITAL GAINS TAX ON APPRECIATION

If held for investment purposes (generally longer than one year), long-term capital gains tax rates are used to calculate the tax on the gain from appreciation. If the property is not held for investment purposes (i.e., held for flip or less than one year), you normally pay short-term capital gains rates, which is usually just the ordinary income tax rate.

RECAPTURE TAX ON DEPRECIATION

Generally, this is 25 percent federally plus whatever your state charges, if anything. The total depreciation you have taken over the years is now taxed, but at a flat rate, not at the rate it saved you during all of those years. Tax rates and laws change, so please consult your advisors.

INCOME TAX ON PERSONAL PROPERTY

If you did a cost segregation and converted some 27.5-year or 39-year property to five- and seven-year personal property and fifteen-year land improvements so you could write it all off in year one, then you may be paying ordinary income tax on that portion of the gain. For this reason, I recommend cost segregation for long-term holds—but not for flips.

How to Make a Decision

Let's bring it all together. Our stabilized NOI was $100,000. Our original annual debt service was $36,768 per year, so our stabilized cash flow, if we didn't refinance, was $63,232. If we did refinance, it was closer to $50,000.

If you're trying to decide whether or not to sell in year five, simply run your two formulas to see what kind of returns you are getting. Let's run it for both scenarios.

If you didn't refinance:

$$\text{Cash-on-Cash} = \frac{\text{Stabilized Cash Flow}}{\text{Capital Invested}} = \frac{\$63,232}{\$223,750} = 28.3\%$$

$$\text{Cash-on-Equity} = \frac{\text{Stabilized Cash Flow}}{\text{SPBT}} = \frac{\$63,232}{\$784,723} = 8.0\%$$

This means we are getting 28.3% per year on the cash we put into the deal and 8.0% per year on the cash we could pull out of the deal (before taxes). This is at the project level. The GP and LP positions would be calculated by determining the splits and then using the cash for flow that position divided by the cash in or potential cash out for each position. Let's look at the numbers if we had refinanced.

If you did refinance:

$$\text{Cash-on-Cash} = \frac{\text{Stabilized Cash Flow}}{\text{Capital Invested}} = \frac{\$50,000}{\$0} = \infty$$

$$\text{Cash-on-Equity} = \frac{\text{Stabilized Cash Flow}}{\text{SPBT}} = \frac{\$50,000}{\$500,000} = 10.0\%$$

If we refinanced, we have no cash in, so we can't calculate a cash-on-cash return anymore. We can adjust our SPBT calculator for the new payoff amount of the larger loan we got when we refinanced, but to keep things simple, I'm using a round number of $500,000 as the SPBT for the refinance scenario assuming a new loan amount of approximately $750,000.

Keep in mind these returns do NOT include principal paydown or other tax benefits.

If we only calculated our cash-on-cash return it would look like we were getting a phenomenal return on the cash we put in because we are—28.3% per year plus principal paydown plus tax benefits! However, take a look at the cash-on-equity. We are only getting 8% on the money we could pull out, per year. We can probably do better in another investment with a similar risk. You would only move that equity into another project if you thought you could do better in another project with the same amount of risk. Most of your projects will yield a 20% IRR or better, so if your cash-on-equity return is under 20% and all of

FREEDOM

your partners are okay with exchanging into a new property, it's probably time to market for your next deal!

Do this task on a regular basis. Decide to sell if you can get a mega premium, think the area is going to decline for some reason, or have another project to move the funds into that would yield a better risk-adjusted return. Have the mindset that anything is for sale at the right price.

Sometimes there is a frenzy, and people need your property for their own use or to meet a 1031 exchange deadline. So let's talk about 1031 exchanges for a minute.

Tax-Deferred Exchange

These are usually called 1031 exchanges because they come from the tax code section 1031. Instead of paying tax on your gains, sometimes you can defer those gains if you reinvest in a new property. You have to meet three criteria to defer 100 percent of the taxes:

1. Same amount of debt or more
2. Same purchase price or more
3. Move all of the net proceeds over

There are also some strings attached.

SAME ENTITY

You have to buy the new property in the same entity you held title in the old property in. If you have a fund with seven people, they all need to stay in the new deal. If any one single person wants out, you can't do a 1031 exchange because you are dissolving the LLC you have to buy the new property in.

> **Pro Tip**
>
> You could buy out that member prior to or after closing to get around this, but for the most part, your partners are coming with you. Another potential work-around is a "drop and swap." This is where you dissolve your LLC well in advance of ever selling and convert all the members to tenants in common. This should be done well in advance of selling to keep Uncle Sam happy and is not recommended by some CPAs.

TIMING 45/180

You have forty-five days to identify a few new properties to reinvest in. There are two options for identification. You can either identify three properties, or you can identify an unlimited number of properties with the market value equaling 200 percent of the price you sold at. In our case, we could identify three properties that were all at least $1.35M (projected sales price for Center Drive), or we could identify any number of properties with market values totaling $2.7M (200 percent of projected sales price).

You have 180 days from the day you sold your asset to close on the new property and finish any work that you want included in the value. You can also do a reverse exchange if you want to buy a new property first and then sell your existing one after. A reverse exchange is where you purchase and close on the new property *before* you close on the sale of your old one. You might need some bridge financing to make it happen. This solves your timing dilemma.

RAISING ADDITIONAL CAPITAL

In most cases, your new property is a higher price than the one you sold, so you have to raise additional capital. You can do that from the current members, add more members, or structure a deal where your LLC takes title with an outside investor as tenants in common. Consult your legal and tax advisors for these advanced techniques, but they can work great if done the right way.

FREEDOM

Creative Exit Strategies

Last but not least is the creative exit. There are an infinite number of creative exit strategies, but here are the top ones I use:

- Sell on a contract for deed
- Sell on a master lease with an option to purchase
- Do a seller carryback

Look familiar? These are the same creative methods you used to buy. Most smart sellers are open to these options too. You can get an above-market price and a healthy residual income if you sell with creative seller terms. Go back and review the "Present Your Offers" chapter where we cover each of these strategies in detail. Start thinking creatively on the sell-side too.

When it comes to selling, be reluctant, but always be open to creative ways to exit and lock in your profit. Buy from motivated sellers, but don't be one yourself. Also, remember that refinancing is only freeing up your capital, but it doesn't lock in your profit.

I recommend entering deals with the intent to hold long term, but if someone wants to take it off your hands before you close for a wholesale fee, let them have it. If you close on it, hold it long enough to refinance and pay off partners, or hold it long term until you can move that equity over and do better somewhere else.

You may not formally list your property, but if someone makes an offer, calculate what your SPBT and SPAT would be and then decide if that equity is best moved somewhere else.

Make sure you stick with the program here until you get your first deal done on the exit side. It won't be easy, but when you walk out of closing with a fat six- or seven-figure check, I guarantee you'll call me and offer to buy me a steak dinner.

Key Takeaways

- ☐ Always be willing to sell, but always be reluctant.
- ☐ SPBT is the check you would walk out of closing with if you sold.
- ☐ Distributable profit is the SPBT minus the capital you have into the deal.
- ☐ SPAT is the SPBT less taxes for capital gains from appreciation, depreciation recapture tax, and ordinary income tax on personal property gains. It will be different for each investor based on their personal tax situation.
- ☐ Systematically analyze the return you are getting on your cash into the deal and the cash you can pull out of the deal, and see if moving that cash elsewhere would yield you a higher return.
- ☐ Think of creative exit strategies to avoid tax, increase price, and maintain passive income.

Action Items

- ☐ Find a local 1031 exchange intermediary in your area, and ask them to educate you on 1031s.
- ☐ Interview your partners and see if they are open to exchanging into a new property.
- ☐ If they are, get a new deal under contract, compare the returns and the risks, and decide if moving your money into this new project makes sense or not.

FREEDOM

Conclusion

I hope by now you can visualize yourself living your ideal life and doing the things you were called to do. In this book, I laid out a very simple, seven-step process for getting you to real freedom, well beyond the money.

Let's recap what you learned.

In the first half of the book, you formed your strategy. You faced your fears and recognized the benefits that commercial has to offer. You learned how to understand risk and how to structure it away by adopting a multi-tenant, Value-Add strategy in an asset class and area that has the most potential. You learned how NOI and NOI multiple are the keys to creating value, and you learned clear-cut strategies to increase both.

In the second half of the book, you learned the 7 Steps to Freedom—a proven system for increasing your net worth and creating residual income. You learned how to find deals, figure out what to pay for them, and then fund them by structuring an equity partnership. Then you learned how to fix them, fill them, stabilize the financials, and free up your time, capital, and profit.

Let's do a recap of what you learned in each of the seven steps:

1. Find

You created a broker and property owner prospecting list and rolled out a comprehensive marketing strategy that included gathering, hunting, fishing, and farming to schedule tours.

2. Figure

You learned how to tour a property, measure the building, and find the seller's hot button. You talked to brokers, pulled market reports, and researched other properties to figure out the rent rates, vacancy rates, and cap rates to use in your analysis.

You learned how to use the MACO worksheet to project your income and expenses to figure out your stabilized NOI, and you also learned a workaround using a net rent approach to estimate that NOI even faster. You translated that stabilized NOI to a projected sales price, the as-stabilized value, using a market cap rate or Market Multiple.

Then you deducted your costs and desired profit to back into the Max Allowable Cash Offer, your MACO. To do this, you learned how to use the renovation, leasing, and closing cost worksheets to calculate your costs to stabilize. You even learned how to calculate your Magic Multiple, which allowed you to figure out how much you could invest per square foot in any property quickly—your max allowable investment per square foot.

Finally, you figured out how much more you could pay if the seller gave you favorable financing by using the price multiplier tables. You learned how to present a few different offers and negotiate until you got a property under contract.

3. Fund

You learned a simple system to structure away as much risk as possible by doing proper due diligence. You also learned how to raise debt and equity effectively. You can now complete a sources and uses worksheet and structure a joint venture or fund with a preferred return and a waterfall that shows how you get paid during the operating years, at refinance, and at sale. You know what type of banks and investors to target and how to approach them to get the best terms. Lastly, you learned how to complete the nitty-gritty items to get your deal across the finish line.

4. Fix

Then I showed you how to estimate repairs for the purpose of making an offer using the renovation cost worksheet. You learned the big categories of expenses, and then I showed you how to expand that estimate into a full scope with specifications and drawings and request bids from qualified general contractors or subcontractors. You made some decisions about whether you wanted to be your own general contractor or hire someone else. You learned how to keep your project on schedule and on budget, and how to submit draw requests.

5. Fill

I also taught you a leasing process that is sure to get your properties filled with the best tenants in the shortest amount of time. You learned the importance of a world-class listing with top-notch media. Then you learned how to drive traffic to that listing to generate leads, conduct showings, take applications, screen tenants, and sign leases. You learned the difference between a net lease and a gross lease and what clauses to include in your lease. You also learned how to use creativity to get your lease deals done when other landlords couldn't.

6. Financials

You learned how to hire a property manager and structure their compensation creatively to incentivize them to drive up the NOI for you. You know how to work with them to onboard your property correctly. You learned that smart utility billing and accounting practices make all the difference in the world, and that a good property management software is worth its weight in gold. Finally, you learned the tricks to driving up the NOI and the NOI multiple: raise rent, increase occupancy/collection rates, bill back proper square footages, decrease operating expenses, and sign longer-term leases with better credit tenants.

7. Freedom

You know how to refinance like a pro and how to get the best terms. You can decide to return capital or buy membership units back. You learned how to calculate your

SPBT, SPAT, cash-on-cash, and cash-on-equity returns so you could decide when to sell. And most of all, you learned you're not alone.

> **I have done this over and over and over, and you can too.**

You have everything you need to achieve the freedom and adventures you crave—not in the next thirty years, but in the next one to three years. You can get excited and challenged again by moving from residential into this crazy world of commercial. I hope by filling in some of the knowledge gaps, you have gained the confidence you needed to proceed forward boldly.

The best part is that if you walk down this pathway and never quit, you are guaranteed to arrive at your destination eventually. The speed at which you travel along your journey will depend on your commitment and your willingness to enlist a coach or mentor to help you along the way. That's why I'm inviting you to contact me personally. You can find me at our website, Podcast, or YouTube channel. I want to hear your story and be a resource to help you get where you want to go.

In other words, the only thing holding you back from living your ideal life is your willingness to take action on this system.

Your life is ultimately just the sum of the individual days you lived. The decision you make today to commit or just let it be another regret is up to you.

No amount of money can buy back the things you have lost. I can't save my mom. But if this system allows you to buy back your *time*, so you can spend it blessing others and doing the things you were called to do, then my own purpose will have been fulfilled. I'm counting on you. Please don't waste this opportunity. Become who you were called to be, and find your true freedom.

You're just seven steps away.

Appendix

Due Diligence Document Addendum

This is the list we include as an addendum to our purchase agreement so the seller contractually agrees to provide these items. It's important to ask for and review all of these documents.

We prefer the seller delivers a link to an online folder that contains all of this information, like Dropbox, Google Drive, or OneDrive. Review the list for the specific deal and remove anything that doesn't apply to this deal. Add any items that you want to see specific to this deal.

- Tenants
  - Rent Roll
  - Tenant contact List
  - Lease documents
  - Leases
  - Amendments
  - Extensions
  - Estoppels
  - Abstracts
  - Subleases
  - Any verbal agreements

- Vendors
  - Vendor contact list
  - Vendor contracts
  - Most recent vendor invoice/statement
- Financials
  - Bank statements
  - Last three years P&L transaction detail in Microsoft Excel
  - Last three years partnership tax returns or schedule E if single member LLC
  - Annual reconciliations/charges for net leases or expense stops
  - Copies of last twenty-four months of utilities bills
  - Operating budget, if any
  - Capital improvement reserve schedule, if any
- Building
  - CAD file
  - Floor plan PDFs
  - Space measurement study
  - Detailed parking schedule and map indicating any assigned spots for any of the tenants—hand draw if needed on a Google map image
  - Plat/Survey
  - Print a floor plan of the building and mark up the locations for utility meters for gas, electric, water etc., indicating what meters run what units and meter numbers if available.
- Signed Statements
  - Any options to purchase or right of first refusal the tenants have
  - List of delinquent tenants, if any
  - Status of any and all deferred maintenance issues or capital improvement projects needed that you are aware of
  - Description and security/life/fire safety systems with written information on how they work
  - List of any and all code violations, non-confirming use, zoning, encroachment or any other issues you have with ANY authority that you are aware of, if any
  - Any pending or past litigation involving the property? If so please describe and attach any supporting documentation.

- Any pending or past insurance claims processed? If so please describe and attach reports.
- Reports
  - PCAR—Property condition assessment reports
  - Environmental Phase I or Phase II
  - Reports of any kind
  - ADA Report
  - Mold or Hazardous reports
  - Roof report
  - Mechanical/Engineering reports
  - Infrared survey
  - Structural
  - Warranties still in place
- Legal
  - Current title policy
  - Copies of construction contracts in progress, if any
  - Property tax appeals, if any
  - Association documents, if any
- List of personal property to transfer at closing on a bill of sale, if any
  - Cleaning and janitorial
  - Office furniture
  - Equipment and supplies
  - Tools
  - Spare parts
  - Motors
  - Building plans
  - Internet systems
  - Security or automated systems
  - Desktop and laptop computers

CPSIA information can be obtained
at www.ICGtesting.com
Printed in the USA
LVHW021133180723
752377LV00004B/242

9 781544 520988